THE WAUGH TWINS

The Cricketing Story of Steve and Mark Waugh

KERSI MEHER-HOMJI

Foreword by Bob Simpson

Kangaroo Press

Dedicated to Beverley Waugh,
one of cricket's most influential mums,
for her help and inspiration

THE WAUGH TWINS

First published in Australia and New Zealand in 1998 by Kangaroo Press
an imprint of Simon & Schuster Australia
20 Barcoo Street, East Roseville NSW 2069

A Viacom Company
Sydney New York London Toronto Tokyo Singapore

© Kersi Meher-Homji

National Library of Australia
Cataloguing-in-Publication data

Meher-Homji, Kersi
    The Waugh twins: the cricketing story of Steve and Mark Waugh.

    Includes index.
    ISBN 0 86417 921 9.
    1. Waugh, Mark, 1965– . 2. Waugh, Steve, 1965– .
    3. Cricket players – Australia – Biography. I. Title.

796.3580922

Front cover photograph: Allsport/Shaun Botterill
Back cover photographs: Allsport/Shaun Botterill (left), Allsport/Mike Hewitt (right)
Designed and typeset by DOCUPRO

Set in 11/14pt AGaramond
Printed in Singapore by Kyodo Printing Co. Pte Ltd

10 9 8 7 6 5 4 3 2 1

Contents

Foreword

I am honoured to have been asked to write this Foreword. First, as the book is by Kersi Meher-Homji, I know it will be accurate, honest and a very good read. Secondly, the Waugh twins were a major part of my life for over a decade and I had the good fortune to be able to see and perhaps oversee their development from talented youngsters to champions.

I first met Steve and Mark when I was appointed coach of NSW in 1984 and was immediately struck by their natural talent and contrasting personalities, builds and styles. They share a huge talent for the game, but otherwise there is not that much similarity between the Waugh twins. They had always been highly successful at whichever sport they tackled, but at 19 Steve produced a little more than Mark and made the state team first. Their natural talent was unique, whether it was batting, bowling or in the field.

They introduced new ideas to fielding with sleight-of-hand throws either through or under their legs, or around their bodies, which added a new dimension to the game and danger to the batsmen. These skills were learnt in indoor cricket, which they played brilliantly.

While they were abundantly blessed with great natural skills, Steve appreciated that natural talent alone was not going to take him right to the top of Test cricket. Even with such rich gifts, Steve realised there were flaws in his game which, if unchecked, could have threatened his international career. Cricket is filled with great natural players who did not make it because they lacked the brains, the common sense or application to make the most of their gifts. Steve has the brains to match his outstanding talents.

In his early days, Steve was a purely instinctive player, thrilling to watch as he unleashed a string of breathtaking strokes and ultimately frustrating when he fell attempting shots which just were not on. He was a classic example of a player with bags of natural talent, who had not taken the trouble to couple it with technique. There is no point in having all the talent in the world if you are sitting back in the pavilion!

Mark on the other hand is the perfect but rare example of a player who can win a match off his own bat. In this regard he is up with the great Doug Walters, whom I felt achieved more victories for Australia off his own bat than any batsman since Sir Donald Bradman. While Doug's style often looked brutal and a little crude, Mark's is full of casual grace. Mark has been criticised for appearing not to care, but this is absolutely incorrect. His desire to succeed is equal to Steve's but his body language is different. Perhaps the greatest strength of the Waughs is their great cricketing brains. Too often over-talented players are not blessed with the greatest asset of all—a thoughtful incisive view of the game. Such players wither on the vine when something goes wrong. Not the Waughs. They analyse and decide to go to Plan B.

This attribute makes both of them good captaincy material. Steve has the nod at present, but I have no doubt that Mark would also make an excellent skipper. He is full of flair, good ideas and good old-fashioned nous. In so many ways they are complete cricketers. Steve's brisk medium-pace kept him in the Test team for some years and his fearless bowling during the death (final) overs in one-day internationals earned him the nickname of 'The Ice Man'. Always thinking and experimenting, he was the first to develop and introduce the change-of-pace leg-spinner into the limited-overs game.

If Mark did not bat so well he could have held down a spot as a pace bowler or off-spinner. In the early days I thought so highly of his pace bowling that I convinced the selectors and captain that he was good enough to open the bowling. He proved his worth by taking four wickets in an innings at the Gabba against Queensland. He went on to grab 5–24 against the mighty Windies in a World Series Cup international in front of about 70,000 wildly cheering Melburnians in 1992–93. These days he is a fine off-spinner, as good as any going around in Australia, and he should bowl more often for Australia.

And of course both Mark and Steve are also in the top bracket in the world in fielding. Mark, I believe, is the best all-round fielder about. His catching in any position is brilliant and he has easily the safest pair of hands in cricket, either in slips or the outfield. Steve is equally adept and hits the stumps when run-outs are on.

Bob Simpson, dressed in 1857 gear, during a Heritage match in Sydney's Domain to recreate an historic event.

It has been suggested that they are not close. Not so. Certainly they do not run together socially but, as they say, 'We saw plenty of each other when we shared the same bedroom for twenty years.' Their off-field interests are totally different so they go different ways. They are, however, fiercely protective of each other and outsiders who criticise either one in the presence of the other do so at their own risk.

Both have been ornaments to the game and have given great pleasure to cricket lovers throughout the world. I know Kersi's book will add to this pleasure.

Bob Simpson

Bob Simpson
May 1998

Acknowledgments

It is my pleasure to thank Bob Simpson for his perceptive Foreword, and the Waugh family—especially Beverley and Rodger Waugh and Dion Bourne—for their long interviews. I am most grateful to Ross Dundas for providing detailed statistics and checking some of mine. My thanks also to Rick Smith (Apple Books), Beverley Waugh, Alan Crompton, and Mark Ray for the loan of photographs and Tony Rafty for caricatures; Tricia Ritchings for her word-processing skills, advice and encouragement; and Carl Harrison-Ford for editing the book and giving it a smooth finish.

I also thank Mike Whitney, Alan Crompton, Gavin Robertson, Geoff Lawson, Dirk Wellham, Doug Conway and Peter Roebuck for their critical appraisals of the Waugh twins and providing some original stories; Mike Gately and Pan Macmillan Australia for their permission to quote from *Waugh Declared*; and David Rosenberg, Karen Williams, Brigitta Doyle and others from Simon & Schuster Australia for their help.

For photographs supplied, I acknowledge Mark Skarschewski from the Allsport Australia, Andrew Foulds of the *Sydney Morning Herald*, Rick Smith, Mark Ray, Beverley Waugh, Alan Crompton, Ronald Cardwell, Denise Franks and Gulu Ezekiel.

I would like to thank the following journalists, newspapers and magazines for material quoted in this book: Greg Baum, Peter Roebuck, Bill O'Reilly, Phil Wilkins, and Malcolm Knox from the *Sydney Morning Herald*; Danny Weidler and John Benaud from the *Sun-Herald*; Mike Coward and Malcolm Conn from *The Australian*; John MacKinnon from *Wisden Cricketers' Almanack*; Ken Piesse from *Australian Cricket*; Jim Tucker and Mark Waugh from *Inside Edge*; Robert Craddock, Ray Kershler and Ron Reed from the *Daily Telegraph* (Sydney); my friends Doug Conway and Ian Jessup from AAP; Allan Miller from *Allan's Australian Cricket Annual* and Jim Maxwell from *ABC Cricket*.

Books consulted and quoted include: *Waugh Declared* by Mark Gately (Ironbark Press, Pan Macmillan Australia 1992); *Solid Knocks and Second Thoughts* by Dirk Wellham with Howard Rich (Reed Books, 1988); *Steve Waugh's Ashes Diary* (Ironbark Press, 1993); *Steve Waugh's West Indies Tour Diary* (HarperSports, 1995); *Steve Waugh's World Cup Diary*

(HarperSports, 1996); *Steve Waugh's 1997 Ashes Diary* (HarperSports, 1997); *A Year to Remember* by Mark Waugh with Grantlee Keiza (Random House, 1997); *Wisden Cricketers' Almanack*, several volumes (John Wisden & Co. Ltd); *The Wisden Book of Test Cricket*, Vols I and II, compiled and edited by Bill Frindall (Macdonald & Jane's Publishers Ltd, 1979, and Headline Book Publishing, 1995); and *Whiticisms* by Mike Whitney (Ironbark, Pan Macmillan Australia, 1995).

Every effort has been made to contact the owners of copyright.

Preface

With so many cricket books being released every year, adding one more needs an explanation—especially one on the Waugh twins.

Steve Waugh has been writing his interesting Tour Diaries every year from 1993 to 1997 and last year brother Mark penned a season's summary (with some help). Just as Mark was five years behind Steve in making his Test debut, he was four years behind in his literary bow. Also, Mark Gately has written an authorised and well-researched biography on the twins titled *Waugh Declared* which was published in 1992. So why another book on the Waughs when they are still playing?

Although replete with dressing-room stories and personal opinions, the Tour Diaries represent detailed summaries of five separate tours with no mention of home seasons and other tours undertaken by Steve.

Waugh Declared by Gately had assessed the twins' careers until the end of the 1992 season. However, much has happened since then. By September 1992, Steve and Mark had played only two Tests together and 58 in all. By August 1998 they have played 60 Tests in tandem and 181 in all—helping Australia reach the top in the Test arena. They had clearly shown promise of greatness in 1991 but achieved it later; Steve after his masterpieces in Sydney 1993, Kingston 1995, Delhi 1996, Johannesburg and Old Trafford 1997; Mark in Melbourne 1992, Edgbaston 1993, Kingston 1995, Port Elizabeth 1997, Adelaide and Bangalore 1998—to name just a few of my favourites. Thus, their previous biography was like a book on Sydney before the Opera House was built, or on Agra before the Taj Mahal was erected.

The Waugh Twins does not claim to be an in-depth biography. It is, rather, their cricketing story from birth until the present with their achievements highlighted, along with lesser known trivia, opinions of their colleagues and detailed, never-before-published statistics. Personally knowing their parents Beverley and Rodger before the twins had broken into Sheffield Shield was a privilege and is the inspiration behind the book.

It is also the story of the rise, fall and rise of Australian cricket from the 'no-hopers' tag in the mid–1980s, when Steve made his rather premature international debut, to their Test championship status in the mid–1990s and the role the Waugh twins—along with Bob Simpson, Allan Border, Shane Warne, David Boon, Mark Taylor, Ian Healy, Geoff Marsh, Craig McDermott, Glenn McGrath et al.—played to bring about this elevation.

Who would have thought in 1984 that in the next decade Steve and Mark Waugh would become household names in the cricketing world by virtue of their performance and sportsmanship, or that they would be internationally ranked as number one and two batsmen in April 1997, and, at the time of writing, among the top six?

Introduction

It was a partnership to cherish; the partnership that destroyed the wall of superiority of the West Indians. For 15 years and 29 Test series they were the undisputed kings of cricket. The spectacular strokeplay of Lloyd, Richards, Greenidge, Haynes and Lara, the tenacity of Kallicharran, Gomes and Logie, and the intimidating pace of Roberts, Holding, Garner, Marshall, Croft and Ambrose had not just defeated their opponents but pulverised them.

However, 3 May 1995 saw the changing of guard at Sabina Park, Kingston. Australia, who had lost their last eight Test series to the Windies since 1978, suddenly staked claims as world champions of Test cricket by defeating them by an innings and regaining the Frank Worrell Trophy 2–1. The heroes of this remarkable victory were the low-key high achievers Steve and Mark Waugh. In reply to the Windies total of 265, Australia amassed 531, thanks to an incandescent 231 runs added by probably the greatest twins the sporting world has seen. On 30 April 1995, Mark knuckled down to score 116 of the best and Steve was unbeaten on 110, playing with an air of invincibility.

Big Curtly Ambrose, with whom Steve had an on-field altercation in the previous Test, bowled only 11 overs that day and his partner-in-pace Winston Benjamin sat weeping during the drinks break and had to be cajoled to continue bowling. Such was the heady domination of the twins from the Sydney suburb of Canterbury Bankstown. Steve continued the next day in the same vein and was unremovable until he hit his maiden Test double century.

Robert Craddock wrote in *Wisden 1996*: 'He [Steve] was last out batting for close on ten hours and 425 balls, more than 150 short-pitched, and had 17 fours, one six and six aching bruises at the end of his greatest innings.' Trailing by 266 runs, the Windies were bowled out for 213 and lost the Test, the series and their world-beating image by one gigantic KO punch. 'It was the pinnacle in the cricketing lives of Steve and Mark Waugh,' added *Wisden*.

In the series, Steve totalled 429 runs at the Bradmanesque average of 107.25 and Mark 240 at 40. No other Australian could average 30 and no West Indian 45. Steve topped both the batting and bowling averages and was the undisputed Man of the Series. This was nothing new for him as he had topped batting and bowling averages (and was the Player of the Series) against South Africa in 1993–94—both at home and away.

Further triumphs awaited the twins in South Africa in 1997, where Steve added 385 winning runs with Greg Blewett in the Johannesburg Test which Australia won by an innings. Not to be sidelined, Mark etched out a masterly 116 in the next Test at Port

Elizabeth which enabled the Aussies to win the series. This victory enhanced the claim that Australia were champs, as *Wisden Cricket Monthly* had only a month previously rated South Africa as the number one nation at Test level. Following this conquest, the Waugh twins were ranked as the two best batsmen in the world by the Coopers & Lybrand rating system. Steve had been ranked number one since his Kingston masterpiece in 1995 and Mark leapfrogged over Brian Lara and England's Alec Stewart after his heroic 116 at Port Elizabeth.

The rise of Steve, which had started at Headingley in 1989 and of Mark in Adelaide in 1991 reached a peak in South Africa in 1997. At 32, Steve was appointed as Australia's vice-captain and as captain of Australia in limited-overs internationals, and he is recognised as the hardest batsman to shift. Internationally known and respected as 'Ice Man', 'Asbestos Fire-Fighter' and 'Rock of Gibraltar', he is there when his country needs him even if this involves him removing all elegant but risky shots from his armoury. 'In 1985 Steve Waugh was Australia's batting Porsche . . . a young thrasher,' wrote Robert Craddock in Sydney's *Daily Telegraph*. 'Now he is a trusty Bentley who might not break speed records but invariably goes the long journey.'

Adds Steve just before playing his 100th Test in 1997: 'If I played the same way I did when I was 20, I wouldn't be playing now. I was flashy and good to watch, but like so many other players who have played that way for Australia, would have been out of the team.'

Mike Coward wrote in *The Australian*: 'The most complete person in the Australian first-class game, [Steve] Waugh has had a profound effect on countless Test, Sheffield Shield, grade, schoolboy, parkland and backyard cricketers. And like Border before him, he is a hero not only to kids but to many of the men who play alongside him under the baggy green cap he considers so sacred.'

Mark is trying hard to be tougher in his approach without divorcing his wristy and at times risky flicks and glances. He is one of the most fluent stroke players Australian cricket has seen since Stan McCabe, Neil Harvey and Greg Chappell. To quote the Indian captain Mohammad Azharuddin, a silken stroke player himself: 'I just love watching Mark Waugh bat. I enjoy it even when he scores runs against us. He is great.' And 1998 has seen the emergence of a new Mark Waugh. He proved that he can now bat all day without loss of concentration or a rush of blood. He showed Border-like doggedness against the South Africans on the kill in Adelaide, and against belligerent Indians in Bangalore, to rescue Australia on each occasion from the brink of disaster.

Despite occasional failures and frustrations, the rise of the Waugh twins continues. Having written, to the best of my knowledge, the first feature article on them in a national magazine in 1984 (published in *Cricketer*, February 1985) before they had even made their Sheffield Shield debut, somehow makes me feel paternal about them. I get traumatised every time a duck walks with them on the TV screen and get vicarious thrills when they lift their bats to acknowledge spectators' cheers as they reach another milestone.

❶ Back to the Future

It all started in an Indian restaurant in George Street, Sydney, on 19 November 1984. That was the day NSW had humbled the mighty Windies (Lloyd, Richards, Greenidge, Garner, the lot) on the SCG, and a dinner was organised that evening by the Cricketers' Club of NSW.

I was surrounded on my table by past, present and future cricket personalities, amongst them a beaming Bob Simpson with his daughter Debbie, Steve Smith, the dashing NSW opener who had scored 33 and 8 in that match, and a tallish, handsomish, youngish man. He appeared elated when he got up to receive the Richie Benaud Award for the Best Under–19 cricketer and I whispered to Debbie: 'He does not look under–19 to me.' 'Shh, he's not Mark Waugh,' she whispered. 'It's his dad accepting on behalf of Mark, who's representing NSW 2nd XI in Melbourne.'

That was the beginning of my friendship with the Waugh family. The years that followed saw the emergence of two world-class cricketers with more records under their belt than Elizabeth Taylor had husbands or Queen Elizabeth has corgis, and of two promising players in younger brothers Dean, 29, and Danny, 22. Danny is the only left-hander in the family and a leg-spinner.

Back to 1984, when people asked 'Mark who?'. The hot lamb curry and pappadams were forgotten as Rodger Waugh talked about his teenage twins, Mark and Steve. Their performances for Combined Schools, NSW colts, Australia Under–19s, NSW 2nd XI and Bankstown in Sydney's first-grade matched the spiciness of the food. Only two batsmen had recorded centuries in the Youth test series against Sri Lanka in 1983. One was Mark Waugh scoring 123 runs as an opener in Adelaide and the other was Steve Waugh who smacked 187 off 216 balls in the final test in Melbourne. Steve topped the batting aggregate and average in the series which was to become a familiar occurrence in the years to come.

A few days later I received a fat envelope from Beverley Waugh, the twins' sports-loving mum and their guiding light. It included clippings from local papers of their achievements. The highlight was Steve Waugh's unbeaten 127 (eight sixes, 10 fours) in 95 minutes for Bankstown v. Sydney University which was described by former Test opener John Dyson as one of the strongest centuries he had seen.

It was nostalgic reliving that November 1984 night when I contacted Rodger after Steve's marvellous 160 in the 1997 Johannesburg Test and Beverley after Mark's series-winning 116 in Port Elizabeth a fortnight later. Both Rodger and Bev were proficient tennis players who made their sons' climb to the top easier by discipline, inspiration and good old-fashioned hard yakka.

Steve (rt.) and Mark Waugh, NSW cricket's star twins.

THRILL is being surrounded by the past, present and future of top class cricket on a dining table.

It was November 19, 1984, the day NSW had humbled the mighty Windies at the S.C.G. A function was held the same night by the Cricketers' Club of N.S.W. at an Indian restaurant.

Sitting opposite me was Steve Smith, the dashing N.S.W. opener. On my right was Debbie Simpson, the daughter of a very happy Bob Simpson and on my left was Roger Waugh.

I can imagine you saying, "Roger who?" But one day he could be as well known as Martin Chappell or Lou Benaud. He appeared elated as he stood up to receive the Richie Benaud trophy on behalf of his son Mark, who was then in Melbourne to represent the N.S.W. second XI.

The hot lamb curry and papadams were forgotten as Roger started talking about Mark, 19, and his twin brother Stephen. Their performances for Combined High School, N.S.W. Colts, Australia under 19s, N.S.W. second XI and for Bankstown in Sydney's first grade cricket, matched the spiciness of the food.

Only two batsmen had scored centuries in last year's Youth Test series for Australia v Sri Lanka. One was Mark Waugh, 123 in the second 'Test' at Adelaide and the other Steve Waugh, 187 in the third and final 'Test' at Melbourne. Australia won the series 2-0, thanks to the all-round contributions of these teenage twins.

Mark's 123 as an opener at Adelaide enabled Australia to declare at 8 for 409. Steve, at No 6, made 55.

In the next 'Test' at Melbourne, Steve turned on a devastating batting display, his 187 coming off only 216 deliveries. In the series he had the best batting aggregate and average. He also took eight wickets and eight catches.

That season was prolific for Steve, hitting four unbeaten tons; 200 in the schoolboy carnival, 170 for N.S.W. Combined High School v Great Public Schools, 161 in a 60-over match for the Australian carnival and 127 for Bankstown-Canterbury v Sydney University in first-grade competition.

This 127 not out at the Sydney University Oval came in 95 minutes and included 8 6's and 10 4's. It was described by Test player John Dyson, as one of the strongest centuries he had seen. With Mark scoring 65, Bankstown declared at 5-236. But Sydney University replied with 8-237 (Steve 3-46, Mark 2-54) to win the match.

Mark, six feet tall, is an opening batsman and a first change bowler. Steve, 5ft 10in, bats at No 4 and opens the Bankstown attack. At the half-way mark of the season Steve was close to the lead in the "Sydney Morning Herald's" grade cricket player of the year award with a string of impressive performances for Bankstown:

  110 and 5-50 v Waverley
  68 and 2-20 v St George
  92 not out and 2-23 v Western Suburbs
  5-40 v Petersham
  4-75 v Balmain
  38 and 6-53 v Sydney

Not to be outdone, Mark shone out with 48 and 47 v Northern Suburbs, 48 and 3-70 v Western Suburbs and 72 v Balmain.

As both are keen fielders, c Waugh b Waugh is a familiar line in Bankstown's first-grade scorebooks.

Season 1984 has so far proved to be a memorable year for the Waugh twins. Steve was made Player of the Series in both Indoor Cricket and Australian Schoolboy Soccer, subsequently selected N.S.W. Sportsman of the Year, and made his debut for NSW against Queensland in Brisbane.

And Mark was recently awarded the Richie Benaud Trophy as the best Poidevan Gray (Under 21) player of 1983-84.

The Waugh family is highly sports-conscious. Their father Roger is an "A" grade tennis player and mother Beverley an "A" grade squash player. Their uncle Dion Bourne had captained Bankstown and was a capable middle-order batsman.

Younger brother Dean, 16, is a lower-grade cricketer with Bankstown and a member of N.S.W. Under-15 team. Youngest brother Daniel, 9, is a left-arm spinner who represents Bankstown's Under 10 Team.

— KERSI MEHER-HOMJI

Cricketer (Aus.) February 1985. (Edited by Ken Piesse.)

'I stayed up till 2.30 a.m. and could not go back to sleep, I was that excited,' said Rodger recalling the 385-run partnership between Steve and Greg Blewett. 'It was the same story when the boys were in the West Indies in 1995. I became a zombie watching them on TV all night. Steve deserves his ranking as the number one batsman in the world. I was disappointed with Brian Lara in Australia [in 1996–97]; he looked vulnerable. And Mark [Waugh] is often unlucky, getting out when on top. Even when it came to selection, the equally gifted Mark missed out for many years. In fact, he had played some 100 first-class matches and scored over 7000 runs before he was picked for Australia, and what a great century he hit off the Pommies on his debut in Adelaide!'

Rodger runs a newsagency in Revesby, a suburb of Sydney. He strongly feels that Dean

Waugh, who played a Sheffield Shield match in 1996 should be in the NSW Mercantile Mutual Cup team on a regular basis. 'He is the hardest hitter of the ball in NSW. Yes, a bigger hitter than Mark and Steve.'

Bev was disappointed that she saw only the last part of Mark's magnificent innings in Port Elizabeth on 17 March 1997. 'I was playing a squash tournament match at the time and finished just in time to see Mark hit his ton then lose his wicket shortly after,' she said.

'As I am involved in sports, I noticed that they had a very good eye-ball co-ordination when barely 18 months old and I said to myself: "Wouldn't it be wonderful if they were to represent Australia in a sport!" All four boys were very similar and mad keen on many sports—cricket, golf, tennis, football, baseball, soccer . . . I think they would have shone out in any sport.'

Bev, who teaches in the Department of Education, explained: 'I work a fair bit with "special" children (mentally and/or physically handicapped) and in dealing with them there are many lessons to learn about life. I made the boys aware of how fortunate they are being healthy, able and fairly bright.' The Waugh twins owe an enormous amount to their sports-loving parents and the next chapter is devoted to them, as also to Dion Bourne, Bev's brother and a gifted cricketer. Between them they set Steve and Mark on the road to fame by example, encouragement and sporting genes.

② A Matter of Genes

Call it sporting heritage or a matter of genes. Beverley and Rodger Waugh were outstanding tennis players, and it was through tennis that they met and fell in love. Rodger, 52, remains a good tennis player at the Masters level. As a teenager he played in the same group as Tony Roche and Allan Stone, and, as a junior, was once ranked among Australia's top ten. In an Australian Under–17 doubles final in Sydney he had a victory over a pair including the great Roche. Despite his obvious talent, promise and performances, doors did not open for Rodger when it came to selection and representation, and lack of money in tennis forced him to take up a career in banking.

Beverley, cricket's most influential mum along with Martha Grace, the mother of E.M., W.G. and G.F. Grace, and Amir Bee, the matriarch of the famous Pakistani brotherhood of Wazir, Raees, Hanif, Mushtaq and Sadiq Mohammad, had defeated Evonne Goolagong-Cawley in a doubles match in tennis when she was 13. Evonne and Bev were together in a coaching clinic at Cowra in NSW, and they came to Sydney at the same time. Bev won the South Australian Under–14 Singles title. At 19 she gave up competitive tennis to concentrate on motherhood and her teaching career. On a typical day she would drop Mark off at her Mum and Dad's place and then Stephen at Rodger's parents' place, go teaching, pick up the babies, and some afternoons also coach tennis (when the boys were a little older).

Later, when 38, she took up squash to keep fit and excelled at competitive level. Starting in F grade at Panania, it did not take her long to reach first grade—the highest level short of joining the pro circuit. Bev competed in World Squash Championship held in Queensland a few years ago and won the Australian Women's 50–55 years age group championship in 1996 and again in 1997. Not bad for a grandmother! She is delighted that her name is on the trophy next to that of the legendary and invincible World Champ of the 1970s, Heather McKay.

Bev and Rodger married when they were 18 and had the twins a year later; Steve four minutes before Mark. The parents observed that the twins had excellent hand-eye-ball skills when barely 18 months old. Rodger was particularly impressed with the way they took catches on the tennis court. 'They were barely four but seldom dropped a catch,' he remembers. 'I couldn't believe it. At that stage I thought to myself that we have some talent here.'

Rodger enjoys telling this story. A visiting friend from Lloyd's of London told Rodger that he intended having a substantial bet with his company about his talented daughter winning the Wimbledon ladies' event one day. That was over 20 years ago when the twins were 10 or 11. 'You've been telling me how promising your twin sons are, how they'll play Test cricket,' the friend said. 'If they're so good why don't you bet on them with Lloyd's that they'll be Test cricketers? You'd get 10,000 to one.'

The odds would have been astronomical had Rodger bet on each hitting ten Test hundreds or on them playing 50 Tests together. But even at 10,000 to one to become Test players, a $100 bet would have made him a millionaire. 'I kick myself for missing the bet of a lifetime,' he remarked.

Not that he ever doubted his sons' potential. When I first met Rodger in 1984, Steve and Mark were 18 and already making names for themselves in first-grade cricket and in Youth tests, but they were still apparently not close to Sheffield Shield contention. Yet he said, without a touch of arrogance, 'The *Sydney Morning Herald* correspondent is always pushing for Mark O'Neill and other youngsters, completely ignoring my lads. But they will go places—sooner than the so-called experts think.'

And go places they did. Within a month, Steve made his Shield debut (Mark followed a year later) and, in December 1985, Steve played in the Melbourne Test against India. Steve took a long time to hit his first Test ton but made up for the delay by hitting two big unbeaten hundreds in successive Tests in England in 1989—at Headingley and Lord's.

Rodger's joy was still incomplete. 'Mark should be in the Australian team. Look at all his big scores for Essex—especially his century against the touring Aussies.' The genie granted Rodger his second wish a couple of seasons later when Mark made his Test debut memorable by scoring a magnificent century against England in Adelaide in January 1991. However, the genie has not yet granted him his third wish. 'Dean [son number 3] should be a regular for NSW in the Mercantile Mutual Cup. He is a terrific hitter of the ball.'

There was sport in the family for both Rodger and Beverley. Rodger's grandfather, Arthur Johnson, was a talented lawn bowler, and his father, Ned, a rugby league player who had represented Country against City. But Rodger's biggest inspiration is his mother Ella. A promising tennis player, Ella contracted poliomyelitis when 18. She was a beautiful girl who loved to dance and swim, but after the polio she was told that she would never be able to dance, swim or play tennis again—or have children. A brave woman, she persevered and did not rest until she walked again. Ella then took up lawn bowls. Even in her eighties, she refuses to use a wheelchair. More pertinent, she defied doctors' orders and had a son, Rodger.

Bev's bloodline in sports is equally impressive. Her father Keith Bourne, a teacher, was a very good club cricketer and tennis player. He remained cool at all times and never spoke badly of anyone. He was patient, never lost his temper and was universally liked. 'I had a really special dad,' Bev recalls. 'He was always there. He always supported me. He might have criticised me a little bit, but only if he thought it was going to help and I knew I was never going to get in trouble. I just felt his kind support and I swore that I would carry that through with my children. And I always told them to try their hardest, that is, how to be proud of yourself.'

Bev's mother Dorothea is one of those fitness-obsessed grannies. She plays tennis regularly, goes for long walks and enjoys life even though approaching 80. She loves to communicate with people of all ages and has a great interest in life.

Dion Bourne was an outstanding first-grade cricketer for Bankstown in Sydney's grade competition. He made his debut, for Manly, in 1959–60 as a 17-year-old and remembers his initial first-grade match was against Test great Norman O'Neill and Tom Brooks (former Test umpire and NSW fast bowler). 'Coincidentally, my debut coincided with Tom's last first-grade match,' Dion recalled. After just one year with Manly, Dion played for 21 seasons with Bankstown. An opening batsman and an inspiring leader, he holds the club's run-scoring record and was unlucky not to represent NSW. His 8149 runs at 28.29 for Bankstown from 1960 to 1981 is still a club record for first-grade. (In all he scored 8243 runs at 28.03 in first-grade matches—including the season with Manly.) He captained Bankstown when they had two of the wildest and fastest bowlers in Australia— Jeff Thomson and Len Pascoe. It was Dion who harnessed their talent in grade cricket which ultimately saw them play for Australia and terrorise opponents with their pace like fire.

Currently, Dion is state selector for NSW and treasurer of Bankstown Cricket Club, and the scoreboard of that club is named after him. Not only that, but Dion shone out at an early age. For Tumut Intermediate High School in the early 1950s, he played an innings that has no parallel. He scored 177 runs out of a total of 179 (that is, 99%) hit off the bat. There were eight ducks, one nought not out and 11 sundries; the other batsman scored 2 runs. The newspaper clipping describing his feat ends with: 'Bourne is an unspoilt lad, proud of his achievements but humble to acknowledge his great talents, a quietly spoken lad who is anxious to learn and advance.' Dion's most prolific seasons for Bankstown were 1971–72, when he scored 800 runs at 40.60, and 1967–68 (752 at 47.00), but his finest achievement was his committed and competitive grooming of Bankstown youngsters.

Although reticent about his own achievements, Dion talked about his nephews. 'When Steve and Mark were 12, I could see talent in them. They were obvious first-grade cricketers even then, no doubt about it. I was very keen for Lennie Pascoe to meet them and help them. Lennie agreed but returned soon, saying, "Look, they can teach me more than I can teach them!"' That was the honest opinion of a (then) current Test cricketer on boys who were not even in their teens. Dion was always worried that some coach might change them and take away or diminish their talent.

'When 16, Steve hit 136 in the third grade,' added Dion. 'It was an exceptional innings. Mark played first-grade before Steve—which many don't know—and scored 98 as an opening batsman in 1981–82. The only reason he did not get his century was that afternoon tea was taken at that score and he was out soon after.

'For success in cricket, you need talent and commitment. Fortunately they had both. They held high value on their wicket, even when young—as they do now. Both are fairly reserved—especially Mark who keeps his thoughts to himself. They don't smoke and are respectful of others. And team-mates have a lot of respect for them. I did not coach them but watched them with interest. With Bev, I encouraged them to take up cricket. Mark could well have become a tennis champ and Steve could have represented Australia in soccer. They were that good. But cricket was the sport we wanted them to take up—it being a team game and character-building.'

Although both the parents and their uncle were behind the emergence of the twins as top cricketers, Bev was the beacon of strength and inspiration. Call her the glue or the rock, but she was the one who completed the jigsaw puzzle when a few pieces went missing.

As Steve Waugh told Mark Gately in *Waugh Declared*: 'I suppose we saw more of Mum and she took us to more of the games, but that was probably because Dad was always coaching tennis at the weekends and playing a lot of tennis himself so Mum sort of had to take a back seat with her tennis career. She probably took us to more sporting events but I'd say they were both equally keen and both gave us a lot of encouragement.'

Mark Waugh added that if Bev started anything she would always finish it. 'Often she trained harder than us, running round the block and going to the gym.'

The best thing Bev has tried to teach her sons is to care about others—especially those less fortunate than themselves. 'You don't need to go and carry on, and make a fuss if things don't go your way,' she told them when they were children. 'Give credit to your opponents if they played better than you. The most important thing you can give your child is your time.'

On very rare occasions, Steve throws his bat or tells a charging Ambrose where to go, and Mark used to get aggressive when bowling. But by and large the twins are role models for youngsters to follow by providing engrossing, entertaining cricket—match in and match out. Bev has no favourite amongst her sons. There was a time when she had to go to four different grounds to see each of them perform. She was exhausted but would not have it any other way.

The twins invited Bev to watch the first three Tests in the Ashes series in England in 1997. The third Test at Old Trafford was a milestone for the Waughs as Steve became the first right-handed Australian to score centuries in both innings in an Ashes Test. Mark scored an elegant 55 in the second innings. More than just scoring, these runs were vital in Australia's winning the Test and subsequently retaining the Ashes.

'It was a huge achievement, quite spectacular,' Bev stated. 'It was a special moment, Stephen batting on in the second innings practically one-handed—due to an injury to one of his hands. It was a dream come true, just to sit and watch.' Her proudest moment came in April 1997 when the twins were ranked numbers one and two in the world. 'Even if they didn't achieve anything else, that would remain a treasured memory.'

To my question as to whether she still feels nervous when they go out to bat in a Test (live or on TV), she replied: 'Not any different now than before. It's exactly the same feeling for any parent. You tell yourself, whatever will be will be, but sometimes, at a crucial moment, for example, on 99, I can become very anxious, almost holding my breath, in anticipation. It seems there is not enough oxygen! I feel exhausted by the end of such a day. Generally, I try to relax and enjoy their cricket because I know that is what the boys would be wanting. The boys are talented but that's just a gift. It's how you use the talents you have that is the thing to be proud of. To see your children—whatever their age—perform, be it ballet, music or sport, you want them to achieve their best. And when they do, it is one of the greatest thrills in life.'

However, Bev's horizons are wide and not restricted to the success of her own boys. She gets some of her biggest sporting kicks not as a cricketing mum or as a squash champion but as a swimming teacher for the Education Department in Sydney. Her message for the handicapped children she helps is never to give up. At first some of them are too scared to even go near the water, but Bev gently persuades them.

'What seems a small achievement to some, like a child swimming one metre, is absolutely huge to that child and to me. You hear kids say, "I can't do this" and it's such an achievement when eventually you hear, "I didn't think I could do it and you told me I could." And I say, "There is no such word as can't. You are just great." Every child must have self-esteem.'

As AAP reporter Doug Conway remarked in the *West Australian*: 'It's Bev Waugh talking but it sounds like Steve Waugh batting.'

③ Teenage Triumphs

Stephen and Mark Waugh arrived in the world after a few false alarms. Beverley went into labour every night at about 1 a.m. for about two weeks. She would pack up her bags and Rodger would panic, but it was another 'maiden over'. Nothing happened until 2 June 1965—their exact due date. The doctor involved was as nervous as everyone else because it was his first time for twin delivery. He considered the event so special that he brought in medical students. Perhaps daunted by the large audience, the low-profile twins refused to 'pad up' and emerged before the doctor and students arrived. A young nurse delivered them and ran around the hospital to show off her first-ever two-in-one package.

'Forget Shane Warne, this was the delivery of the century,' AAP's Doug Conway wrote some years later in the *West Australian*.

'I can still see the clock on the wall: 8.14 and 8.18 on a Wednesday night,' recalled Beverley of the arrival of the twins who together have now scored 28 centuries and over 11,000 runs in 181 Tests. 'I was in labour every night for a week. I remember it as an absolute miracle. People would say, "You poor thing, you've got twins," but I thought I was just absolutely blessed.'

Steve was the 'prettier' of the two with a crop of black hair and visitors thought he was a girl. Mark was almost bald and looked every inch a boy. They grew up as quiet and happy boys; they were slow talkers but fast movers and communicated in their own language. When infants, they called each other 'Mooney' and 'Gooley'. Steve was nicknamed 'My Little Rabbit' by Bev's mother because he used to run fast. He was always the ringleader, the messier and more mischievous of the two. His first sentence included a swear word 'bloody fool truck' when he couldn't manoeuvre his toy truck up the back steps. Mark was more timid and clumsier. Rodger was a disciplinarian and the boys were on the whole well-behaved, but there were exceptions. When practising with a golf ball, Steve swung wildly and broke the window of a neighbour's toilet—with the neighbour in it! Just as well Rodger wasn't at home!

Bev cannot remember their fighting much over toys. This was due to the fact that they received similar gifts or presents they could share. 'Mostly they innovated play-

Holding the future of Australian cricket: Rodger with three-month-old Steve, Beverly with Mark. (*Beverly Waugh*)

things like boxes, saucepans, etc.,' Bev recalls. More than the toys, the twins enjoyed watching sports—any sports—on TV and then playing it out in the backyard.

On odd occasions they did get into mischief, for which they were punished, although at times they were too quick for their mum to catch them. Bev recalls one incident when Steve, about 12, ran around the house to avoid punishment, saying 'You can't catch me!'. But, when taking a flying leap over a chair, he hit his head on Rodger's favourite tennis trophy—a clock. The clock stopped and Steve received the punishment he deserved. Fortunately, the stricter parent was at work and remained unaware of why his clock had mysteriously stopped ticking.

Was it a problem being a twin? Looking back, Steve believes that it was an advantage. As both of them were shy, it was handy to have someone you knew when going away to a new place to play cricket or soccer. 'I suppose you felt a bit safer going away,' he said.

Mark (left) and Steve with their loving great-grandfather Arthur Johnson. (Beverley Waugh)

A hypothetical question: Would Steve and Mark have been as proficient if they were not twins? We shall never know for sure, but with the talent each one has, the answer would probably be 'yes'. However, with both of them equally interested in a wide variety of sports, and living in the same home, they had the opportunity to play together in the backyard all the time—honing each other's skills. This possibly gave them an impetus to excel, and it certainly made them more competitive. To quote Mark Waugh from *Waugh Declared*: 'I suppose being twins has helped. We always had someone to play against. It gave us the competitive edge.'

The twins played baseball, tennis, soccer, golf and cricket at competitive level, shining in each sport. Mark had shown exceptional talent in tennis and Steve had as much talent as a goal-kicker in soccer as he displayed in cricket.

Twins on the beach, Steve on left. (Beverley Waugh)

Nonetheless their first game of cricket in 1972, when they were seven, was a disaster for both. They did not have a coach and were 'managed' by a few mothers who did not know the right pad from the left, and the protector or the 'box' was a complete mystery to them. Their team was shot out for 9—all sundries; Mark being clean-bowled first ball by a full toss. And Steve walked in—pads on the wrong legs and the 'box'o n his knees behind the pads! He remembers this incident as the most embarrassing moment of his life. He blocked the first ball and was bowled by the second.

Alan Dougherty was their first coach (from age 7 to 14) and he remembers the twins as excellent fielders and quick learners. 'If you showed them once, they could do it,' he remembers. He also thought very highly of Mark as a leg-spinner. 'He had good control, bowled a terrific wrong 'un and turned the ball really fast off the pitch,' Dougherty told Gately, author of *Waugh Declared*. 'We didn't have a keeper who could handle him sufficiently to get the full results. He was made to give it up. He could have been as good a leg-spinner as you'd get.' Mark regrets giving away his leg-spin. 'I'm now hopeless with leggies,' he says, and bowls an assortment of medium pace and off-spin.

When they were 10, Dougherty told everyone who would listen that he had two kids who were going to play for Australia. But success did not come instantly to Steve or Mark and they were made to realise that you have to work hard to reach the top. They scored ducks and tons, won awards and tasted failures. Their first award was Slazenger bats (one for each) as weekly winner of the New South Wales Cricket Association—*Sunday Telegraph* Encouragement Award. They were 11 then.

The next year, 1977, they had success in cricket, tennis and soccer, representing NSW at school level in all three sports. They won the Torch Roselands Sports Star Award for leading their Panania Primary School in the Umbro International Schools soccer, overcoming a strong challenge from Cardiff South, Newcastle, and winning 3–1. Steve kicked two of the goals, and Mark the other. Mark captained his school in the State Tennis Carnival when they lost in the final.

Cricket's famous brotherhood in the making: Steve (left), 11, Dean, 7, Danny, 1, and Mark. (*Beverley Waugh*)

The school, captained by Mark and vice-captained by Steve, won the State Cricket Carnival in 1976–77. The highlight was a 150-run partnership by the twins. Another match to remember was a 15-over clash between Panania East Hills and Villawood for Under–14s. Villawood scored 124 at a daunting 8.3 runs per over but Panania passed the score with five overs in hand, Steve smashing an incredible 112.

Steve captained his side in the A.W. Green Shield (Under–16) and so mature was he in his outlook that coach Ian Gill let him run the team. 'Steve had the knowledge to set fields and made his own decisions,' recalled Gill. 'He read the game and made changes accordingly. Only when he was unsure, would he ask me.'

In the 1980–81 season, Steve, 15, amassed more than 1500 runs in Green Shield and grade cricket. The run-spree included five centuries, four of them unbeaten. Not that Mark was a silent partner that season. In a fourth-grade match he scored 124 to Steve's 123.

Ian Jessup of AAP remembers a third-grade match between his team, Macquarie University, and Bankstown in 1981. Macquarie Uni looked confident when they scored 280 runs and the opponents were 3 for 70. Their confidence soared when two 15-year-olds came together. But soon they smashed the ball here, there and everywhere, scoring a century each and winning the game. You guessed correctly. They were Steve and Mark Waugh. Coincidentally, the day Jessup told me the story, Steve (202 not out) and Mark (74, including a massive six out of the ground) added 156 runs for NSW v. Victoria on the North Sydney Oval in October 1997, when the talk of the day was whether players would go on strike for a pay dispute with the Australian Cricket Board.

Their uncle, Dion Bourne, remembers another epic grade match when the twins were in their teens. On the first day of a two-day match between Balmain and Bankstown at Drummoyne Oval, Balmain totalled 210 by tea. During the tea interval Steve announced: 'We'll get those runs by stumps.' Steve Small, the former NSW opener and currently their coach, got out early. Steve Waugh came in at no. 3 and was soon joined by Mark. 'For the last session, Drummoyne Oval rocked to a cyclone at one end and a hurricane at the other,' reported Phil Wilkins in the *Sydney Morning Herald*. The twins raced to 211 in just 108 minutes. 'The best thing I did that day was to get out early,' Small recalled with a smile.

'I have never seen anything like it in grade cricket,' remembers Uncle Dion. 'Their controlled hitting and brilliant running between wickets were a revelation. I was reminded of this partnership when they came together at Sabina Park in Jamaica and shared their double-hundred stand for Australia to beat the West Indies for the Frank Worrell Trophy in 1995.'

With such talent in excess, they did not need formal coaching. Former Test cricketers Len Pascoe and Ian Davis thought the twins could teach them, and not the other way around! They attended Barry Knight's coaching nets on Thursday evenings but that was more to gain confidence than to receive expert advice—and to gorge on McDonald's burgers at the end!

The young Waugh twins scythed through the opposition as a chainsaw runs through tree trunks until they encountered Brad McNamara. He bowled fast and was probably the first bowler they faced who could keep them quiet. Later on they became close friends and Brad was the best man at Steve's wedding in 1991.

Mark (left), 14, with Danny, 5, and Steve. (*Beverley Waugh*)

Steve and Mark enjoyed playing sports anytime—even two sports in a day, or two cricket matches (Under–16 and then grade) on a Saturday. To them, school offered a way to play more sport. What about studies? They did not see the point of going home and studying for two hours when they could be out playing a sport. Why sit at home with their noses in books when there were heavenly abodes like soccer ovals, golf links, tennis courts and cricket pitches? They did, however, do the necessary school work, and with very good results.

They were nothing if not competitive. Even a social game could become a razor's edge. If they were going to have a game of tennis or whatever, they would like to play their best and beat someone. The school reports in their final year were eye-openers. Bev recalls that they read something like this: for Mark, exemplary work always completed, high achiever, well behaved, always punctual, eager to please; for Steve, very good results but at times a little disruptive, sometimes late and laid-back.

For work experience, Mark was positioned as a laboratory assistant at British Paint and Steve had a week's experience at the Picnic Bowling Club as a greenkeeper. Despite a relaxed attitude to studies and occasional wagging, Steve did surprisingly well at the HSC, scoring more than 300 marks out of 500. A slightly jealous—and a bit more studious— Mark could not believe this. 'He copied from me all year,' Mark told Gately. 'I think they got our papers mixed up. It's not that he is dumb but he shouldn't have got more marks than me.'

Seasons 1983 to 1985 were memorable for the twins as success came big and fast. Steve was made Player of the Series in both Indoor Cricket and Australian Schoolboy Soccer and was selected as NSW Sportsman of the Year. Mark was awarded the Richie Benaud Trophy as the Best Poidevin-Gray Shield (Under–21) Player of 1983–84.

Both were selected in the Youth test series for Australia against Sri Lanka in 1983. Mark's century in Adelaide and Steve's 55 (at no. 6) enabled Australia to declare at 8 for

409. At Melbourne in the following test, Steve turned on a devastating batting display, his 187 coming off only 216 deliveries. Before that Australia was in trouble at 4–181, chasing Sri Lanka's total of 356. By the time Steve left the crease Australia was well-placed at 7–470. In the series he also took eight wickets and eight catches.

The 1983–84 season was a prolific one for Steve, who hit four unbeaten flamboyant centuries: 200 in the Schoolboy Carnival, 170 for NSW Combined High School against Great Public Schools, 161 in a 60-over match in the Australian Carnival and 127 for Bankstown v. Sydney University in first-grade. His 127 came in just 95 minutes of awesome high hitting. It included ten fours and eight spectacular sixes. With Mark chipping in with 65, Bankstown declared at 5–236. However, to their disappointment, Sydney Uni replied with 8–237 (Steve 3 for 46, Mark 2 for 54) to win the match.

That season Steve had strings of impressive all-round performances in first grade for Bankstown: 110 and 5–50 v. Waverley, 68 and 2–20 v. St. George, 92 not out and 2–23 v. Western Suburbs, 5–40 v. Petersham, 4–75 v. Balmain and 38 and 6–53 v. Sydney. Not to be outshone, Mark scored 48 and 47 v. Northern Suburbs, 48 and 3–70 v. Western Suburbs and 72 v. Balmain. As both were outstanding fielders, a local paper titled one of their stories as 'c. Waugh b. Waugh'.

NSW selectors could no longer ignore Steve Waugh's all-round ability and picked the 19-year-old for the Sheffield Shield match against Queensland at the Gabba.

In Sharp Contrast

Before proceeding to their forays in first-class cricket, it is timely to show a glimpse of the non-cricketing side of the Waugh twins.

They are not identical, Mark (180 cm in height) is taller and broader than Steve (174 cm). Mark is nicknamed 'Junior' (born four minutes after Steve whose initials are S.R.) and 'Afghan' (the forgotten war/Waugh). Mark enjoys punting on horses and the trots—a love he has inherited from his father Rodger—and owns a few racehorses. However, gambling on cards and in casinos does not interest him.

Steve (Mark, mother Beverley and wife Lynette call him Stephen) is nicknamed 'Drobe' (for wardrobe) and, more recently, 'Tugga' (from tug-of-war). His favourite drink is Southern Comfort and coke. He enjoys movies, music and travelling; his ambition is to see the seven natural wonders of the world.

Mark is a homebody and, when on tour, prefers to stay in the hotel watching television or raiding the mini-bar. Steve is more adventurous and likes to explore—to see new places, meeting interesting people. One of his biggest moments during the 1996 World Cup in the Indian subcontinent was to talk with Mother Teresa. He was totally uplifted. 'I now hold her in even higher esteem than before,' he wrote in his 1996 *World Cup Diary*, a year before she died. A man of compassion—a kind heart ticking within a tough exterior—Steve was moved by the plight of children of leprosy sufferers during the tour of India in 1998. He has pledged support for the uplift of the female children of the unfortunate, stigmatised victims in a village near Calcutta (see Chapter 19).

As teenagers Steve was a better soccer player and Mark was superior in tennis. Mark does not enjoy running and training hard. Steve used to love a mess as a glance at his 'coffin' (cricket bag) would convince any non-believer. Steve is a leader, Mark more of a follower. Steve was selected in Sheffield Shield cricket a year before and in Test matches five years earlier, but Mark was picked in Sydney first-grade ahead of Steve.

Both love food and gobble it fast. 'They're dreadful eaters,' Mark Taylor once said. Steve has learnt to cook well, Mark would rather order takeaways. Mark adores tomato sauce on anything and everything. Steve hates butter and pickles with a passion. Both are 'mechanical morons' with cars and are musically tone-deaf.

Steve is married to Lynette and has a two-year-old daughter Rosalie whose smile makes him feel as if he has scored a double century. He was a shy schoolboy when introduced to Lynette at a school dance and they barely talked for a few minutes, but the chemistry seemed to have worked alright. When the school formal was approaching, Steve rang her and invited her to be his partner. Romance did not bloom straightaway with Lynette hating cricket and Steve determined to play cricket for Australia one day, which looked an outrageous ambition then. But bloom it did and Lynette has been a great influence on Steve who relaxes much more these days and has an improved dress sense. What's more, Lynette no longer hates cricket! The two tied the knot on 16 August 1991 with Brad McNamara as the best man. For this privilege, Brad travelled thousands of miles in four days as he was then a professional cricketer with Oldham in the Lancashire League in England, and in the middle of a Cup final.

Susan Porter, Mark's partner, has made him appreciate the finer things in life apart from bats and bets. 'Sue has been good for me,' Mark says. 'She spoils me a bit but I think I've matured since I met her—in dress sense especially. She is organised and I've grown up quicker than I would have normally . . . She understands that cricket is very important to me and since it's my livelihood I've got to spend a lot of time on it.'

Steve has developed a keen interest in the history of cricket and its lofty traditions. He collects cricketiana and has a room in his home to keep all his cricketing memorabilia; autographed bats, caps, stumps, bails, balls, ties, cigarette cards, etc. Mark tends to fall asleep out of nervousness before going out to bat and is occasionally seen yawning when batting.

Steve is the author of five well-written and unghosted *Tour Diaries*: Ashes 1993, South Africa 1994, the West Indies 1995, World Cup 1996 and Ashes 1997. Mark wrote his first book, *A Year to Remember*, in 1997. Both Steve's Ashes 1997 Diary and Mark's book were launched on the same day, 12 November 1997; Steve's in Sydney, Mark's in Melbourne.

A perfectionist, Steve jots down his mistakes and his modes of dismissal, and is the better player for it. Both are intense on the field but pranksters off it. Steve also has a subtle sense of humour. When *Cricketer* (Australia) magazine asked him what his favourite animal is, he replied with a deadpan expression: 'Merv Hughes'. His good luck charm is a red rag which he carries in his pocket when on a cricket field.

Mark had a habit of drawing little stick men on his thigh pad after scoring a first-class century. The origin of this custom has nothing to do with superstition, explains Mark. When playing for Essex in 1989, a bored Keith Fletcher, the former English captain and later Essex manager, sketched about ten stick men on Mark's thigh-pads. Mark decided to give these stick men some significance and turned them into symbols for centuries. That thigh pad is currently in retirement after almost a decade of hits and runs, but the centuries keep flowing.

4 First-Class Forays

The climb to the top is often paved with crenated rocks and slippery lichen, crawling with dragons and abominable snowmen and—if you are a batsman—ducks, head-high bouncers and Curtly Ambrose. Although Steve and Mark Waugh jumped grades from fifth to first with effortless ease, success in Sheffield Shield was not an overnight hop. Both struggled and were dropped after their initial two matches. Nonetheless, they persevered with their grandma Ella Waugh's never-say-give-up spirit.

Steve's Sheffield Shield debut was promising but in no way sensational. Against Queensland at the Gabba on 7 December 1984, he went in at no. 9, scoring 31 runs in NSW's total of 357, adding 44 runs with Greg Dyer for the ninth wicket. The Queenslanders were bowled out for 315. Steve Waugh, bowling medium pace as first-change bowler, had steady figures of 23–12–34–0.

His next match against Tasmania in Newcastle a month later was rather forgettable. He scored 4 and 2 but took his first Shield—and first-class—wicket, trapping K. Bradshaw lbw for 63. After being dropped against Victoria on the Melbourne Cricket Ground, Steve reappeared against Queensland on the Sydney Cricket Ground. It was another sterile outing for the future star as he made a duck and did not get a bowl on a spinners' paradise. Luckily for Steve, NSW won by an innings and the selectors persevered with the teenage tyro with safe pair of hands and a strong arm for throwing from the boundary.

He did not let the selectors down as he hit a stylish 94 (including a towering six) against the Vics on the SCG. He cut and drove beautifully, added 178 vital runs with Greg Matthews in just under four hours, and later bowled opener Dav Whatmore for 30. NSW again won outright to top the Shield table and qualified to play the final against Queensland with home-ground advantage. Matthews later commented that young Steve had more talent in his little finger than he (Matthews) had in his entire body. Steve's dynamic stroke-play reminded critics of Doug Walters.

The holding of a Shield final between the two best teams was inaugurated the previous season, but the 1984–85 final against Queensland was something special. It was an epic encounter with a thrilling climax. Experts described it as one of the most exciting matches in the 93-year-old history of the competition. Steve was lucky to play in this epic, due to a last minute injury to fast bowler Geoff Lawson. 'It was my luckiest break,' he said. Batting first, Queensland totalled 374, Trevor Hohns at no.7 top-scoring 103 while skipper Allan Border and 'keeper Ray Phillips chipped in with valuable fifties. The visitors' fears of a turning top SCG pitch were ill-founded as speedsters Imran Khan and Dave Gilbert took seven wickets between them while Steve dismissed a well-set Phillips.

NSW fell 56 runs short despite a handy opening stand of 98 by John Dyson and Steve Smith and a well-chiselled 71 by Steve Waugh coming in at no. 8. Imran then showed his class as a world-class speedster by claiming five wickets in the second innings (and nine in the match) and Queensland collapsed for 163. The pitch showed signs of wear and tear and NSW's 220-run target on the fifth day looked difficult. With quickies Carl Rackemann (6–54) and Jeff Thomson (3–81) bowling their hearts out to try to win Queensland its first ever Shield, NSW were on their knees at 6–140. At this stage, Steve Waugh joined a confident Peter Clifford and the two added 33 runs before Steve was caught off Rackemann for 21. It soon became 8–175, with 45 runs still needed for an unlikely win with only rabbits to come. But the rabbits, Bob Holland and Dave Gilbert, stayed with Clifford (83 not out) and the target was reached with the last pair together. Gilbert surprised himself by cover-driving Rackemann for a winning four.

So poignant was the moment that big Carl Rackemann, over 6 feet tall and strong as an ox, was seen sobbing in a corner. He was exhausted and heartbroken. What more could he have done? He had bowled 60.2 overs with barely a bad ball and captured eight wickets.

The final, attended by over 24,000, demonstrated to new boy Steve the toughness of first-class cricket with tension mounting every session and climaxing with a strong man breaking down and weeping. Steve had contributed 92 valuable runs, taken a vital wicket and accepted catches from Greg Ritchie and Glenn Trimble. His 71 and 21 in this match so impressed Bill O'Reilly, Australia's legendary leg-spinner and later a hard-hitting columnist, that he proclaimed: 'This boy has what it takes.'

In the off-season, 1985, the twins sampled English cricket, signing to play with Bolton League club Egerton—Steve as a professional and Mark as an amateur. However, as the rebel South African tour had weakened the Australian side, NSW pace bowler Dave Gilbert, who was playing with Essex as an Esso scholar, was called up to play for Australia. Steve took his place at Essex in the second XI and Mark became the professional with Egerton. Steve started off with 100 from 29 balls for Ilford against Chelmsford. He struck 10 enormous sixes and eight fours in his 112. Phil Wilkins reports of another match that season against Brondesbury when Steve hit a savage 184 not out, including eight sixes, for seven of which the ball was never seen again. Steve's most pleasant memory was recording a double century in a 50-over Under–25 match against Sussex. He was dropped first ball in the slip but did not put a foot wrong from then on. Meanwhile, Mark proved an inspiring professional by completing 1000 runs and 50 wickets that season, and his captain (who happened to be a dentist) crowned his troublesome teeth for nothing as a reward.

Mark made his Sheffield Shield debut against Tasmania at Hobart on 25 October 1985. With regular NSW openers John Dyson and Steve Smith joining the rebel tour to South Africa, Mark Waugh opened with Mark Taylor in both innings and scored 13 and 28. By now a Shield regular, brother Steve went in at no. 5, registered his initial first-class century (107), and added 174 breezy runs with Greg Matthews.

The following match against Victoria at Newcastle was disappointing for both brothers; Mark making 0 and 4, Steve 15 and 11. Steve's one consolation was clean-bowling Dean Jones for 19. Mark was dropped for the next two home matches but Steve played a dashing and unbeaten innings of 119 against South Australia, bowled Glenn Bishop for a duck, caught Peter Sleep and ran out Warwick Darling. This useful all-round performance was noticed by the national selectors and they included him in the squad for the Melbourne

Test in December 1985. He was earmarked for the 12th man spot but last minute injury to Greg Ritchie enabled Steve to make his Test debut.

To play Test cricket for Australia had been Steve's dream ever since he was a boy playing backyard battles with brothers Mark, Dean and Danny. But the reality almost frightened him. To play on the magnificent MCG against legendary stars Sunil Gavaskar, Kapil Dev and Dilip Vengsarkar, with almost 300 Test appearances between them, would unnerve the best. Steve had by then played only eight first-class matches. Like his Shield debut exactly a year previously, his Test bow was unimpressive, with scores of 13 and 5, although his medium pace dismissed the experienced Ravi Shastri and 'keeper Syed Kirmani. The first ball he faced was from Shastri and it turned viciously. Steve feared that his first Test could also be his final one.

Steve's inclusion in the Test team at 20 raised a few eyebrows, but Bill O'Reilly was delighted. 'His promotion to the Test team for Melbourne was a foregone conclusion,' he wrote in the *Sydney Morning Herald*. 'To me he made an instant appeal as Sid Barnes, Arthur Morris and Doug Walters had done the first time I had set eyes on them. [Steve] Waugh is a natural. Success lies ahead of him in large lumps . . . No young Australian has impressed me half as much in recent years as this youngster.'

Inclusion in two Tests against India and then touring New Zealand (where he played all three Tests with moderate success) forced Steve to miss the last six Shield matches including another thrilling final. However, his absence enabled Mark to play the last four Shield matches, batting at no. 6. But it was Mark's medium-pace bowling which kept him in the team. He took 4–130 in the first innings against Queensland in the away game, including the scalps of Test players Robbie Kerr and Kepler Wessels. In the return game, he shared the new ball with Mike Whitney and grabbed four wickets in the match.

The Sheffield Shield final between NSW and Queensland on the SCG was another nerve-tingler. As NSW topped the points table, they gained a double advantage. They played at home and needed only a draw to lift the Shield. In other words, Queensland had to win outright. Surprisingly, they batted slowly in the first innings, skipper Wessels scoring a dour 166 and Glenn Trimble a none-too-spectacular maiden hundred. Queensland declared at 9–436 in 165.4 overs at an unsatisfactory rate of 2.6 runs per over. Whitney was the outstanding bowler with a 6–65 haul and Mark provided admirable support by taking 1–71 off 27 steady overs.

The only hope for the Queenslanders was to bowl out NSW for under 236 and force a follow-on. They were on the way by the time NSW had nosedived to 5–124 and Mark Waugh emerged—yawning with nervousness. Mark O'Neill was sixth out at 149 with NSW still needing 87 to make Queensland bat again. The home team was gasping for breath but Mark Waugh (41) and Greg Dyer (88 not out) added 99 crucial runs for the seventh wicket and NSW reached 294. The dreaded follow-on was avoided. Jeff Thomson, playing his final first-class match, captured three wickets, including Mark's.

With a lead of 142, Queensland went for quick runs and declared at 7–133, setting NSW 276 to win. All NSW had to do now was to play for a draw. It was up to Queensland bowlers to dismiss the home team. Mark made a dogged 21 but NSW were in trouble at 8–254 with nine overs still to go. Murray Bennett and Bob Holland were exceptional spinners but had no pretensions as batsmen, and the Queenslanders had visions of the elusive Sheffield Shield in their boardroom followed by a tickertape parade on the streets of Brisbane. Bennett and Holland, however, had no such vision. They defended for 54 balls, did not score a run but refused to budge. For not losing, NSW retained the

Shield—winning it for the 40th time. The Queenslanders had to wait nine more years before bringing the Sheffield Shield home for the first time.

After a disappointing home season for both the twins in 1986–87, Mark Waugh became the co-winner of the Sheffield Shield Player of the Year Award, with Queensland's Dirk Tezelaar, the following year. In ten first-class matches that season, Mark hit four centuries, scoring 833 runs at 64.07. Steve was less prolific, making 517 at 36.92 with only one hundred.

Mark 'entranced spectators all over the country with his uninhibited stroke-play and brilliant fielding', wrote John MacKinnon in *Wisden 1989*. The highlight of the season was NSW's match against Victoria on the SCG in December 1987 when Steve scored 170 in almost seven hours and Mark a more aggressive 114 not out in barely three hours. This was the first time the twins had both scored centuries in the same first-class innings. In fact, they became the only twins to notch a hundred each in the same innings. Oddly, they were engaged in big partnerships only with other players; the two added an unimpressive 26 runs for the fifth wicket.

The second occasion the twins both recorded hundreds in the same match was in Chelmsford, England, in August 1989 when they played against each other. For the touring Australians, Steve made one and 100 not out. Mark hit 100 not out and 57 for

Mark Waugh is still awaiting a Test call despite his 3000 runs in 1990. (*Rick Smith*)

Essex, but the home team lost by 150 runs. For the Australians, Steve totalled 1030 runs in 16 first-class matches at 64.37, hitting four centuries. For Essex the same season, Mark totalled 1537 runs in 24 matches at 43.91, also making four hundreds.

Back home, Mark enjoyed a run-spree in 1989–90 when he amassed 1009 runs at 77.61, topping batting averages and belting five centuries. His highest score was an unbeaten 198 against Tasmania and he was again voted Sheffield Shield Cricketer of the Year. Yet there was no Test call for him. No wonder the media nicknamed him 'Afghan'— the forgotten war.

The following season, on 20 and 21 December 1990, the twins rewrote history on the WACA ground in Perth in a memorable Shield match. They combined to produce the highest partnership in Australian first-class history. Both recorded unbeaten double hundreds and they added 464 runs—a world record for the fifth wicket in first-class cricket, and the highest for any wicket in Australia. On a pitch with a reputation for bounce and swing, Western Australia's captain Geoff Marsh—currently the Australian coach—sent NSW in to bat. In Terry Alderman, Bruce Reid, Chris Matthews and Ken MacLeay he had the best bowlers to exploit WACA's first-day 'juice'. Marsh was pleased with his decision as NSW tumbled to 4–137, Reid looking particularly dangerous with figures of 3–25 when Steve joined Mark.

Mark had gone in 38 minutes earlier and had not found his rhythm yet. As neither had scored a fifty on the WACA before, both started carefully. Soon, however, they were in top gear, pressing the accelerator pedal to the limit and leaving Marsh questioning the wisdom of his decision. At stumps, NSW was in full command, the scoreboard reading NSW 4–375, Mark Waugh 128 not out, Steve Waugh 112 not out. The twins had added 238 runs in 244 minutes and looked hungry for more.

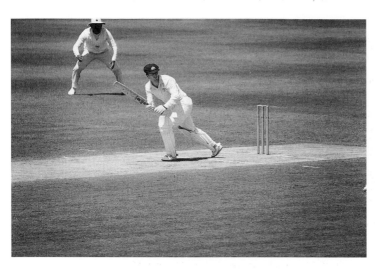

Steve places the ball deftly against the Sri Lankans in Hobart in 1989–90. (*Rick Smith*)

Once they got together, the nasty pitch suddenly looked a paradise for batting. The outfield became lightning fast and the first 50 of the partnership came in even time. The next 50 came in barely half an hour. The run-flow continued the next day. Marsh tried every ruse to slow down the awesome twosome—even asking wicket-keeper Tim Zoehrer to bowl five overs of leg-spin. Nothing worked as the brothers continued their assault on Australia's most feared fast/swing bowlers. Not only did they play without offering a chance, they hardly mishit a ball in seven hours. To quote Greg Growden from the *Sydney Morning Herald*: 'The best bowling attack in Australia was reduced to a gibbering rabble because of the pair's inexhaustible batting talents.'

Many milestones were reached as the Waughs amassed double hundreds. The landmark of 600 and a world record fifth-wicket stand of 464 runs were reached simultaneously. Of the many spectacular shots, Mark's big six off MacLeay, which cleared 15 rows of seats in the pavilion, remains etched in one's mind. The twins' partnership is the 13th highest in the world and the highest in Australia. It was 53rd time that a first-class innings had contained two double centuries, but the first time that brothers were involved.

Geoff Lawson declared at 4–601, to the annoyance of Steve who must have been eyeing the world record partnership of 577 by India's Vijay Hazare (288) and Gul Mahomed (319) for the fourth wicket for Baroda v. Holkar at Baroda in 1946–47. Drenched with sweat as he took off his pads, Steve looked at Lawson, and Mike Whitney remembers him telling his skipper, 'Hell, we could have put on 600'. Mark's 229 had come in 446 minutes off 343 deliveries and he hit 35 fours and a huge six. Steve's 216 took 407 minutes off 339 balls and he belted 24 fours.

'There were so many records happening we didn't know what was what,' said a weary Mark Waugh. 'We didn't know about the record until Michael Bevan, our 12th man, came out and said, "Wait till we get to 600—that's a record".'

Rodney Marsh, the most successful Test wicket-keeper (355 dismissals in 96 Tests) who saw many brilliant batting displays from close quarters, ranks the Waugh batting extravaganza on the WACA as the greatest ever. He opined that their batting display was superior to that of Barry Richards, the masterful South African stroke player, when he scored 325 runs in a single day on the WACA for South Australia v. Western Australia at Perth in 1970–71.

To test his stamina, Lawson threw the new ball to Steve after Whitney's opening over. The home team replied with 314 and 7–475 and the run-rich encounter ended in a draw. It was Mark's third double century of his career—all of them achieved in 1990; the other two for Essex in the English County championship. But it was Steve's maiden double ton.

In his second full season for Essex in 1990, Mark had played 21 matches and scored 2009 runs at 77.26, only second in averages to skipper Graham Gooch, and Essex finished as runners-up. *Wisden 1991* wrote: 'Mark Waugh, with an elegant ease bordering on arrogance, displayed a rich talent, and even when confronted with the pitch giving encouragement to bowlers, he showed an ability to gather runs fluently. He hit eight championship hundreds including double centuries against Gloucestershire and Yorkshire.'

England's captain Gooch added: 'I think he has the potential to be one of the best players of his generation . . . I'll be surprised if he does not end up with a very very good Test record . . . He has been absolute pleasure to play with. He's tried his bollocks off and he's done well for us.' What about Mark's reputation to give away his wicket when well set? Gooch did not think that Mark was 'soft'. 'I think "pure elegance" would be a better way of putting it than saying "casual",' said another Essex colleague, Paul Prichard.

Peter Roebuck, the noted cricket writer and then captain of Somerset, considered Mark one of the best two or three overseas players in county cricket and an undoubted match-winner. 'In England Mark is regarded as a very hungry batsman—hungrier than Dean Jones,' he wrote.

Mark is pleased with his county cricket experience with Essex. Because he played so many games in a short time, it quickened up the process of learning to play the right stroke at the right time. It also taught him to play under pressure, since overseas players are expected to excel and set examples. As he was replacing Allan Border, he realised he had a hard act to follow.

In 1990, Mark scored 3079 runs at 81.02 for Essex and NSW, to become the tenth Australian to amass 3000 runs in first-class cricket in a calendar year. The others were Victor Trumper in 1902, Charles Macartney (1921), Sir Donald Bradman (1930, 1938 and 1948), Arthur Morris (1948), Neil Harvey (1953), Bob Simpson (1961), Bill Lawry (1961 and 1964), Bill Alley (1961—in English country championship matches only) and Mark Taylor (1989). All of Mark Waugh's centuries in 1990 came in the first innings, and his average of 81.02 is the highest in this group apart from Bradman's 112.88 in 1938, 99.78 in 1948 and 97.06 in 1930.

Statistical Landmark—1
Australians Scoring 3000 Runs in a Calendar Year in First-Class Cricket

Batsmen	Year	Runs
V.T. Trumper	1902	3130
C.G. Macartney	1921	3147
D.G. Bradman	1930	4368
D.G. Bradman	1938	3838
D.G. Bradman	1948	3193
A.R. Morris	1948	3011
R.N. Harvey	1953	3506
R.B. Simpson	1961	3081
W.E. Alley	1961	3019
W.M. Lawry	1961	3015
W.M. Lawry	1964	3122
M.A. Taylor	1989	3092
M.E. Waugh	1990	3079

Statistical Landmark—2
Partnerships of More Than 400 Runs by Australians

Runs	For wkt	Batsmen / Match / Venue	Season
464*	5th	M.E. Waugh (229*) & S.R. Waugh (216*), NSW v. WA, Perth	1990–91
462*	4th	D.W. Hookes (306*) & W.B. Phillips (213*), SA v. Tasmania, Adelaide	1986–87
456	1st	W.H. Ponsford (248) & E.R. Mayne (209), Vic v. Qld, Melbourne	1923–24
451	2nd	W.H. Ponsford (266) & D.G. Bradman (244), Aust. v. Eng., The Oval	1934
433	8th	A. Sims (184*) & V.T. Trumper (293), Australian XI v. Canterbury, Christchurch	1913–14
431	1st	M.R. Veletta (150) & G.R. Marsh (355*), WA v. SA, Perth	1989–90
428	6th	M.A. Noble (284) & W.W. Armstrong (172*), Australian XI v. Sussex, Hove	1902
424	4th	I.S. Lee (258) & S.O. Quin (210), Vic. v. Tasmania, Melbourne	1933–34
405	5th	S.G. Barnes (234) & D.G. Bradman (234), Aust. v. Eng., Sydney	1946–47

* = unbroken or not out

Statistical Landmark—3

- Steve and Mark Waugh became the first brothers to score double centuries in the same first-class innings.

- Both recorded their highest score in first-class cricket.

- The total of 601 was the highest by NSW in a Sheffield Shield match against Western Australia.

- It was the highest score by any team playing Western Australia at the WACA.

- The 464-run partnership was the first by two NSW batsmen to go beyond 400. The previous highest was 397 by Warren Bardsley and Charles Kelleway against South Australia at Sydney in December 1920 which was also for the fifth wicket.

- The unbroken quadruple century stand by the Waugh twins is a world record for the fifth wicket in first-class cricket, breaking the previous record of 405 by Sid Barnes (234) and Don Bradman (234) in the second Test against England at Sydney in 1946–47.

⑤ Steve's Struggles

The twins were getting restless, but for contrasting reasons. Steve received a Test call early on but did not really get going until four years later in 1989. As it happens on occasions, after the run feast in England there was a drought back home. Mark kept scoring consistently and prolifically but could not get into the Test team. When he was finally picked for Australia (against England in the Adelaide Test of January 1991), he had scored 7501 runs at 55.15 in 100 first-class matches, with 25 centuries and 33 fifties. He was 25 then but his entry was at the expense of Steve, who was dropped.

Compared with this long apprenticeship Mark had to serve, Steve had entered the Test arena five years earlier and with far fewer credentials. Because of the rebel tour to South Africa there were a few vacant positions and Australia needed an all-rounder. Was Steve thrown to the wolves too soon? Did the sudden promotion help or hinder his development? 'When I was first picked for Australia, I was excited but scared,' he recalls. As described in the previous chapter, he performed moderately in his Test debut but the selectors saw his promise and retained him for the next Test. In fact, he played 42 Tests without a break. Apart from bowlers Kapil Dev and Ravi Shastri, what worried Steve was the interest the media showed in him. The low-profile Bankstown boy was overawed by requests for interviews from print and electronic media.

It was marvellous getting a chance to represent his country. However, as a realist, he felt in retrospect that it would have been better if he had been hardened with a couple of more years in Sheffield Shield. He is grateful to his NSW colleagues Greg Matthews and Dave Gilbert for help and support during his first few traumatic Tests, but others had enough worries on their own plate. Later on, coach Bob Simpson was a big help to Steve, giving him confidence and convincing him that he was good enough at Test level. 'It was obvious from the very start he was somebody special,' said Simpson. 'I can't remember seeing a batsman who hits the ball so hard or sweetly. He is a very rare, even unique talent . . . He has to be in that area of excellence we saw with young Doug Walters and Greg Chappell.'

Bert Sutcliffe, the great New Zealand batsman of 1950s, was also impressed with young Steve. 'He could

Steve is all concentration during the famous Madras (now Chennai) tied Test of 1986. (*Gulu Ezekiel*)

21

It's a TIE! Jubilant Australians immediately after the Test; from left: Steve Waugh, Allan Border, Bruce Reid and Tim Zoehrer. (*Gulu Ezekiel*)

be anything. I've seem them come and go over the last 40 years or so and it is a long time since I've seen anyone so good, so young,' he raved in 1986. 'He has all the patience and application to succeed. There is nothing wrong with Australian cricket that a few young guys like Waugh cannot fix.'

All the same, Steve's performances did not do justice to his talent. In his first eight Tests he averaged only 17.20 with the bat and 31.33 with the ball. He realised that he was not cementing his place and was just hanging on because of good performances in limited-overs matches. But after that his performances started improving at Test level. Against the touring Englishmen in 1986–87, he did reasonably well with 71 in the second Test at Perth, an

unbeaten 79 in the next Test at Adelaide exhibiting crisp driving, and 73 in the final Test at Sydney, including a 98-run stand with Peter Taylor which, to a small extent, contributed to Australia's only Test win in the series. This victory, in his 13th Test, was the first he had tasted and it delighted the seldom-smiling Steve.

Bill O'Reilly was so impressed with Steve's batting in the Perth Test that he was moved to write in the *Sydney Morning Herald*: 'Waugh, going at his best, has a lesson to teach every batsman engaged in this first-class season on either of the two sides. The intriguing power he can deliver to his off-side shots from a firmly planted back foot immediately captures one's imagination . . . His poise on the back foot reminds me nostalgically of Stan McCabe. I never knew a better performer in this area. One would need to be blind to fail to recognise the amazing ball sense of [Steve] Waugh. The speed with which he can swing on to his punching hook shot is almost as eye-catching as the tradesman-like footwork that allows him to come right down and over a square-cut that leaves fielders stranded.'

But always a self-critic and self-analyst, Steve realised that three seventies without a century fell short of his and his admirers' expectations. There were cruel comments about how lucky he was to retain his Test position. Steve's lack of Test tons became an obsession with journalists, although he hit six centuries in 15 matches when playing for Somerset in the English county championship of 1988. He received accolades from Peter Roebuck and others and *Wisden 1989* honoured him as one of its Five Cricketers of the Year.

Then came his most disappointing tour, to Pakistan in September–October 1988. Disasters followed debacles: the death of Pakistan's President; ethnic violence and talks of general elections (which resulted in the cancellation of the first two one-dayers); some dubious umpiring; Australia losing the first Test by an innings and the series 0–1; and, personally for Steve, a measly total of 92 runs at 18.40 in the series. The only saving grace for him was a disciplined 59 in the final tension-filled Test at Lahore.

A bitter controversy erupted on the third day of the first Test in Karachi. Australians felt robbed because of many questionable decisions by umpire Mahboob Shah. They were struggling against the left-arm spin of Iqbal Qasim and, when Steve was given out lbw for nought to make them 5–54, the team and the management exploded. Manager Col Egar, a former Test umpire himself, and coach Bob Simpson, angrily protested to Pakistan Board officials. In a hastily arranged press conference, Egar and Simpson criticised the pitch and challenged the umpire. The Australians felt so strongly about it that there was a possibility of their packing their bags and returning home mid-tour.

Captain Allan Border described the Karachi pitch as the worst he had seen anywhere. 'It would seem like sour grapes after losing the Test, but ultimately someone has to make a stand,' he said. Australians probably had genuine reasons for their rage, but a diplomatic manager such as Alan Crompton would have handled the situation coolly and tactfully. Despite rising temperatures and discontent spreading, the tour went ahead and Australia came close to winning the final Test at Lahore to draw the series. Steve played with composure to register his only fifty, but injury to Bruce Reid thwarted the tourists.

Steve considers this tour as the nadir of his career. It was not just his lack of runs or the tough decisions he got. It was the way people back home criticised the team for their lack of sporting spirit. He was very much cut up by the way the Australian press reported the incidents—especially when Channel 9's *60 Minutes* painted them as a bunch of spoilsports. Steve fumed when Lynette—later his wife—showed him the clippings. 'That's the only time I've seen him angry,' she said.

Steve struggled against India's legendary pace bowler Kapil Dev early in his career. (*The Fairfax Photo Library*)

Australia's struggles continued back home when Clive Lloyd, with his ferocious band of express bowlers Malcolm Marshall, Curtly Ambrose, Courtney Walsh and Patrick Patterson, landed in Australia. So overwhelming was the Windies' superiority that they won the first three Tests by big margins and retained the Frank Worrell Trophy before New Year 1989 was ushered in. One Australian batsman to emerge with credit was Steve Waugh. In the second innings of the Brisbane Test he fought valiantly to score 90 in 250 minutes, hitting nine fours and adding 92 in 115 minutes with Allan Border. In the next Test at Perth, Australia once again looked doomed at 4–167 in reply to the West Indies total of 449 when Steve joined Graeme Wood and added 200 runs for the fifth wicket. So well were they negotiating the Windies pace battery that there were chances of an honourable draw. But once the two W's were dismissed it was a downward slide for Border's boys. Steve again fell in the nervous nineties.

Those narrowly missed hundreds frustrated Steve. The Brisbane pitch was not easy to bat on, and, as he had scored only four in the first innings, he had to score or disappear from the Test scene. He was dropped at 20 and still considers the missed chance as the turning point of his Test career. Steve took this as a good luck charm and attacked with gusto. The stroke that cost him his wicket was the sweetest one he had played all day, but it went straight to Desmond Haynes at cover point.

Steve was more frustrated with the way he fell at 91 in Perth. It was a lazy shot off Ambrose, and 'keeper Jeffrey Dujon was delighted at what landed in his glove. More than these two nineties, what stopped selectors from

Dirk Wellham, the twins' first captain for NSW.

dropping Steve was both his immense value as a limited-overs specialist with ball and bat, and his steadying influence during crises.

Dirk Wellham on the Waughs

Studious, brainy and articulate, Dirk Wellham was the captain of NSW when Steve and Mark Waugh made their Sheffield Shield debuts in the mid–1980s. His assessment:

I have always admired Steve Waugh's talent as an athlete. However, a Test cricketer needs more than ability, and I have enjoyed his capacity to stay calm and isolated away from the game's short-term emotions of stress and fear of failing—most cricketers' main weaknesses. Whenever I played with or against him, he was always a performer and not a talker. In the New South Wales team we had pride that we looked after our own personal game, so that the match outcome would not be as a result of your failure. I never heard him sledge anyone; rather he was ruthlessly quiet. He would always stay in control of the game when he was batting, and I think that's why he has stood up to other internationals' attempts to manipulate the Australian team's stresses in Test cricket confrontation. His photograph from the West Indies, confronting a rampant Curtly Ambrose, provides a terrific summary of the man and his control of emotion and his strength in threatening situations.

Steve's ability not to be distracted from his task is also shown in his batting, which has often recently been dogged and relatively unattractive. At the same time, it is the most effective batting in Test cricket by anyone in the world—a fantastic achievement. Occasionally he has loosened up, so that his great attacking flair is also shown, such as in his wonderful partnership with brother Mark during the SCG Test against South Africa, his 100th, where the twins took control of what had previously been a tough, tense match. It is a fair reflection of his skill, that he has been so single-minded about performing to the best of his ability that he has seemed unconcerned by his appearance as a batsman, sacrificed in the pursuit of runs, victory and power over all other teams.

In his book *Solid Knocks and Second Thoughts*, Wellham wrote in 1988 (which demonstrated what a sound judge of a player he is):

I first met Steve Waugh when he was selected in the Australian Schoolboys' team of 1982. Steve was one talent who always looked the goods. However, it was his twin brother, Mark, who actually appeared the better prospect of the two. The difference was that Steve worked harder at his game.

Steve and Mark are different characters and different types of players. When Steve was first picked to play for NSW against Queensland in 1983 [1984], he was batting 9 or 10. His approach to the game was what impressed me most; he always looked professional, he made no noise and was competitive and dedicated—pretty good ingredients for a future, regular Test cricketer. Steve failed with the bat in his first match for NSW and I could sense, quite naturally, that he was displeased. But he did bowl well, taking a few wickets. The turning point with his batting was a brilliant 60 against Victoria where he revealed immense timing and power—somewhat surprising for such a slightly built man.

Bill O'Reilly, writing in his column for the *Sydney Morning Herald*, rated Waugh an outstanding prospect after his first few games for NSW, and he was proved right.

Such words of praise for a 19-year-old could quite easily have gone to the head of many a cricketer—but not Steve. He was naturally quite pleased with the plaudits, but he was level-headed to boot.

The only Test match in which I played with Steve was the fifth Test in Sydney against England in early 1987. Until that match, Steve had played some 15 Tests [12 to be exact] without being on the winning side. So it was a very relieved and delighted young man who raced off the field at the dismissal of John Emburey by Peter Sleep to give Australia a stunning victory. Steve's bout of depression was over just as it was for the other regulars in the Test team.

Although a potentially magnificent player since making his Test debut in 1985, it is fair to say that Steve's confidence in Test matches had been sapped by Australia's recent poor record. He was playing in a team that wasn't expected to win and consequently that tended to curb much of his brilliance. That last win against England [in Sydney] was an end to all the frustration and a just reward for a fine cricketer.

There is no doubt that Steve is a real pressure player who will continue to develop with experience. I believe he is a better batsman than bowler. His bowling performances will pale into insignificance against the accolades he will receive for his batting.

Steve has developed greatly under Australian coach Bob Simpson. In his former role of NSW coach, Simpson advised Steve to go for his shots and use his talent to the full. The result was a brilliant century against South Australia, which destroyed the attack, including Peter Sleep, who was bowling on a spinner's dream.

As a bowler, Steve's strength is as a very handy change bowler—better than Doug Walters in that regard. Steve bowls straight at the stumps and possesses a good bouncer. He often hits the seam and is capable of catching the batsmen unaware with his gliding pace. Unlike Doug Walters, who was a brilliant striker of the ball off the back foot, Steve is more a front-foot player. He is a more technically correct and disciplined player than Walters. Both players have an enormous amount of natural talent as their common ground.

I feel Steve can become as good as Allan Border over a long-term career and by 1989 should be in the top of world class Test players.

6 Limited-Overs Virtuoso

Australian cricket was at a low ebb in the late 1970s and 1980s. First the Packer revolution, then the simultaneous retirement of Dennis Lillee, Greg Chappell and Rodney Marsh, and finally the rebel tours to South Africa, had clipped Australia's wings. By 1989 Australia had lost to just about every country: the West Indies, England, Pakistan, New Zealand and India. So low was Australia's morale that few expected them to make the semi-final of the 1987 World Cup in the Indian subcontinent—let alone win it. Channel 9 ignored the event, considering Australia as rank outsiders.

However, just one victory, by one run, over India in Bombay (now Mumbai) in the Cup opener, changed everything. The man behind this fairytale morale-booster was Steve Waugh. Australia scored 6–268 in the allotted 50 overs, but at lunch break the score was adjusted to 270 when it was agreed that Dean Jones had hit a six and not a four.

As Australia won by a single run, the lunchtime adjustment very sportingly agreed upon by the Indian captain Kapil Dev, made all the difference. Still, the match was heading for an easy Indian victory when they needed only 15 runs in the last four overs with four wickets intact. However, two were run-out and, in the heart-stopping final over, India needed six runs with the last man, Maninder Singh, on strike. The bowler chosen for the final over was 'Ice-Man' Steve Waugh. He conceded two runs from each of the first two balls, but bowled the bearded Maninder off the fifth. This splendid win was a big confidence-booster for Australia, reckoned Steve. The team partied all night as if they had already won the World Cup. For the first time they had the self-belief that they could lift the World Cup.

Their next match against New Zealand at Indore was almost an action replay of the Bombay thriller. Steve bowled another pressure-cooker final over when the Kiwis needed seven runs with four wickets in hand. Their master batsman, Martin Crowe, was in full flight, having blitzed 58 runs off 46 balls, but Steve dismissed him first ball—caught at deep cover by Geoff Marsh. The next ball was a yorker which bowled wicket-keeper Ian Smith, and Steve was on a hat-trick. He ran out Martin Snedden and Australia won their second cliffhanger by three runs.

By winning five of the six preliminary games—losing only to

Mike Whitney credits Steve Waugh for his most outstanding Test figures by encouraging him to bowl 'Irish'. (*Mike Whitney*)

India in the return match at Delhi—Australia qualified to meet an over-confident Pakistan in the semi-final at Lahore. Pakistan was expected to win, which made it easier for Australia because they were under no pressure. An unwise and cocky prediction by former Test great Zaheer Abbas brought the best out of Australia. He stated that the Australians were no better than a schoolboy side. Stung by this insult, Border's men were determined more than ever to win. 'When Zaheer Abbas called us a bunch of club cricketers, I knew we would be sparkling. Our boys take a fancy to that type of talk,' commented Border.

'We knew that we were a chance,' recalls Steve. 'No-one fancied us but I really thought we were going to win. It was just a great team atmosphere.' Australia scored 8–267 in 50 overs, David Boon top-scoring with 65. Steve's unbeaten 32 included 18 off one over from Saleem Jaffer beginning with a six over long-on. Although Pakistan sizzled at the start with 70 quick runs from Javed Miandad, they fell 18 runs short—Craig McDermott snatching 5–44.

Now to the final at Calcutta, watched by over 70,000 (one estimate says 90,000) against old foe England. As England had defeated India in the other semi-final, most of the 70,000 (or 90,000) present supported Australia. With Boon again top-scoring, Australia totalled 253. England's reply was a nail-biter. Channel 9 will forever regret not fully televising this epic final. After McDermott clean-bowled Tim Robinson for a duck off his fourth delivery, Graham Gooch, Bill Athey, Mike Gatting and Allan Lamb scored at will. Just then Athey was run-out by a throw from Steve, who also bowled Lamb in the 47th over. Earlier, Gatting was caught behind off Border, going for a suicidal reverse sweep.

Philip De Freitas gave England some hope by belting McDermott for 14 runs (4, 6, 4) in the 48th over, but Steve conceded only two runs in the 49th over and had danger man De Freitas caught. That left England a daunting task of scoring 17 runs in the final over from McDermott. He allowed only nine and Australia won another thriller and, with it, their first World Cup.

It would have been a different story had Gatting not gone in for the reverse-sweep shot or if Waugh had not dismissed De Freitas when he was on the kill. In bowling, batting and fielding, Steve was one of the chief contributors to Australia's surprising but well-merited victory. He scored 167 runs at 55.66 and took 11 crucial wickets at 26.67.

'I like to bowl the last few overs . . . Bowling-wise, I never feel under too much pressure,' Steve recalled. 'I'm not the world's greatest bowler but if it gets down to the last couple of overs, I'll back myself against any batsman.'

According to Greg Matthews, 'Steve carried the Australian side during the 1987 World Cup. The resurgence of the team as a one-day side dates back to him.' Phil Wilkins concurred: 'In the environment of limited-overs cricket, Steve Waugh is more than a batsman. He is an all-rounder whose confidence in his medium-paced bowling extends to an enjoyment of competing against the destructive force that is Ian Botham.'

Whitney after gaining another Test victim with his reverse or 'Irish' swing. 'Although very competitive, the Waughs would never cheat,' Whitney said. (*Mike Whitney*)

Mike Whitney on the Waughs

Former Test cricketer and current Channel 7 (Sydney) television personality, Mike Whitney played with both Steve and Mark for NSW and Australia. His assessment:

Easily Steve and Mark Waugh are two of the most gifted cricketers I have laid my eyes on. They are both natural cricketers and persons although their physical skills and mental make-ups are vastly different. I think of them as genuine all-rounders.

Much is said about their batting but they were in the top echelon in bowling as well. Often we bowled together, so I know. In his early days Mark was pacey, believe me. In a Sheffield Shield match against Queensland in Brisbane his speed and bounce frightened a few guys.

Not many know, but Steve contributed to my most important Test performance; 7–89 against the West Indies at Adelaide in 1989. In the nets a day before the game, I was bowling with an old ball and moving it in the air just a little from the right-handers, with what we call 'Irish' or reverse swing. Steve told me that if I bowled like that in the Test, keeping line and length, middle-leg and 'Irish', I'd get wickets. And I did. It was such a turning point in my career thanks to Steve's advice.

Steve is my favourite cricketer, even his defensive shots are a treat to watch and an object lesson for all budding batsmen, mate. His back foot remains anchored just inside and parallel to the crease, his bat close to the front foot and parallel to his back-foot thigh. It epitomises technical and visual perfection.

Mark is one of the best technicians I've seen. I enjoy watching him; even a low score of 15 from him will include two sparkling fours. He has natural reflexes when batting and fielding. He also has unbelievable ball skill, running out an unsuspecting batsman by just flicking back a defensive prod to the wicket-keeper. He is the best slip fielder I've seen.

As cricketers they are positive in all they do, but as persons they are very different. Junior [Mark] is laid-back and quiet, Tugga [Steve] loves challenges, having had to prove his ability time and again. The extrovert side of Steve is on the field. He has a wicked sense of humour, he once put prawns in Tim May's cricket bag during a Sydney Test against India. The pong a week later was beyond belief, mate.

Mark is often in a world of his own and is passionately fond of horseracing. There's a TV in the dressing room at the SCG and it is forever on Sky Channel, the horseracing network. The twins are very protective of each other. Once Mark got out after playing a reckless shot and I spat out: 'What a bloody stupid way to go.' Sitting next to me was Steve who roared at me, 'Hey, don't you bag him. You never complain when he plays those shots and they go for four.' He later apologised for flying off the handle and said, 'You've got to understand that we're very close.'

One of the greatest days of my life was to see them put on 464 runs against Western Australia in 1990. I just sat and cheered at this Bradman-like mastery; not a false shot between them. As I have totalled only 415 runs in my entire career spanning 14 years, you can understand my admiration.

I feel honoured to have played with the Waughs. They are very special persons and play the way cricket is meant to be played—properly, aggressively and fairly. Although they are very competitive, they would never cheat.

7 Hurrah Headingley

Despite his successes in limited-overs cricket, Steve Waugh had yet to establish himself at Test level. After playing 26 consecutive Tests, he had not scored a century despite making ten fifties. This changed dramatically on the triumphant Ashes tour of 1989.

He had earlier experienced English wickets and conditions when he played for Essex second XI in 1983 and for Somerset in 1987 and 1988. Somerset was then recovering from a bitter conflict with superstars Ian Botham, Vivian Richards and Joel Garner. Their overseas professional for 1987 was New Zealand great Martin Crowe. However, after two early centuries, the next season he developed back trouble involving stress fractures of the spine which ruled him out for the entire season.

Steve was then playing as a professional in the Birmingham and District League in Smethwick. Somerset summoned him in desperation and Steve came to their rescue in a dramatic 'stranger than fiction' match. He drove to Southampton and arrived just before lunch in the match against Hampshire when Somerset was reeling at 4–64. He went in at no. 7 and scored an unbeaten 115 (nine fours and a six) in the team score of 308. He also took three catches in Hampshire's first innings of 156 and was an overnight hero.

He had to leave Somerset in mid-August to prepare for Australia's tour of Pakistan, but by then he had scored 1286 runs at 80.37 in 14 matches, topping the averages for Somerset, and was the only player to reach 1000 runs. In all first-class matches, he was second in the national batting average and hit six centuries. Just as he had started with an unbeaten hundred, he signed off with 83 and 112 not out in his final match against Middlesex. 'Not even Crowe or Richards had achieved such a level of consistency,' wrote *Wisden 1989*.

'The players still talk about him,' recalls Peter Roebuck, his captain. 'He was very highly regarded as a cricketer and a team-mate. He didn't say much, but when he spoke people listened. There were things that were not very obvious to me at the time and he would spot them very quickly . . . Give him a situation and he'd react to it.' Roebuck remembers an unfinished partnership of 179 runs in 43 overs he had with Steve, both scoring unbeaten hundreds. He also recalls with admiration a Steve Waugh masterpiece the previous season against the West Indies fast bowler Sylvester Clarke on a green, bouncy and nasty pitch.

Thus Steve had more than a nodding acquaintance with English conditions and looked forward to the Ashes series in England in 1989. The series established him as a Test batsman when he not only hit the elusive hundreds but also finished with a century average. Prior to the first Test at Headingley, Leeds, his form was patchy with only two fifties against the counties and not one in the three Texaco Trophy one-dayers. However, his consistent batting and steady bowling in those one-day-internationals had earned him the Man of the Series award.

The real Steve Waugh stood up at Headingley and fulfilled all he had promised for so many years and not quite achieved. To quote John Callaghan from *Wisden 1990*: 'Wearing a cap instead of the familiar helmet, Waugh reminded many spectators of a bygone age, despatching the ball stylishly through the gaps and timing his forcing strokes so well that he brought an effortless quality to the proceedings.' His majestic and unbeaten 177 came in 309 minutes off 242 balls and included 24 fours, most of them driven on the back foot to the off—his signature tune which he has all but given up these days for the sake of scoring consistently.

'I went in with a positive attitude and had a bit of luck early in that innings,' Steve recalled. 'From there my confidence just grew. I was a different player after that innings.' Whatever doubts he had about his being Test-class disappeared after that mighty hundred. It seemed as if there was a magnet in the middle of his bat and the 'iron-coated' ball was attracted to it. After his fifty, he made a special effort to convert it to a ton. As he approached the magical three figures he thought of the two nineties against the Windies a few months ago. His mind was in turmoil. 'I had no saliva. I thought if I don't get it [a century] now, I'm going to collapse.' When he did reach his hundred he was so ecstatic that he forgot what he had wanted to do when he got his first Test ton: to kiss his bat. Australia declared at 7–601 and won the Test by 210 runs.

Steve continued in the same vein in the next Test at Lord's, stroking a masterly unbeaten 152 from 249 balls and hitting 17 fours. Batting at no. 6, he looked after the tail so well that the last four wickets added 263 runs. Number 10 batsman, Geoff Lawson, contributed his Test best of 74 and added 130 runs for the ninth wicket with the ever-vigilant Steve. This Lord's hundred was a dream come true for Steve and the English press gave him the full treatment with sometimes punny headlines: 'Declaration of Waugh', 'Post-Waugh Depression', 'The New Aussie Ace', 'The New Don Bradman'.

A no-frills realist, Steve only smiled when compared to Sir Donald. 'They were writing me up as the next Bradman but that's bull,' he said. Steve continued to scintillate in subsequent matches as Australia won the six-Test series 4–0. He scored 506 runs at a Bradmanesque average of 126.50, after averaging an incredible 393.00 midway through. In the fourth Test at Old Trafford, Manchester, he top-scored with 92 but failed to score in the next Test at Trent Bridge, Nottingham.

As he wrote in the Foreword of my earlier book, *Out For A Duck*: 'A duck is a leveller. After two unbeaten hundreds at Headingley and Lord's and a 92 at Old Trafford, I started my innings in the Trent Bridge Test with confidence. Any why not? The score was 4–543 when I went in and my series average a hot 242.50. But soon I was back in the dressing room—c. Gower b. Malcolm for a duck.'

Just as well that Steve has that occasional philosophical streak. He soon realised how fickle fame can be. Sixteen months and ten Tests later, he was unceremoniously omitted from the Australian team.

Statistical Landmark

Steve's Unique Record

After the first three Tests in England in 1989, Steve averaged an awe-inspiring 393.00. Is this a record? It is, as shown below:

Averages of Batsmen After First Three Tests in a Series
(Average of 140.00 or more)

Batsman	Series	Batting average
S.R. Waugh	Aus. v. Eng. 1989	393.00
R.J. Shastri	Ind. v. Aus. 1986–87	231.00
S.R. Waugh	Aus. v. N.Z. 1993–94	216.00
Zaheer Abbas	Pak. v. Ind. 1978–79	194.33
G.S. Sobers	W.I. v. Pak. 1957–58	183.00
B. Sutcliffe	N.Z. v. Ind. 1955–56	164.66
Javed Miandad	Pak. v. S.L. 1985–86	153.00
D.G. Bradman	Aus. v. Ind. 1947–48	152.33
E.D. Weekes	W.I. v. Ind. 1948–49	146.25
J.V. Coney	N.Z. v. Aus. 1985–86	146.00
D.G. Bradman	Aus. v. Eng. 1930	145.60
E.H. Hendren	Eng. v. W.I. 1929–30	144.25
S.M. Gavaskar	Ind. v. W.I. 1970–71	143.33
S.M. Gavaskar	Ind. v. W.I. 1978–79	141.75

England's Graham Gooch holds the record of scoring most runs in the first three Tests of a series: 752 runs at 125.33 v. India in 1990. Next best is Don Bradman's 728 runs at 145.60 for Australia v. England in 1930. Everton Weekes (1948–49) is the only cricketer to hit four centuries in the first three Tests. In the two-Test series against India in 1996–97, Sri Lanka's Sanath Jayasuriya scored 571 at 190.33. And in the two-Test series *v.* Sri Lanka in 1995–96, Steve Waugh scored 362 runs at 362.00.

8 Come In, Junior

It was the paradox that intrigued Steve Waugh and his supporters. He was a national hero in July 1989, at one stage averaging almost 400 in a series and a 'new Don Bradman'. In January 1991, he was dropped from the Test team. Not that he had completely lost his form in the ten Tests following the tickertape parade to mark the 1989 Ashes triumph. In the two Tests against Sri Lanka he hit 60 and 57 in Brisbane and an unbeaten 134 in the inaugural Hobart Test, to average 89.00 in the series.

After that he had a poor series against the Pakistan speed quartet of Wasim Akram, Waqar Younis, Aaqib Javed and Imran Khan, with just 44 runs in three Tests at 11.00. Then followed a disappointing one-off Test at Wellington which Australia lost and to which Steve contributed 25 and 25. As an anti-climax, the hero of Headingley and Lord's was dumped from the Test team. He had struggled in the first two Tests against England but looked in fine touch in the next Test in Sydney where he made a confident 48. However, he fell cheaply in the second innings and half expected the axe, especially after his inability to bowl due to stress fractures in his lower back.

'That's it, I'm going to be dropped,' he told himself after he was caught behind off a careless stroke. However, when he was actually dropped he was devastated. In retrospect he reckons that his exclusion could be attributed to his batting at no. 6 in over 100 one-dayers. 'I couldn't seem to get a decent opportunity in the shortened game and was continuously sacrificing my technique (and often my innings) trying to score as quickly as possible. The limited-overs game really is made for the top three or four batsmen in the order.' His depression lifted somewhat when he heard that his place was taken by Junior—his twin brother Mark. In fact, it was Steve who broke the news to his family.

He came round to his parents' home and told Mark, 'Congratulations, you're in the Test team.' Mark: 'Oh what, the Test team! Great! Who got dropped?' When Steve answered, there was stunned silence. After a while Mark said, 'Oh, bad luck.' Silence again broken by Steve who mumbled, 'Don't worry about it.'

No-one quite knew what to say. Beverley congratulated Mark but could not say much. Steve was the one who kept talking. It was a poignant moment of mixed and unrehearsed drama when emotions ran riot.

Mark later elaborated. 'It was a hard situation because I took Stephen's place. Naturally you have feelings for your family. Mum and Dad were obviously upset for Stephen and happy for me, so it was bit of a tricky situation. But once I got over that I knew I had to do the job for myself and the team. I had waited so long to get a chance and wanted to make the most of it.'

What followed the next week was something out of Boys' Own fiction. After waiting five years in the wings while Steve played 42 Tests, Mark achieved in his first Test what Steve had in his 27th Test. The confident debutant scored a magnificent century. In describing Mark's batting, John Thicknesse raved in *Wisden 1992*: 'He produced an innings which a batsman of any generation would have been overjoyed to play any time in his career, let alone in a first Test appearance and in a situation which verged on crisis.'

When Junior stepped in about an hour after lunch on the opening day, Phillip De Freitas had sent back Allan Border and Dean Jones in four balls and the score was 4–104. It became 5 –124 when a well-set David Boon (49) fell to speedster Devon Malcolm. Mark did not have time to be nervous. If he was, he did not show it. He started off with a flowing Greg Chappell-like drive for three off his second ball. He reached his 50 in 74 balls and his 100 in 126. His footwork and stroke play were dazzling and he added 171 runs with his NSW team-mate Greg Matthews for the sixth wicket. With fours flowing from his bat after tea, he scored 95 runs in the final session as partner Matthews watched, clapped, backed up and marvelled from the bowler's end.

Come in 'Junior'—all set for another ton. (*UPPA/Australian Picture Library*)

Mark was dismissed the next morning—Australia Day—for a bewitching 138. He became the 15th Australian and 54th cricketer to notch a century in his Test debut. He remembers the encouragement he had received from England's Robin Smith, who said on his arrival: 'Now's the time to release the handbrake, champ.' Coming from an opponent, it was very inspiring. He played his natural game and got on top of bowlers on an easy pitch. He did experience some initial difficulty against left-arm spinner Phil Tufnell but soon went on the attack, smashing him for five fours in 11 balls. 'It was an incredibly impressive first Test innings,' wrote Henry Blofeld in *The Weekend Australian*: 'One can pay him no greater compliment than to say that he made the art of batting incredibly easy.'

Lightning struck again in the final Test against the West Indies at St John's, Antigua, three months later. Although Mark did not score prolifically in the first four Tests, 'he looked a class cricketer through and through', wrote West Indies cricket critic Tony Cozier. Mark kept the adrenaline flowing in the final Test which Australia won by 157 runs. He hit an adventurous 139 not out with three sixes and 11 fours and added 187 for the fifth wicket with Dean Jones in 163 twinkling minutes. This was achieved against a four-pronged pace-attack of Curtly Ambrose, Patrick Patterson, Malcolm Marshall and Courtney Walsh. The only chance Mark offered was when he was 97, a sharp caught-and-bowled off skipper Vivian Richards.

It is interesting to find out which of the two centuries Junior ranks higher, his debut 138 in Adelaide or his unbeaten 139 in Antigua. As the Windies had an intimidating battery of pace, he considers the Antigua ton as much harder. 'But being my first Test, I thought my innings against England was a better innings,' he said.

Mark had played many risky shots in Antigua and a fair bit of luck was involved. Technically, his Adelaide innings was superior; it was not only chanceless but also faultless. However, as Australia had only drawn the Adelaide Test but had defeated the then world champions at Antigua, Mark—forever a team man—has happier memory of the Caribbean ground.

As Mark Waugh was going full-steam ahead in his belated Test career, much like a genie released from a bottle after some 3000 years, Steve—one of the architects of Reliance World Cup win in 1987 and the regaining of the Ashes in 1989—was trying desperately hard to reconstruct his Test career. A stoic introvert, Steve took his disappointment on the chin. The support shown by his family, friends, team-mates and fans was a solace to him and his wife Lynette. He pressed on regardless at grade and Sheffield Shield levels and refused to take on his brother's 'Afghan' mantle. A back injury, which hindered his bowling, further frustrated him.

To his relief, Steve was picked in the squad to tour the Caribbean in 1991 where he played in all five limited-overs internationals which Australia won 4–1, scored an unbeaten 96 against West Indies Cricket Board President XI, and was included in the third and fourth Tests at Port-of-Spain in Trinidad and Bridgetown in Barbados.

The Port-of-Spain Test is unique as Steve and Mark played together. They were the first—and so far are the only—twins to play together in a Test for men. It may be added that twin sisters Elizabeth and Rosemary Signal had played for New Zealand against England in the first Test at Headingley, Leeds, in July 1984. The Signals were not successful, totalling nine runs between them in four innings and bowling nine overs without taking a wicket. Nor did the Waughs set Trinidad on fire. They added 58 runs for the sixth wicket, Mark scoring 64 and Steve 26. Australia took a 67-run lead but unseasonal rain restricted play and the Waughs did not bat in the second innings.

What were their emotions when Steve joined Mark in the middle during that Test? In two words, nothing special. They had played too many backyard battles, under-age competitions, grade matches and Shield games with each other to make a song and dance of this Test togetherness. All Steve wanted to do was to cement his place in the Australian team and help his country to win.

In the following Test at Bridgetown, Australia lost by 343 runs despite leading by 15 runs in the first innings. Gordon Greenidge's 226 in the second innings annihilated the Aussies. Between them the Waughs could total only 29, and Steve was dropped again.

Mark blazed in glory in the final Test at Antigua, but encountered problems against the visiting Indians in 1991–92. He always looked in fine touch but just could not get runs; only 83 at 13.83 in four Tests. On the Adelaide Oval, the scene of his triumph exactly a year ago, Mark made 15 and 0 and was dropped for the final Test at Perth. At the time of writing (August 1998), the Perth Test of 1992 remains Australia's only Test without at least one Waugh brother since December 1985.

Misfortune comes in five ('Panchvati'), says an Indian superstition and Mark tasted all five within five months. In a thrilling, topsy-turvy Test at Colombo in Sri Lanka, Australia was 291 runs behind Sri Lanka's first innings but won by 16 runs, thanks to Shane Warne's 3–11 blitz in 5.1 overs on the final day. Mark was back in the Australian team and scored a valuable 56 in the second innings. That was when his luck really ran out. In the subsequent two Tests he scored 0 and 0, 0 and 0—a pair of pairs. Enough to send a man into a state of acute depression or self doubt. On the positive side, failure of this magnitude would reassure lesser batsmen that such disasters can happen in the best circles and that there is life after ducks.

'Four ducks . . . you can't imagine it can you?' he later wrote in *Inside Edge* magazine. 'I know I just didn't think it was happening at the time. I knew my concentration was gone when I was bowled for the third duck off an inside edge by a ball I thought was a no-ball. I could hear myself saying, "it doesn't matter, it's a no-ball" as I was hitting the shot. What I imagined as a no-ball call halfway down the wicket was actually the bowler grunting. I was out . . . I couldn't believe it.' Steve was then in the USA and Lynette remembers his waking up one night and saying that he dreamt that Mark had made a pair in Sri Lanka. Next day Mark did.

Fortunately, Mark left his jinx behind him in Sri Lanka and the new season was less traumatic for the twins. Back together, they played against the West Indians and each registered a hundred. Mark started off the season with an unbeaten double hundred for NSW against the tourists. It was the first-ever double century by a New South Wales man against the Windies.

Still, he was a worried man as he faced his first ball in the first Test at Brisbane. He desperately wanted to score a run after four successive noughts in his last two Tests in Sri Lanka. He broke the sequence to make 39 and 66, then returned to his best form with 112 in the Melbourne Test which Australia won—thanks to Shane Warne's deadly spell of 7–52 on the final day. Mark and Allan Border had contributed handsomely by putting on 204 runs for the fifth wicket.

Steve was again playing for his cricket life in the third Test at Sydney. He had scored only 10, 20, 38 and one in the previous Test innings, and one more failure could have seen him relegated to the Shield circuit. The memory of the Sydney Test two years ago where he got the axe was still haunting him. He concentrated to his utmost and worked diligently for four and half hours to score his fourth Test century, which included only five fours. He added 94 runs with Mark before the latter was run out for 57. This was not the first time one of the twins had run out the other, nor was it the last. Anyway, their father Rodger considers Steve's 100 in this Test as one of the best innings he has seen from Steve.

Everything in this Test paled into insignificance compared with Brian Lara's fantabulous 277. That was the work of a maestro, even granting the easy-paced pitch. The rain-affected Sydney Test was drawn and Australia was one-up in the series. On the fourth and final day in Adelaide, Australia needed a mere 186 runs to win the Test, the series and, with it, the Frank Worrell Trophy—regardless of what happened in the final Test in Perth.

But things went wrong, woefully wrong, for the Australians. They lost both the openers for 16, then the Waugh twins failed and Australia was 8–102 and staring at defeat. Test debutant Justin Langer (54) at no. 3 played a lone hand until he was ninth out at 144. Then came the biggest twist of the fluctuating Test. The last pair of Tim May (42 not out) and Craig McDermott (18) added 40 gallant runs. But with just two runs needed for a win to clinch the series, McDermott gloved a catch to Junior Murray off a Courtney Walsh bouncer to lose the Test by one run. It was the first time a Test had been lost by this narrowest of margins, and it left the series locked one-all.

Shattered and demoralised by this wafer-thin loss, the Australians capitulated in the following Test at Perth—losing by an innings in two and half days. In the last two heart-wrenching Tests for the home team, Curtly Ambrose captured 19 scalps and Border and the two Waughs between them recorded four ducks. Australia rued not getting those two runs in Adelaide which would have given them a series win against the Windies for the first time in 17 years.

9 In Top Gear

In more ways than one, the 1993 tour to England was an action replay of the 1989 Ashes series. Prior to both visits, Australia had plenty to forget. In 1989 it was the humiliating defeats by the West Indies and Pakistan. In 1993 it hurt even more because the Australians were superior to the Windies for all but the last few days, yet lost. On both these Ashes tours, the Australians rejuvenated themselves and returned home winners.

Steve and Mark Waugh were the batting successes in a team full of prolific scorers, namely David Boon, Mark Taylor, Allan Border and the new sensation Michael Slater. Steve topped the Test batting averages at 83.20 and Mark Waugh—on his first official tour to England—was second on aggregates; 550 runs at 61.11. Only Boon, with whom Mark had five century partnerships in the first five Tests, scored more runs; 555.

It was success and more success for the rampaging Aussies who won the Texaco Trophy for limited-overs matches 3–0 and the Test series 4–1. Mark 'Junior' Waugh played a dominating part in the second Texaco Trophy match. England looked on top after scoring 5–277 in 55 overs, Robin Smith being in magnificent touch with an unbeaten 167 (three sixes and 17 fours). Australia lost 3–95 before a 168-run stand between Mark Waugh (113) and Border (86 not out) enabled them to win with nine balls left.

On the morning of the first Test at Old Trafford, Manchester, Steve woke up feeling as if he had gone 'five rounds with Mike Tyson'. 'My head was throbbing and the rest of my body was aching,' he wrote in his *Ashes Diary*. The highlight of the second day—in fact, it set the tone for the entire series—was Shane Warne's first ball in an Ashes contest. It pitched some 15 centimetres (six inches) outside the leg stump, spun viciously past Mike Gatting's half-formed forward stroke

A rasping square cut by Steve Waugh during his unbeaten century for Australian XI against the Windies at Hobart in 1993. (*Rick Smith*)

and hit the off-stump almost on the top. Years will roll by and viewers will still remember that delivery, except that the 15 centimetres outside the leg stump will become 35 or 40 by the year 2013!

Australia expanded on their 179-run first-innings lead by scoring briskly in the second. Mark Waugh (64) added 109 runs with Boon (93) for the third wicket, and Steve (78 not out) had an unfinished 180-run partnership with Ian Healy (102 not out). As Healy had never hit a century in first-class cricket, he asked Steve when on 93: 'What do you do when you're in the nineties?' The no-frills Steve replied: 'Stuffed if I know. I've only buggered up half a dozen hundreds myself.'

To an outsider this would indicate that Steve did not care about his partner's fears. Far from it. He wanted Healy to consider the approaching milestone of a century as a normal event and not to tense up or 'choke'. England were set a huge target of 512 in a day and a half and started confidently with skipper Graham Gooch scoring an authoritative 133 before given out 'handled the ball'. He accidentally touched a ball with his hands to stop it hitting the stumps. The English tail wagged but Australia won easily.

The second Test at Lord's was a batting bonanza for the tourists who declared at 6–632. Slater played a scintillating innings of 152 in his second Test and his opening stand with Mark Taylor (111) piled on 260 runs. Boon at no. 3 chipped in with an unbeaten 164 and had a big partnership of 180 with Mark Waugh before the latter was bowled by Phil Tufnell for 99.

To quote Steve from his *Ashes Diary* (1993): 'They say twins have some form of ESP or that they are affected by events that happen to each other. Well, on this occasion it felt as if I had been dismissed one short of 100, such was my disappointment. I'm sure Mark's disappointment would be magnified many times over. That one delivery will surely be replayed in his mind a thousand times tonight [18 June 1993] and all the while he'll be hoping for time to turn back and give him another shot at history.'

Mark's dream of recording a Test century at Lord's remains unfulfilled as he could make only 33 on this hallowed ground in 1997. England was never in the fight for the 1993 Lord's Test despite Mike Atherton's 80 and 99 run out, and lost by an innings.

The next Test at Trent Bridge, Nottinghamshire, was a high scoring one and ended in a draw. Boon scored his second successive century and was engaged with Mark Waugh in another entertaining century partnership at more than five runs an over until Junior threw away another chance at a hundred when sweeping Peter Such recklessly.

Headingley again proved a happy hunting ground for Steve. He followed his unbeaten 177 in 1989 by hitting 157 not out and added 332 in an unbroken fifth-wicket partnership with Border (200 not out). Nearly half of Steve's score came in boundaries. The two Aussie battlers were closing in on Don Bradman and Sid Barnes' record for the fifth wicket (for 405 runs) when Border, with a view to wrap-up the series, declared at 4–653.

To Steve, a big stand with Border is a masterclass. 'Batting with Border makes you

Allan Border congratulates Steve on his century against the Windies in the 1993 Sydney Test. (*Allsport/Joe Mann*)

concentrate that little bit extra because you can see how much it means to him to give his wicket away. You play accordingly as anything less than hundred per cent is not expected or accepted.' Things went well till Steve reached 90. He always felt a bit edgy in his nineties and was not helped by the rain which caused the players to leave the ground twice with his score on 93 and 98. But on reaching his hundred he never looked back until the declaration. He felt 'about 60 years old' after this marathon and headed straight for the spa.

Earlier, that faithful pair of David Boon (107) and Mark Waugh (52) had shared their fourth successive century stand. It was Boon's third consecutive hundred but Junior had a lapse of concentration and let go a Mark Ilott delivery that clipped the top of his off-stump. Australia won by an innings and retained the Ashes with two Tests still to play. As per his promise, Gooch resigned as captain although he had top-scored in the first innings. England's new captain Atherton started well at Edgbaston, Birmingham, by winning the toss and top-scoring in both innings. But their totals of 276 and 251 were not sufficient to prevent an eight-wicket loss.

For once Australia started badly, losing 4–80, and would have been in big trouble had wicket-keeper Alec Stewart stumped Steve when he was on nought. A 'born again' Steve (59) added 153 with Mark (137), who scored his initial Test hundred on English soil. This was the first century partnership between the twins in 13 Tests together and was watched by their father Rodger in the Members' Stand. Now no-one could accuse him of jinxing his sons.

This was Mark at his brilliant, elegant best, picking the ball off his toes, and hitting wherever his fancy took him. His wristy, whiplash-like leg glances were a joy to behold as he streaked 18 fours. Meanwhile, Steve—to quote himself—was endeavouring to locate the middle of his bat. This has been Steve's strength, as it was Ian Chappell's late in his career. They miss balls, they mishit, but they stay there even though they look anything but convincing—which frustrates the opposition. The twins went along well in their contrasting fashion, despite two mid-wicket collisions which almost ruled out the theory that they have extrasensory perception. Talking of ESP, Steve had a premonition that Mark would be caught behind square of Ilott. And the next ball Mark was caught behind square by Graham Thorpe off Ilott.

Another easy win for the Aussies was followed by another resignation by an English 'heavy'. The chairman of selectors, Ted Dexter, resigned after Australia led 4–0. The final Test at The Oval was an anti-climax for the Australians but ecstasy for Atherton's Englishmen. It was their first victory in 19 Ashes Tests. Their last had been in Melbourne in December 1986; almost seven years earlier. The selection of three new-ball bowlers; the speedy Devon Malcolm, the never-say-never Angus Fraser and the resilient Steve Watkin was probably responsible for the victory. Or it could be the now-familiar FDTDS (final dead Test defeat syndrome) for the Australians.

The Test started well for Steve Waugh who dismissed both the openers Gooch and Atherton—Gooch being his 50th victim in

And take that! Another slashing cover-drive by Mark during his 56 in the 1993 Manchester Test. (*Allsport/Adrian Murrell*)

Test cricket. Trailing England by 73 runs, the Australians were set 387 runs to win. The three English pacemen found a hole in the 'Au-zone layer' and dismissed the top five Australian batsmen for a sub-hundred total. Junior top-scored with 49 but the rest were panic-stricken and Australia lost the Test by 161 runs.

Despite the final Test debacle, it was a memorable tour for most. Even Matthew Hayden and Damien Martyn, who were not picked in the Test series, scored a mountain of runs against the counties. Four batsmen—Boon, Mark Waugh, Hayden and Slater—topped 1000 runs on the tour in first-class matches. The reason Steve did not was that he often batted at no. 6 and there were times the innings were declared before he could get in.

England 1993 remains a favourite tour for both Steve and Mark. It was here that Steve first started writing his Tour Diaries, which are unghosted, and he has continued with these in subsequent major tours. They have all been popular among cricket fans, providing them with not only the on-field performances but also off-field dramas. After the Headingley Test, which decided the series, Steve wrote: 'It's moments like these when the camaraderie is so evident that you wish time would stand still. These occasions only happen once or twice in a cricketer's lifetime.'

⑩ Player of the Series

Steve Waugh does not wear his heart on his sleeve. He keeps his emotions pretty much to himself and lets his bat do the talking. Yet, after returning from England, we saw a different side to his character. The cool guy was stung and showed it. A few critics had rated his performance in England in 1993 as unimportant, and claims that he did not scale the heights of 1989 because there was no need to, that the runs were generally made by the time he came in, and that his bowling was ineffectual until the last Test, irked him. After all, in batting he had averaged 83.20 in six Tests and 67.30 on the tour.

He pondered and he seethed, the iron entering his soul. 'It's the first time in nine years that I've really been angry about what's written about me. Not because it affects me, because I know I'm doing well, but it does affect my family and in this case it was completely unfair. It's the power of the media and I think some people have to think more before they make judgments.'

Having bared his soul, Steve continued from where he had left off in England when New Zealand and South Africa toured Australia in 1993–94. He averaged 216.00 in three Tests against the Kiwis. He also topped batting and bowling averages against South Africa at home and away and was adjudged Player of the Series both times. The flamboyant Steve Waugh of the past had by now become a percentage player—removing all fancy but dangerous shots—and he was recognised as cricket's Mr Consistency. Below are presented his statistics in four consecutive series where he outpointed both his colleagues and his opponents.

Against	Season	In	Steve's batting average	Next best from both sides
England	1993	England	83.20	David Boon (Aus.) 69.37
New Zealand	1993–94	Australia	216.00	Mark Taylor (Aus.) 95.33
South Africa	1993–94	Australia	82.50	Peter Kirsten (S.Af.) 60.50
South Africa	1993–94	S. Africa	65.00	Andrew Hudson (S.Af.) 58.60 Mark Waugh (Aus.) 58.25

After the first Test against New Zealand was drawn, Australia won both of the next two by an innings. The second Test at Hobart was highlighted by centuries from Michael Slater, David Boon and Mark Waugh, and crafty spin bowling from Tim May and Shane Warne. In the final Test in Brisbane, Boon (89) and Mark Waugh (68) added 125 runs for the third wicket, their sixth century partnership in nine Tests. Later Steve (147 not out) put on 159 runs for the fifth wicket with Border (105 runs in his 150th Test), and 142 for the unbroken seventh wicket with Shane Warne (74 not out).

Compared with the cakewalk win against New Zealand, the series against South Africa was more like a barefoot hop on burning coal. The series went right down to the wire and Australia had to fight hard to level the series one-all. Steve realised that he had to prove himself against the tough-as-nails Springboks whose captain, Kepler Wessels, had earlier played for Queensland and Australia and knew the weaknesses of Border's men.

Steve psyched himself up and was mentally ready to fire, but, when taking a quick single during a Benson & Hedges World Series match against New Zealand at Melbourne, he tore a hamstring and missed the first two Tests against South Africa. His place in the team was taken by Damien Martyn, a free-scoring batsman from Western Australia. Had Martyn got going, Steve would have found it difficult to get back in the Australian team which was rich in batting. Also a torn hamstring can take up to six weeks to heal.

'When I had that injury, I just had to accept it. Damien Martyn got his chance and it was a case of good luck to him, but you have to believe in yourself,' Steve said. However, Martyn failed, scoring eight runs in Melbourne and 59 and six in Sydney. He seemed to freeze with fright in the second innings, taking 106 minutes to score six unimpressive runs, and Australia lost narrowly.

By exercising sensibly and having over ten hours of intensive treatment per day, Steve recovered in just two weeks. He gives credit for his quick recovery to NSW physio Peter Farquhar who sacrificed his Christmas and New Year's Eve to treat Steve's injury. Steve proved his fitness by captaining NSW in the Sheffield Shield matches against South Australia and Tasmania, winning the first game and scoring an unbeaten 190 in the second.

Lanky NSW off-spinner Gavin Robertson, who later toured Pakistan in 1994 and India in 1998 with the Waughs, thinks very highly of Steve as captain. 'Stephen Waugh is a born leader and like all born leaders he has the ability to bring out the best in a player and to understand the individual,' he said. 'As he was recovering from a torn hamstring injury, Stephen made himself available to lead us in a Shield match against South Australia in Adelaide. After we struggled for the first three days and were ahead by only 265 runs the next day, Stephen told us that he was declaring the innings and we were going to bowl them out. I scanned the dressing room to see looks of disbelief on the boys' faces.

'As we were thrashed in a day and five hours in our previous match in Perth, our confidence was pretty low. But since our captain said we were going to win, we believed him and became positive. I still remember tying my shoelaces when Stephen came over to me and said, "Robbo, have you ever bowled with a new ball before?" I said, "No, why?", and he replied, "Well, you are going to now." Exactly four hours and 15 minutes later, the Blues [NSW] walked back into the dressing room as winners by 109 runs [Robertson grabbing 5–43]. It was elation as I had never seen and will never forget.

'Our captain stood up after the singing was over and asked team manager Neil Marks if he could cancel the team bus and our flights for that night, and re-book our rooms at the Park Royal so that we could celebrate like a team. After the biggest night out and dancing to a band organised by Stephen, the Blues turned their fortunes around from the Perth debacle to win both the Sheffield Shield and Mercantile Mutual Cup. There is only one way to describe Stephen Waugh as captain—inspirational.'

By the time Steve was selected to play in the final Test at Adelaide, Australia was one-down in the series. The first Test in Melbourne had been ruined by rain but not before Mark Taylor scored 170 and Mark Waugh 84.

The second Test in Sydney was a cliff-hanger highlighted by Shane Warne taking 7–56 on the opening day. After leading by 123 runs, the Australians needed a token 117 runs to win. Incredibly, panic set in and they were bowled out for 111 and lost by five runs despite a rearguard action by fast bowler Craig McDermott. He went in at no. 10 and top-scored with 29 not out. Steve's doggedness was surely missed. According to Dr Ali Bacher, the former captain of South Africa and one of the strongest opponents of apartheid, 'It was our finest achievement ever.'

Steve returned in the third Test in Adelaide and made an immediate difference. He scored 164 authoritative runs, hitting 19 fours, and shared a 208-run partnership with Border. It was Border's last Test in Australia and he became the only player to reach 11,000 runs in Test cricket. South Africa replied strongly and were 2–173 when Steve trapped opener Andrew Hudson for 90. He went on to clean bowl Jonty Rhodes and Daryl Cullinan and had Brian McMillan lbw—in all capturing 4–26 in 18 overs. The visitors trailed by 196 runs in the first innings and lost the Test convincingly. Steve was the unanimous choice as Man of the Match and Player of the Series despite playing only one Test.

Australia's historic tour of South Africa—their first in 25 years—produced engrossing cricket with Steve dominating. So close were the two teams that the Test series was drawn 1-all and the one-day series 4-all. According to Jack Bannister in *Wisden 1995*, Steve 'played the best cricket of his life, excelling in the field as well as with bat and ball'.

Steve was made Man of the Match in the second Test at Cape Town for his all-round excellence. First, he brilliantly ran out Hudson when he looked unstoppable at 102. Then he scored 86 and added 108 runs with Healy to help Australia gain a valuable first-innings lead of 74. With four days gone, there was little hope of a result, but Steve thought differently. He took a sharp return catch from Hansie Cronje and trapped Hudson lbw and the South Africans were reeling at 6–100. The next morning he dismissed big hitter McMillan cheaply, had the pugnacious Peter Kirsten caught by Border and bowled Alan Donald for a duck. He ended with match-winning figures of 22.3–9–28–5, his best bowling figures in a Test innings. The last three wickets fell at the same score of 164 and Australia won by 9 wickets with more than a session in hand. The series was now locked 1-all, the home team having won the first Test in Johannesburg.

In the final Test at Durban, Mark Waugh was the Man of the Match. 'If it's not one Waugh, it's the other', the opponents must grumble. Sent in to bat on a grassy wicket, Australians were bowled out for 269 (Steve 64, Mark 43, Healy 55). South Africa reached 100 without loss and appeared in a strong position. All they had to do was score briskly.

Surprisingly, skipper Kepler Wessels made no effort to force the pace as his team pushed and prodded to total 422 runs in 205 overs. Trailing by 153 runs, Australia did well to save the Test, Mark Waugh remaining unbeaten on 113, his sixth Test hundred.

In the exciting limited-overs international series, Steve scored 291 runs at 48.50 (making 86 at Verwoerdburg and a scintillating 67 at East London) and took five wickets, including 2–48 in the final match at Bloemfontein which Australia won by one run to level the series. This led to Steve being adjudged Player of the One-Day Series, apart from his earlier Player of the Test series award—a rare and well-deserved honour for the Aussie battler.

The series in South Africa marked the end of an era as it included Border's final Test appearance. He had played the most number of Tests, captained his country in most Tests, scored most runs and fifties, and accepted most catches.

The season ended on a high note for Steve but it could well have gone the other way.

His successful Ashes tour of 1993 was played down by critics and his big scores against the New Zealanders were treated too lightly by some—'Ah, but then anyone can score against those Hadlee-less Kiwis.' Steve had to prove himself against the unrelenting South Africans and he did so in a masterful manner. He was the top performer from both sides in Australia, as he was a month later in South Africa. His batting was back to its best, with backfoot square-drives predominating, and his apparently innocuous bowling grabbed 10 wickets at 13.00. He had topped both the batting and bowling averages.

'I like to be involved,' he said after the tour. 'When I was just batting I felt something was missing. The South African wickets helped me [in bowling]. I wouldn't expect to have so much success with the ball as that, but it was great to get the results.'

⏸ Mission Unaccomplished

Even before a ball was bowled, the new Australian cricket season of 1994–95 bristled with controversies. After keeping the Australian Cricket Board, the media and his fans in suspense, Allan Border decided to retire from Test cricket. The choice of his successor became a hot national issue. Mark Taylor had proved himself an able deputy to Border since 1992 and had an impressive record as the captain of NSW. However, there were other candidates with interesting curricula vitae. Ian Healy was a strong motivator and an indefatigable fighter. Steve Waugh was a deep thinker and was respected by his colleagues and opponents alike.

Steve had only recently demonstrated his credentials as a future Australian captain by leading NSW with imagination and verve against South Australia and Tasmania in December 1993–January 1994 when recovering from a hamstring injury between the second and third Test against South Africa. The cares of captaincy had not affected his batting concentration as he scored 73 and 46 at Adelaide and an unbeaten 190 in the next match against Tasmania at Hobart. But when Taylor got the Australian captaincy with Healy as his deputy, Steve showed neither surprise nor disappointment.

Australia's next destination was Pakistan—not exactly their favourite haunt. Their mission was to win a Test there for the first time in 35 years and improve Aussie–Paki relations which were at rock-bottom a few summers earlier. The last time the Australians had defeated Pakistan in Pakistan was way back in November 1959 at Dacca. The 1994 tour was planned in advance to prepare the selected players physically and mentally. They were given detailed fitness programs, nutritional advice and lessons in different cultures to help avoid the acrimony of 1988. They were also relieved to learn that, during Test matches, one of the umpires would be from a neutral country.

The series started badly for Mark Taylor. He became the first debutant Test captain to make ducks in both innings, and he lost a 'can't lose' Test in Karachi by one wicket. It was an epic gut-wrenching, fluctuating Test with an ever-increasing final day's crowd chanting 'Allah-o-Akbar' (God is Great).

Australia held the upper hand for the first four and half days. After leading by 81 runs in the first innings, they set Pakistan a win-target of 314. The Aussies had the match in their pocket when Pakistan lost the ninth wicket at 258, and tail-ender Mushtaq Ahmed joined Inzamam-ul-Haq. The latter played a charmed innings of 58 not out against a depleted attack—strike bowlers Craig McDermott, Glenn McGrath and Tim May being injured.

Shane Warne bowled superbly and all but sealed up the Test, but for an amazing mistake by the ever-vigilant wicket-keeper Healy. With three runs needed for a Pakistan victory, Inzamam jumped out to attack but missed the ball. Healy fumbled, the ball went for four leg-byes and Pakistan won. Healy was devastated. 'I missed the one that counted,' he said. 'There's no doubt that was a chance we had to take to win the Test. I feel very, very responsible for the loss.'

Umpire Dickie Bird later said that it was the best Test match he had umpired. The Waughs had contributed solidly in this cliffhanger, Steve with 73 in the first innings. He was engaged in a century stand with debutant Michael Bevan. Mark scored 61 in the second innings, adding 122 runs with his favourite partner, David Boon.

The next Test at Rawalpindi was equally frustrating for the tourists. Sent in to bat, they declared at 9–521 (Michael Slater 110, Steve Waugh 98, Mark Waugh 68). There was an enthralling duel between Steve and Wasim Akram, the latter intimidating Steve with a barrage of chest-high lightning-fast bouncers. When all set to reach his first century in Pakistan, Steve was yorked by another fast bowler Waqar Younis—thus becoming a victim of the nervous nineties once again.

Gavin Robertson, although not selected in any Test on the tour, remembers Steve's gallant knock in Rawalpindi: 'Much is written about Stephen's blood-and-gore encounters with Curtly Ambrose and Allan Donald, but few remember his fierce combat with Akram. The Paki quickie was off the field for three hours on the opening day of the Test and was not allowed to bowl for three hours the following day. This infuriated him, and when allowed, he bowled with venom and fury.

'Stephen was about 30 then and for some 90 minutes Akram bowled at an incredible speed, targeting the batsman's chest and head. He ducked and weaved and was hit excruciating blows on the arms and under ribs. It was a very courageous knock and one that I have not forgotten. But when only two short of a century, he was out quite freakily as he deflected a Younis delivery from bat to arm to pad to foot and finally to the stumps. I think Allah had the final say.'

Pakistan was forced to follow-on 261 runs behind. Two individual performances stood out in their second innings. Pakistan captain Salim Malik scored a match-saving 237 and Australia's fast bowler Damien Fleming took a hat-trick in his Test debut. However, important catches were dropped and the Test was drawn.

Steve missed the final Test at Lahore due to a shoulder injury but Mark scored 71 and was engaged in a century stand with Bevan. Australia totalled 455 and again led on the first innings, but dropped catches at vital stages cost them dearly. The Test was drawn and the superior team lost the series 0–1. The Waughs averaged more than 50 runs each with the bat—Steve 57 and Mark 55—but were disappointed because their mission to win a Test in Pakistan remained unaccomplished.

All the same, Steve got an accolade from his new captain, Mark Taylor. 'I think Steve is the class all-rounder in world cricket at the moment. He and Wasim Akram are probably the two best but Steve's batting over the past 12 months has been astonishing. Not only is he batting with great command and authority, he's getting vital wickets for us too.'

The tour, unlike the previous ones, had gone without any apparent rancour or disharmony. The key word of the previous sentence is 'apparent'. Five months after the tour, Phil Wilkins of the *Sydney Morning Herald* broke the news that three Australian players were allegedly offered bribes by Salim Malik to 'throw' matches. According to Shane Warne's signed statement, he and Tim May were offered US$200,000 on the fourth evening of the engrossing Karachi Test to throw the match on the final day. They rejected the offer straightaway and informed management. Also, Warne bowled his heart out on the final day, all but winning the Test for Australia.

Warne's second charge in the affidavit concerned a conversation between Mark Waugh and Malik at a reception before a one-day international in Rawalpindi three weeks after the Karachi Test. It was alleged that Mark Waugh was 'offered a big amount to four or five Australian players not to play well on the final day'. To keep the record straight, Mark scored an unbeaten 121 in this match, although Australia lost. But they won the Wills Series Triangular Tournament (South Africa being the third nation) by defeating Pakistan in the final by 64 runs.

The Pakistan tour manager Intikhab Alam vehemently denied the bribery accusation. 'There is no truth in it,' he said. 'It is terrible. These are very serious charges against the Pakistan team.' Nevertheless, more than one Pakistani player indicated that bribery and betting activity were out of control and should be investigated. And David Hopps wrote in *Wisden 1996*: 'The International Cricket Council's failure to take a central role by conducting an immediate inquiry—preferring instead to act as a conduit between the two nations involved—identified it as a body hopelessly unempowered to manage the international game convincingly.'

As the ICC failed to take control, the Pakistan Board placed matters in the hands of Fakhrudin Ebrahim, a former supreme court judge and one-time attorney-general and governor of Sindh. His investigation was hampered by Australia's unwillingness to subject Warne, May and Mark Waugh to cross-examination in Pakistan, saying that they feared for their safety and welfare. The Australian Cricket Board suggested that the three players would be prepared to go to London for any ICC inquiry. Thus Ebrahim's investigation was limited. After studying sworn statements by the three Australian cricketers, and after cross-examining Malik at length through his counsel, Judge Ebrahim concluded on 21 October 1995: 'The allegations against Salim Malik are not worthy of any credence and must be rejected as unfounded.'

This angered the ACB and the Australian cricketers. Some of the Pakistani players also alleged that bribery and match-fixing did go on in modern cricket, and the great Imran Khan was quoted as saying that any person found guilty of the above charges should be hanged. Later, he denied this vehemently and added that the word he had used was 'banned' and not 'hanged'.

Although found innocent by the Ebrahim inquiry, Salim Malik was replaced as captain and suspended. He returned as a batsman on Pakistan's tour of Australia a year later. A vengeful Warne had him caught fourth ball in the first Test at Brisbane for a duck. 'It shows there is justice in the game,' he said, full of glee. Taciturn Mark Waugh just yawned at second slip.

⑫ Run Brother, Don't Run!

Mike Atherton's Englishmen landed in Australia in October 1994 in search of the elusive Ashes and started the tour with psychological warfare directed at Steve Waugh. They taunted that he looks good against medium-pacers and spinners but 'jumps and weaves and wets his pants' against real pace and bounce. They pointed out that he could not handle quickie Devon Malcolm in the final Test at The Oval a year earlier.

Steve thrives on insults like these to bring the best out of him. He averaged 49.28 in the series, keeping his upper lip stiff and his underpants dry. Oddly, it was Malcolm who missed the first Test at Brisbane as he contracted chickenpox.

Australia started the series on a high note by scoring 426, Michael Slater (176) and Mark Waugh (140) adding 182 dazzling runs. When 98, Mark edged a Philip De Freitas delivery low to Graeme Hick's left, but the catch was not taken. It was Mark's 50th first-class century and seventh in a Test. He hit a spectacular six off Phil Tufnell and looked set for a big score to silence his critics when a delivery from the unpredictable Darren Gough reared inexplicably shoulder-high and carried to covers from a last-minute prod.

Australia triumphed in the second Test at Melbourne to take a commanding 2–0 lead. Malcolm was back in the English side but failed to shift 'marked man' Steve Waugh. In fact, no bowler worried Steve, who remained unbeaten in both innings with 94 and 26. It was his second frustrating ninety in two months following his 98 at Rawalpindi in October. The Waughs added 71 when Mark carelessly threw his wicket away when 71. This signalled a collapse and Australia nosedived from 5–208 to 9–242. Cometh the hour and in walked Damien Fleming, a tail-ender who refused to budge and tried to enable Steve to reach his hundred. He added 37 invaluable runs with Steve but at 16 was caught off Malcolm, leaving the 'Master Crafter' six runs short of his century. It was an innings of granite stone-walling and gutsy counterattack.

The Melbourne Test is remembered for Shane Warne's hat-trick as England was shot out for 92 in the second innings. All his three hat-trick victims—De Freitas, Gough and Malcolm—fell to his leg-break. In the first innings, Steve had run 30 metres behind square-leg and, diving like an acrobat, caught Mike Gatting.

The third Test at Sydney was fascinating to watch and Australia was lucky to save it thanks to a dour eighth-wicket stand between Warne and Tim May which lasted 77 minutes in the final session. The match continued in semi-darkness and ended at 7.26

Geoff 'Henry' Lawson flanked by author Kersi Meher-Homji and historian Warwick Franks at a book launch. (*Denise Franks*)

p.m. Gough was the Man of the Match with 51 scintillating runs and hauls of 6–49 and 1–72. For the Waughs, it was a match to forget from a personal angle as they scored 29 runs between them. However, the Ashes were retained with two Tests in hand.

The Sydney Test had ignited the series, as England could still tie it 2-all. The visitors, on a high after their Sydney performance, won the Adelaide Test by 106 runs. The highlight for Australia was Greg Blewett's century on debut, but the Waughs again struggled with the bat. Mark had success as a medium-pacer and finished with his best Test figures of 5–40; his only 5-for in a Test innings. The hero for England was De Freitas who scored 88 match-winning runs in two hours, hitting nine fours and two sixes off 95 balls.

Chastened and humbled by the loss in Adelaide, Australia won the final Test in Perth by 329 runs and retained the Ashes 3–1. England's catching was woeful, Slater being dropped at least nine times in his 124. It was a bouncy pitch, all batsmen were at sea for the first few overs and Steve was uncomfortable for most of his innings of 99 not out. This was only the second instance in a Test match of a batsman stranded partner-less on 99. The first one to experience the tragedy was England's Geoff Boycott in 1979–80, against Australia and also at Perth, when he carried the bat—which remains unique in Test annals.

As in Melbourne in the same series a few months earlier, Steve ran out of partners. At no. 11 came Craig McDermott, a capable batsman but hampered by an inflamed back. As he could not run, he used Mark Waugh as a runner.

Imagine the scenario. Steve on 99 not out, his twin brother at the other end as McDermott's runner. Both brothers are on edge but we don't know who is more nervous. To break the suspense and help him reach his hundredth run, Mark attempts a rash single and gets run out through a sharp throw from Graham Gooch. Steve is stranded on 99. If looks could kill! Further doubt about ESP between twins.

Steve recovered his composure soon enough to score 80 in the second innings and added 203 runs with Greg Blewett, who scored his second Test ton in his first two Tests—a rare achievement. It was another successful series for the Waughs, Steve aggregating 345 runs at 49.28 and Mark 435 at 43.50. Mark topped the bowling average, taking eight wickets at 19.62.

Geoff Lawson on the Waughs

Geoff 'Henry' Lawson played Tests with Steve, captained both Steve and Mark in Sheffield Shield and was the NSW coach in 1996–97. His assessments:

To start with, both Steve and Mark were similar players, attacking and attractive to watch. But ever since Steve was dropped from the Test team in early 1991, he changed his style—becoming more dogged and scientific in his approach, and harder to dismiss. In the Sheffield Shield grand final [of 1984–85] he was caught when hooking. This won't happen now.

Steve took long to establish himself in the Test team and until 1989 hung on because of his useful bowling especially in the limited-overs games. Then came his magnificent Headingley Test century.

I have not seen better batting than the 464 runs the twins put on at the WACA in Perth in December 1990. They were supreme. Not only did they record chanceless, unbeaten double hundreds, they did not hit the ball in the air. Mark showed no emotion when I declared at 601, but Steve was upset and angry and told me so. True, the two could have gone on and made 300 each, who knows. But my duty as a captain is to win matches.

In an earlier match in Sydney [against Tasmania in March 1990] I had declared NSW's innings closed with Mark unbeaten on 198 but he did not mind. He is not one to demonstrate much emotion except perhaps when one of his horses is heading for the finishing post at Canterbury or Harold Park! Outwardly, he is almost languid as he comes in to bat, no nervous twitches, pulling of the cap nor constant readjustment of pads and the protector. Coolly, he walks out and takes guard without the ritual scratching of a Dean Jones, David Boon or brother Steve.

Mark has been compared in technique and temperament with living legend Dougie Walters and rightly so. Grace, style and sheer vulnerability are factors that come to mind when looking for the qualities of both batsmen. I would rather watch Mark make 70 than Boon make 200 because that 70 will come relatively quickly and contain a full range of shotmaking; the clip through mid-wicket, the sweetly timed cover-drive, a variety of cuts and the occasional hook. The man looks good just holding the bat.

Mark is as graceful as Greg Chappell but until 1997 had less discipline than Greg. My favourite innings by the Waugh brothers? Steve's unbeaten 177 in the 1989 Headingley Test when he demolished the bowling. [Lawson had an unbroken partnership for the eight wicket with Steve in that innings and added 130 in the next Test at Lord's.] It was the first Test in the series and the Englishmen never recovered from this onslaught. I also enjoyed Steve's 200 at Sabina Park [Kingston] in 1995 against a much stronger attack and on a more lively pitch. For Mark, my favourite is his match-winning hundred against South Africa at Port Elizabeth in 1997; a vital innings in difficult conditions and in a crisis. His debut century in the 1991 Adelaide Test had all the hallmarks of a typical Mark Waugh innings; graceful and effortless.

Steve at Sabina Park and Mark at Port Elizabeth played two of the most important innings for Australia in the last twenty years.

Despite their rise in stature from the rookies of 1985 to champions of today, their attitude has remained unchanged. They have always been easy to play with, easy to captain and easy to coach. Only they are getting increasingly difficult to dismiss!

As persons, Steve is the one whose confidence and trust you have to win. Mark takes people at face value and you have to do something really bad to be on his wrong side. Mark gets upset at getting out and blames others; the umpire, pitch, etc. Steve blames himself more than others, analyses his mistakes and is a better player and person for it.

13 Gone with the Windies

Having pocketed the Ashes for the fourth time in a row, Mark Taylor's Australians packed their 'coffins' (cricket bags) for a tour of the Caribbean to take on the mighty Windies. It was a tour to remember for the Aussies—especially the Waugh twins. To quote Robert Craddock: 'On May 3, 1995, the great wall crashed at last. After 15 years and 29 series, world cricket's longest lasting dynasty was thrown out by the relentless, underestimated Australians—the most distinguished run of triumphant success gone with the Windies.'

The Windies had not lost a series in the Caribbean since the Australians under Ian Chappell had triumphed over them in 1972–73. Although Taylor's men in 1995 lost the one-day series 1–4, they won the all-important Test series 2–1. The Australians had many heroes for this magnificent victory, but Steve Waugh was the hero among heroes, a champion of champions. He scored over 400 runs in the Test series against bowlers of speed and venom whose mission appeared to be: Get Steve Waugh's wicket or head—it doesn't matter which. Mark Waugh was equally gallant in the final, series-deciding Test at Kingston where his century set the tone.

An airborne Steve negotiates a nasty lifter in the Windies.
(*Allsport/Shaun Botterill*)

However, for all the grace of Mark Waugh and Richie Richardson, the flamboyance of Brian Lara and pace like fire of Curtly Ambrose, Courtney Walsh, Glenn McGrath and the two Benjamins, Steve Waugh dominated the series. He scored 189 runs more than the next Australian—twin brother Mark—and 121 more than Brian Lara in the exciting Test series which kept the Aussie supporters back home awake all night.

First, the none-too-successful one-day series. When the West Indies won easily, it appeared that they were all set to wallop the tourists in the Test series to decide the Frank Worrell Trophy. The highlight for the Australians in the one-dayers was Mark Waugh's sublime innings of 70 runs in 56 balls in the final match at Georgetown.

The first Test at Bridgetown, Barbados, was like a sparring contest between two contrasting boxers. Australia, without their opening attack of Craig McDermott and Damien Fleming—both injured and sent home— threw the early punches and the Windies were on the ropes at 3–6 before the crowd had even settled in their seats. Far from defending after this disastrous start, Brian Lara and Carl Hooper counterattacked. Hooper used his feet skilfully and hit Shane Warne for three consecutive fours. At lunch, the score was 3–116. It was exhilarating cricket and, according to John Woodcock, one of the best morning's play he had seen in six decades of watching the game.

The match swung back Australia's way and when Lara was out—caught in a controversial way by Steve—the bottom fell out and the Windies were shot out for 195. The damage was done by Brendon Julian, in the team for the injured Fleming, who took 4–36. He had arrived only a few days earlier after an arduous Perth-Melbourne-Auckland-Los Angeles-Miami-Barbados-Trinidad-Guyana-Barbados trip. In reply, Australia was 2–91 at stumps. Thus 11 wickets had crumbled for 286 runs. The talk of the day, the Test and the series, was that catch Steve took off Lara who was then on 65 and in magnificent form. He hit a Julian outswinger straight at Steve in the gully. To quote Steve from his *West Indies Tour Diary*:

'I clutched at the offering and the ball bobbed out of my hands as I tumbled towards the turf. On the way down I had another two unsuccessful attempts at securing the ball, before a final grab saw the ball come to rest on top of my left wrist. I breathed a sigh of relief and then tossed the ball skyward in celebration.'

Steve and Mark during their epic 231-run partnership in the Kingston Test of 1995. Steve is showing his lucky charm—a red rag. (*Allsport/Clive Mason*)

It never occurred to him for even one instant that he had not made that catch. The TV replays tended to indicate that the ball had hit the ground before it fell on his wrist, but it all happened so fast that Lara, after standing a few seconds, trudged off to the pavilion. Accusations of cheating were levelled at Steve by some—including former Windies skipper Vivian Richards. Steve disagreed. 'If I had doubts I would not have claimed it. I have called players back before.' Ian Healy supported Steve, saying that everyone in the slip cordon thought the ball was taken neatly despite the four juggles. The very fact that Lara walked was some indication about the fairness of the catch, Healy opined.

To digress, during a rain-interruption in the second Test at St John's a fortnight later, Steve had a closer look at that catch on TV. 'As I watched the slow-motion replays from all angles, I couldn't believe my eyes. To me the replay confirmed my impression of the catch, for the ball bounced off my right hand at exactly the same time I hit the ground and then rebounded up and landed on my left wrist, making it a fair catch.' He was astonished to think that the so-called experts could claim it otherwise. I have myself seen the replay of that catch many times without drawing a definite conclusion, but I believe Vivian Richards was wrong in calling Steve a cheat.

'I really find it hard to believe a cricketer of the stature of Richards would create tension in this way,' Steve wrote in his *West Indies Tour Diary*. 'The news of this attack shook me for a couple of hours until I came to realise that it had come from someone who was probably struggling to come to terms with the fact that he is no longer at the centre of attention.'

Terrific together, three maestros in one snap. Brian Lara congratulates Mark as Steve looks on. (*Allsport/ Clive Mason*)

Unperturbed, Steve scored 65 in the first innings of the Barbados Test, starting off with a sweetly timed four off the second ball he received. Mark Waugh chipped in with 40 and Australia led by 151 runs. When Mark was 40, Steve had an ESP that Mark would be caught behind off Ambrose. And he was too, the very next ball. Such a premonition had happened to Steve about six times in the past and he was always right. When he told this to Mark, he sneered, 'Why don't you bloody well tell me when you're thinking those thoughts!'

The West Indies were once again shot out for a poor score of 189. The highlight of the innings was a spectacular catch taken by Steve to dismiss Junior Murray off Warne. He ran from short mid-wicket to the boundary looking at the ball in the sun—never looking away—and caught the ball as he dived. Australia won two days later with 10 wickets and two days to spare. It was Australia's first-ever win in a Barbados Test.

The second Test at St John's, Antigua, is also remembered for a spellbinding catch which cut short Lara's magical innings of 88 in 101 balls. After dismissing the confident Australians for 216 (Walsh bowling like a man possessed to claim 6–54), the Windies were going for the kill with dashers Lara and Hooper in command at 3–186. But Steve Waugh dismissed both of them in a few measly minutes for just one run.

This is how it happened. The pitch reminded him of the Cape Town Test the previous season when he had taken 5–28. It was keeping low, and when Mark Taylor threw the ball to him, he was delighted—especially because Steve thought of Hooper as his 'bunny'. However, his first target was Lara who could influence the Test à la Ian Botham. The game plan was to frustrate Lara into playing a rash stroke, so Steve bowled tightly for two overs. This made Lara impatient and Steve asked for a fielder on the on-side edge of the wicket, next to the batsman at the bowler's end. David Boon, the man with cat-like reflexes, was moved there. In the very next over, Lara clipped a ball uppishly in the direction of mid-on but it was interrupted in mid-flight by Boon, the flying Tasmanian. He leapt in the sky to grab the catch in his outstretched left hand.

In a Test series of fantastic catches, this was probably the most spectacular. Cricket commentators went berserk—describing Boon as a 'Tasmanian Salmon' and 'Flying Pig'. The modest and likeable Boon only smiled, his moustache quivering. 'It started out as a token attempt. At my age [he was then 34] it feels great to take catches like that,' he said. One run later, Steve had Hooper caught by Julian for 11. His job done—getting rid of two stroke-players in six intelligent overs—Steve returned to his gully position. The Aussies trailed by 44 runs.

The Windies quickies were at their intimidating worst, peppering the tourists with bouncers galore. Taylor was repeatedly hit on the body and Mark Waugh, after he had hit Courtney Walsh for a six, received a thundering blow on his back the very next ball. With rain playing hide and seek, Boon and Mark Waugh (61) added another Test century partnership to their impressive list. Steve went for quick runs and was unbeaten on 65 when the declaration came—setting the home team a difficult win-target of 257 runs in a maximum of 36 overs. They could make only 2–80 in 30 overs, Lara scoring a quick-fire 43 and the Test ended in a draw.

The third Test at Port-of-Spain was played on a green top where the first 30 wickets toppled for 369 runs. No team could total

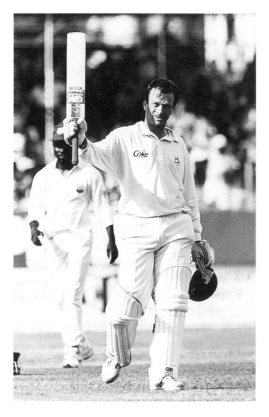

Steve Waugh raises his bat after reaching his double century in the Kingston Test of 1995. (*Allsport/Shaun Botterill*)

140 runs in an innings and there was only one individual fifty—by Steve Waugh. Richardson won the toss and sent in Australia, who were shot out for 128, almost half the score made by Steve (63 not out). With the ball swinging like a happy puppy's tail, Ambrose was in his element as his balls darted alarmingly off the seam and the odd one reared off a good length.

The Test is remembered for a mid-pitch confrontation between Steve Waugh and Curtly Ambrose—arguably the best batsman and bowler of the early 1990s. A bouncer from Curtly cleared Steve's head by more than a metre. After this he followed through to a couple of metres from Steve and stared at him angrily. Without batting an eyelid, Steve asked: 'What the ---- are you looking at?' As later narrated by Steve in his *West Indies Tour Diary*, 'It was at this moment that I realised I had done the equivalent of smashing open a hornet's nest with a large brick.'

The happy twins celebrating their winning hundreds. *(Allsport/Shaun Botterill)*

Beside himself with rage, Ambrose roared: 'Don't cuss me, man.' It was eyeball-to-eyeball stuff and the cricket world waited in anticipation of another Lillee–Miandad kick-and-hit conflict. Fortunately, captain Richardson moved in swiftly to avert a hand-to-hand combat and the game continued. At tea, Steve reached 'the hardest 50 of my career'; a job made more difficult because of the constant booing from a hostile crowd.

With Glenn McGrath bowling superbly (6–47) and Steve again getting his man Hooper, the Windies managed a lead of only eight runs. On a deteriorating pitch, Australia panicked and were bowled-out for a paltry 105 (Mark Taylor 30, Steve 21) and the home team won by nine wickets with two days remaining. The series was now locked one-all with one Test to go. A self-critic, Steve felt depressed. In the second innings, his lapse of concentration had cost him his wicket and his departure signalled a collapse when Australia lost five wickets for two runs in 15 balls. But his 63 not out and 21 in the low-scoring match on a rank bad pitch against a non-stop intimidating attack and a crowd chanting 'cheat, cheat' had lifted him to number two batting rank on the Coopers & Lybrand ratings—with West Indian Jimmy Adams at number one and stars Lara and Sachin Tendulkar at three and four.

In the first three Tests, not a single century was scored, which is especially surprising because both the teams were so strong in batting. Richardson broke the ton-barrier in the fourth and final Test at Sabina Park, Kingston, Jamaica. However, the Windies could total only a modest 265 on a good wicket which *Wisden* described as 'a shiny pitch of rolled mud, as polished as a dance-room floor'. Australia had to win the series. A drawn series was to the West Indies' advantage because, as holders, they would retain the Frank Worrell Trophy. With this in view, the Waugh twins—first Mark who scored a magnificent century, and then Steve who recorded a gutsy double hundred—batted with rare determination, adding 231 runs in 57 overs. It was a partnership which will be forever entrenched in Australian sporting history.

Steve walked in 15 minutes before lunch on day two when the score was a none-too-appetising 3–73. He had hardly slept the night before when a trespasser lurked in his room pretending to be a security guard. He woke up feeling horrible. But after lunch that day, and for most of day three, it was the opposition bowlers and fielders who felt horrible, so rock-solid was Steve's concentration.

Once in the middle, Steve felt totally relaxed. Kenny Benjamin greeted him with a throat-clutching bouncer. Steve stepped aside. There were no nervous butterflies. He felt supremely confident and focused. He got off the mark with a well-struck cover drive. The pitch reminded him of WACA in Perth where both he and Mark had hit double centuries for NSW four-and-a-half years earlier. Bumpers were hurled at the twins' heads, shoulders and chests at the rate of three to four per over. It was not easy but they hung on; swaying, sliding or looking the other way—offering the other cheek or shoulder. They hit only those deliveries which were wide or overpitched, rarely hooking. Luck came Steve's way when wicket-keeper Courtney Brown dropped him with his score on 42. After tea they almost ran each other out—the infamous 'Waugh shuffle'—but the fielder threw at the wrong end.

The pitch had started deteriorating and a friendly off-spinner like Hooper turned the ball sharply. Mark was the first to reach his century, then Australia took the first-innings lead, followed by Steve getting his ton. It was the eighth century for both Steve and Mark. So dominating were the Waughs that the normally aggressive Winston Benjamin looked shattered at the drinks break and sat weeping in sheer exasperation. He had to be urged to continue bowling. Immediately after Steve reached his ton Mark received an unplayable delivery from Hooper. It jumped from a crack, touched his glove and Jimmy Adams snatched up a reflex catch. The brothers had added 231 splendid runs in 233 minutes.

At stumps Australia was 4–321, Steve undefeated on 110. After a promising innings by Greg Blewett, wickets started falling at the other end. The ninth wicket fell with Steve five runs short of his maiden Test double hundred. And who should come in but Glenn McGrath, probably the world's worst batsman, but a favourite among Australian supporters who chanted 'Oo-aah, Glenn McGrath'. Glenn somehow kept his end up and Steve advanced to 196. Then the modest superstar hit Hooper for an all-run four and reached his 200 amid a thunderous ovation. Among those deliriously happy Australians to invade the pitch to congratulate Steve was former Australian Test cricketer Greg Ritchie, alias 'Fat Cat' and 'Mahatma Cote'. 'For the next couple of minutes, everything was a blur,' recalls Steve. He had batted for nearly 10 hours, faced 425 deliveries—a third of them short-pitched ones on the neck-line—received many bruises of various shapes and hues, and hit 17 fours and a six.

Next day was a rest day and Steve recovered with ice-packs, massages and his favourite drink, Southern Comfort, which team mate Carl Rackemann had specially smuggled in for him in a cola bottle. On 3 May, Australia won by an innings and 53 runs, the Aussie dressing room resembling a Friday evening pub during happy hour. Champagne corks were popping, beer and banter flowing, Aussie flags fluttering and Boon conducting the team's match-winning song: 'Under the Southern Cross I stand'.

It was an emotional moment, with neither a dry eye nor a dry glass anywhere. Steve was the Man of the Match and the Player of the Series as Australia proudly held aloft the Frank Worrell Trophy. His winning double ton promoted him to number one in the Coopers & Lybrand batting rankings—displacing Adams. Ian Healy summed up the series with this touching tribute: 'That [West Indies 1995] tour was Steve Waugh's show. He dominated it from start to finish. Without him we'd never have won. He was the rock which held the team together.' Healy describes Steve's double century as 'the best innings I have witnessed in my time in Test cricket'.

'Someone had to put his hand up and make a hundred,' Steve said. 'I was very pleased I was one of them.' He later described this match as 'the biggest Test of our careers' and 'probably my proudest moment'.

Mark, who reached his 3000th Test run in this innings, added, 'To make a hundred against the West Indies in Jamaica is as good a test of yourself as you can get. I just played on natural reaction to where the ball was and today my shot selection was very good. I don't think I played a false shot besides the one I got out on.'

Their father, Revesby newsagent Rodger, was justifiably the proudest dad in Australia. He had always believed that his boys would emulate the Chappell and Mohammad brothers' feats of scoring centuries in the same innings. Unfortunately, he could not see his sons reach their milestones on television as he was throwing newspapers to his clients' driveways. 'But I must admit I was very nervous when making those deliveries,' he said.

ⓘ Batting, Betting and Controversies Galore

The 1995–96 Australian season bristled with thorny controversies which had international repercussions. The bribery scandal during the 1994 tour to Pakistan—mentioned earlier in Chapter 11—came out in the open during the first half of the 1995–96 season when Pakistan played a three-Test series Down Under.

But this was a mere prelude to the real thing when the Sri Lankans visited Australia. In between some brilliant batting displays—especially by Michael Slater, Romesh Kaluwitharana, Ricky Ponting, the Waugh brothers and Sanath Jayasuriya—the visitors were accused of ball-tampering (later exonerated by the International Cricket Council) and their off-spinner Muttiah Muralitharan of throwing. The chucking episode created such a furore that strong letters to the Editor were written even by those not interested in the game. Most of these letters were pro-Muralitharan who had briefly become the underdog the Australian public love to defend. As the tour progressed the bitterness between Australian and Sri Lankan cricketers escalated to such an extent that, in the deciding final of the Benson & Hedges World Series on 20 January 1996, the Sri Lankan players refused to shake hands with the victorious Australians.

Death threats were allegedly made against some Australian cricketers and umpires, leading to a majority of Australians refusing to play their first match in Colombo, Sri Lanka, for the 1996 World Cup. The official reason for the boycott was the civil unrest in Sri Lanka and the bombing of areas close to the hotel where the Australian team was due to stay. The controversies and hostility notwithstanding, Australia remained on top, beating the strong Pakistanis and the talented Sri Lankans. Many contributed, but the men behind these victories were the Waugh twins.

In seven successive Tests from April 1995 to January 1996, they scored seven centuries between them. Mark Waugh had made 126 and Steve 200 in the final Test against the West Indies at Kingston in mid–1995 to start this amazing sequence. In the following Test against Pakistan in Brisbane, Steve hit an unbeaten 112. After neither scored a ton in the Hobart Test (although Mark came close with 88), Mark stroked a gritty 116 against Pakistan in Sydney, followed by an elegant 111 v. Sri Lanka in Perth.

Groin injury forced Steve to miss the Perth Test but he slammed an unbeaten 131 against the Sri Lankans in the Melbourne Test, and 170 and an undefeated 61 in Adelaide. He topped both the batting and bowling averages against Sri Lanka to lift the Player of the Series award for the fourth time in seven successive series. In the combined series against Pakistan and Sri Lanka, Steve had scored 562 runs at 112.40 with three centuries and Mark 555 runs at 61.67 with two tons. Steve also took five wickets and two catches; Mark four wickets and six catches.

Now to the details of the summer of discontent. With the bribery allegation brought out in the open and the arrival of Salim Malik—stripped of captaincy but still in the squad—it was expected to be a quarrelsome and volatile series. The Australians—especially Shane Warne, Tim May and Mark Waugh—were seething with rage that a Pakistani judge had proclaimed Malik's innocence and indirectly called the Australians liars.

The series could well have deteriorated into a slanging match but for the rival captains. Mark Taylor kept the temperature down by advising his players to concentrate on the game and win the

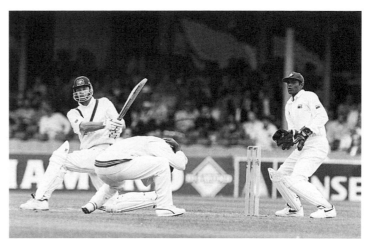

Out of the way, mate. Mark Waugh hooking against Pakistan in the Sydney Test of 1995. (*Allsport/Shaun Botterill*)

matches, although he fully supported his men, saying, 'I think the players feel a little let down'—the epitome of understatement. The new Pakistan captain Wasim Akram deserved equal praise for handling the team with tact and firmness. To quote David Hopps from *Wisden 1997*: 'They [the Pakistan team] had been riven by conflict and mistrust over the allegations of bribery and betting scams but, in trying circumstances, they generally maintained a cordial and dignified air.'

Salim Malik's touchdown in Australia, a week after the arrival of the main party, did spark a media frenzy at the Perth airport. He remained tight-lipped and was escorted everywhere by police. Feeling like a hunted animal, with the press on the lookout for a quote, he remarked, 'I hate Australia; it's hell. I just stay in my room all day watching TV.'

Surprisingly, after all the media hype, the three-Test series was incident-free with Australia right on top in the first two Tests. The home team won the first Test at Brisbane by an innings in little over three days. Australia's total of 463 was built largely on Steve's unbeaten 112 and Mark Waugh's 59. It was not Steve's best innings. He was uncomfortable against the speed and swing of Wasim Akram and Waqar Younis (who isn't?) and offered two chances off Aamir Sohail's left-arm spin when in his eighties. Steve himself called it an ugly innings.

Ugly maybe, but certainly useful, as his 112 was 15 runs more than Pakistan's paltry first innings total of 97 as Warne took 7–23 in 16.1 overs. Warne's joy would have been complete had he dismissed Salim Malik, but Salim had split the webbing on his left hand when accepting a diving catch earlier on. The next day Warne had Salim caught for a duck in the second innings.

The tourists batted more responsibly in the second innings, scoring 240. Aamir Sohail was unfortunate to fall at 99. They looked like putting up a fight at 3–217 with Inzamam-ul-Haq in fine touch, but Mark Waugh changed the scenario in a hurry. Brought into the attack to allow Warne to change ends, he tempted Inzamam to spoon a catch to mid-off which precipitated a collapse during which Pakistan lost 7–23. Warne bowled with a vengeance to claim 11 wickets at 7.00.

In the next Test at Hobart, Mark Waugh top-scored with a fluent 88 in his 50th Test. His first fifty was full of dazzling strokes, despite shooting pains in the right leg, but with wickets tumbling at the other end he played an uncharacteristic, dogged innings. Waqar Younis took only two wickets in the match but made what looked like a match-winning

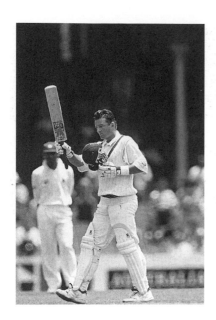

Mark reaches his hundred on the SCG in 1995. (*Allsport/Shaun Botterill*)

contribution. His crushing yorker broke Warne's toe and the legendary spinner could not bowl a single ball in the entire Test. Despite his absence, Pakistan was bowled out for 198 (Steve claiming Inzamam's scalp) in the first innings, and for 220 in the second, to lose by a big margin in four days.

After two successive Test defeats and a humiliating loss to Victoria, the Pakistanis were written off by the critics before a ball was bowled in the final Sydney Test. But the visitors took control, and with Ijaz Ahmed scoring a fine century, and 'googly king' Mushtaq Ahmed claiming nine wickets, they won by 74 runs. This was Pakistan's first Test victory in Australia since 1981–82. Belting eight fours and a six, Mark Waugh scored his first Test century on the SCG and added 83 runs with Steve. At stumps on the second day, Mark was 54 and Steve 26. When play resumed the next day, the umpires were not sure which Waugh should face the first ball until informed by the scorers.

In Pakistan's second innings, Mark had the satisfaction of trapping Salim Malik for 45. Apart from the defeat, a groin injury to Steve was a major worry and he missed the first Test against Sri Lanka at Perth. This Test is remembered for the furore over ball-tampering allegations. After the Sri Lankans were dismissed for 251 on the stroke of 6 p.m. on the opening day, the Australian batsmen were in top gear, hitting balls with gusto. But there was trouble brewing. According to the match referee, Graham Dowling of New Zealand, 'the condition of the ball was clearly altered during the 17th over of the innings by a member of the Sri Lankan team'. He warned that action would be taken if it happened again.

The Sri Lankans vehemently pleaded innocence. No-one even cared to ask them their side of the story before passing judgment. The same ball was allowed to be used as Slater (a dashing 219), Taylor (96), Mark Waugh (111), Ricky Ponting (96 on debut) and Stuart Law (54 not out) flayed the Sri Lankan attack and declared at 5–617. It was an error of judgment by umpires Khizer Hayat of Pakistan and Australia's P. D. Parker not to impound the 'tampered' ball after the 17th over (when they found it was 'doctored') and send it away for investigation. In view of this, the International Cricket Council (ICC) reversed the match referee's decision a fortnight later.

Mark Waugh approached this Test nervously, remembering the four consecutive ducks he had made in the previous two Tests in Sri Lanka in 1992. He almost got his fifth in a row against the visitors but was dropped by wicket-keeper Kaluwitharana. Having escaped this embarrassment, he went on to stroke a majestic 111 off 223 balls, hitting seven fours and a six and adding 156 runs with Slater. It was Mark's tenth Test century and was 'so smooth, it almost slipped by without notice', wrote Trent Bouts in *Wisden 1997*. To watch Mark bat that day was like being chauffer-driven in a Rolls-Royce. It seems you are cruising at barely 60 kph but are actually speeding at 160 kph. Australia won by an innings, it being the fifth time in eight Tests that they were victorious with a day to spare.

Steve Waugh, now fit for the Melbourne Test, made his presence felt by hitting his 10th Test ton, to keep up with Mark. Steve's unbeaten 131 included 11 fours and a five, and he added 115 runs with Ponting. But the talk of Australia—in fact the cricket world—was the no-balling of Sri Lankan off-spinner Muralitharan by umpire Darrell Hair. Murali, as the Australian public called him, was no-balled for 'chucking' twice in his fourth over, three times in his fifth and twice in his sixth. Australia declared at 6–500 and won by 10 wickets.

Steve continued at Adelaide in the final Test from where he had left off in Melbourne, scoring 170 and 61 not out. Australia totalled 500 runs for the third time in three Tests and won by 148 runs to wrap up the series 3–0. It was a dream series for Steve as he averaged a Bradmanesque 362 with the bat and topped the bowling average (8.50) as he took 4–34 in the Adelaide Test, and was deservedly made both Man of the Match and of the Series.

Vociferous Pakistanis appeal against Steve in the Hobart Test of 1995. (*Rick Smith*)

The saving grace for Sri Lanka was Sanath Jayasuriya's 112 runs off 188 balls in the second innings, hitting 14 fours and two sixes. No-one realised then that within two years, he would become a most dynamic player and would revolutionise the limited-overs game strategies.

In the Benson & Hedges World Series that season, the resilient Sri Lankans surprised a divided West Indies team to enter the finals. Steve Waugh had missed the bulk of the World Series through injuries but made up for lost time with his first century in 187 limited-overs internationals. However, his unbeaten 102 in Melbourne was not enough to prevent the Sri Lankans from winning by three wickets in the last over to qualify for the final. In an earlier match in Perth, Mark Waugh seized the opener's spot with a career-best 130, adding 189 runs for the first wicket with Mark Taylor.

Watched by the largest crowd of the summer (72,614 to be exact), the first final on the MCG was full of controversies. The visitors felt that Steve Waugh was lucky to survive an lbw appeal and were irate when the same umpire, Steve Randell, lifted his finger to give dashing opener Kaluwitharana out when he was warming-up with three breathtaking fours in nine deliveries. The acrimony continued in the second final in Sydney. Sri Lanka had to win this match to force a third final and came close to it with a do-or-die policy. There were angry exchanges both on and off the field.

The two Marks, Waugh (82) and Taylor (73), had an opening stand of 135 and Australia made 5–273 in 50 overs; the best total of this tournament. Then came heavy rains which reduced Sri Lanka's win target to 168 in 25 overs—an imposing run-rate of 6.72 on a slippery and heavy outfield. Despite their ferocious hitter Kaluwitharana falling to his arch-enemy Glenn McGrath for a duck, the adventurous Sri Lankans took up the challenge and looked like winning at 6–135 with five overs remaining. But Warne took two crucial wickets, just as he had done in Melbourne two days previously, dismissing the tenacious captain Arjuna Ranatunga for 41 and Kumara Dharmasena in successive overs, and Sri Lanka fell only eight runs short.

During the epic chase in the last few overs, there was an ugly confrontation between Ranatunga and Ian Healy. Podgy and panting, Ranatunga asked for drinks every few overs. Healy objected that this was an excuse to have too many breaks. The Australians also objected when Ranatunga asked for a runner, claiming an injury. 'You can't call for a runner just because you're unfit,' Healy said tersely. The upshot was that the Sri Lankans refused to shake Taylor's outstretched hand after the match or acknowledge the home team who were presented with the Trophy.

Steve Waugh considered this match as the one he enjoyed the least in his decade of international cricket. 'In my opinion the whole episode was an absolute disgrace,' he wrote in *World Cup Diary* (1996). 'Our win meant nothing to me. All I could think of was how little I had enjoyed being involved, and how sad it was when affairs reach the point where opponents can't shake hands after the contest had been won.'

⑮ Wog Twins' World Cup

The acrimony and feuding which had dogged the Australian summer of 1995–96 spilled over the early part of the Wills World Cup 1996, which was co-hosted by India, Pakistan and Sri Lanka. It is not the purpose of this book to go into the rights and wrongs of Australia's decision to boycott their first World Cup match in Colombo. To give their point of view, let me quote Steve Waugh from *World Cup Diary* (1996): 'We were far from happy with what had gone wrong during the Australian summer and, to compound our unease, some of the Australian squad, among them Shane Warne, Craig McDermott and coach Bob Simpson, had received death threats.'

Also, there were horrifying pictures in Sydney's *Daily Telegraph* of 1 February 1996 after a bomb attack in Colombo, a mere five minutes away from where the Australian team would have stayed during their first World Cup match. The bomb reportedly killed 80 and injured over 1000 others. Ron Reed, the Australian correspondent in Sri Lanka, wrote in the *Daily Telegraph*: 'If the directors of the Australian Cricket Board had been in Colombo yesterday morning to accompany me on a grim walk through the horrific aftermath of Wednesday's suicide bomb atrocity, I have no doubt they would quickly arrive at a unanimous decision. Australia must either forfeit the opening World Cup match against Sri Lanka or insist that it be moved to India or Pakistan . . . While Colombo is one of the world's most cricket crazy cities, it is also a war zone. As such, sending the Australian team here represents an unacceptable risk.'

'War zone' notwithstanding, other countries—except Australia and the West Indies—did play in Colombo with no harm to life or limb. Cynics argued whether Australia would boycott a tour of England, where bombing of cars and hotels is not unheard of because of hostility between Britain and the IRA. Or would the repeated rioting on the streets of Johannesburg inhibit the Aussies from playing a Test match there? Also, had the relations between Australian and Sri Lankan cricketers been friendly and there had been no 'death threats', would Australia have boycotted the Colombo one-dayer?

Steve candidly wrote in his Diary, 'I would have been willing to go if the Board insisted on us touring there, even though frankly, I didn't want to.' He was annoyed that there were reports in the media that six senior players—including himself—were threatening to boycott the Sri Lankan leg, 'but these were 100 per cent fabricated. In fact, I took offence that my name was mentioned as one of the six.' His attitude was that 'we were either all in or all out'.

However, once the tournament commenced, politics receded into the background. Steve nostalgically remembered the 1987 World Cup in India and Pakistan when little-fancied Australia had won the crown. Craig McDermott, Steve and coach Bob Simpson were the only survivors of that triumphant World Cup. As Steve sat in the players' area during the Grand Opening ceremony in Calcutta waiting to be introduced to the masses, he recalled the 1987 triumph in that city. 'I could see the massive crowd all willing Australia to victory, the run-out of Bill Athey [of England] I was involved in, Mike Gatting attempting his now infamous reverse-sweep, our victory lap of honour and the buzz of excitement that emanated from the grandstand all day.'

Steve collars the Windies attack during a 1996 World Cup match in Jaipur. (*Allsport/Shaun Botterill*)

Those who label Steve as 'Ice Man' would be surprised at such sentiments. The opening ceremony—despite a few hiccups and flops—made his body cover in goose bumps and 'a surge of pins-and-needles tingled everywhere'.

After forfeiting their first match in Colombo, Australia started their campaign with an easy win over Kenya at Vishakapatnam in India. The 'Wog't wins (a majority of Indians could not get their tongues around 'Waugh') added 207 runs for the third wicket in 32 overs—a new World Cup record for any wicket. Mark scored 130 runs from 128 balls with 14 fours and a six, and Steve—despite stomach cramps—82 in 88 deliveries with five fours and a six. It was Steve's 190th limited-overs international and he passed 4000 runs. Unfortunately, McDermott broke down with injury in this match and returned home.

The next match against India in Mumbai (Bombay) was a thriller. It was the first floodlit international in this cosmopolitan cricket-loving city and was watched by a capacity crowd of over 41,000. They were fortunate to witness two sparkling innings; 126 by Mark Waugh (in 135 balls, eight fours, three sixes) and 90 by India's master batsman Sachin Tendulkar (84 balls, 14 fours and a six). Had Mark Waugh not dismissed Tendulkar, Australia would probably have lost. Freakily, both Waughs were run out. However, Mark became the first player to score centuries in successive matches. Tendulkar's magical 90 made Steve rave: 'He took to our bowlers like crocodiles do to chooks.' On a higher plane, Mark's century in this match inspired an Indian Airlines pilot to compose a poem on him entitled 'Batsman Beyond Compare'.

Mark continued his brilliant form by stroking an unbeaten 76 at Nagpur against Zimbabwe. He was denied a third consecutive hundred only by the modest victory target of 156.

After three successive victories, Australia tasted her first defeat when the West Indies beat them by four wickets in the 'Pink City'o f Jaipur. Stung by their humiliating defeat at the hands of lowly Kenya four days earlier, the Windies were determined to win with pacemen Curtly Ambrose and Courtney Walsh all fired up. Australia, however, weathered the storm and scored 229, Ricky Ponting (102) and Steve Waugh (57) adding 110 runs for the third wicket from 114 deliveries. Mark Waugh, after his 130, 126 and 76 not out (332 runs at 166), was dismissed for 30. To make up, he took 3–38 in 10 overs as an off-spinner, bowling in a yellow floppy hat and sunglasses. His victims were Brian Lara for 60, Shivnarine Chanderpaul for 10 and Keith Arthurton for a duck.

Despite this reverse, and despite forfeiting the Colombo game, Australia finished second in Group A and met New Zealand in the quarter-final at Chennai (Madras). A crowd of around 45,000 saw an epic tussle. New Zealand scored fluently to total an imposing 286, chiefly through their captain Lee Germon (89) and Chris Harris (130) who put on 164 runs, a World Cup record for the fourth wicket. With Australian batsmen's diffidence to chase a big total, the win-target of 287 appeared unachievable but Mark Waugh proved the doubters wrong. He attacked from the first ball to give Australia a thundering start, hitting five fours and two sixes in his 110 from 112 balls. He went from 93 to 99 with a six off Dipak Patel.

Steve suggested to skipper Mark Taylor that he promote 'pinch-hitter' Shane Warne in the batting order and the leggie obliged by hammering 24 runs in 14 balls with two sixes. Later on, the Waugh brothers added 86 runs for the fifth wicket. After Mark Waugh fell in sheer exhaustion, Steve carried on despite having twisted both his ankles. Helped by Stuart Law, he guided his country to a memorable win with six wickets and 13 balls to spare. In the process, Mark became the first player to hit three centuries in one World Cup. Also, he received his third Man of the Match award. Mark himself considers this innings as one of the best he has played under pressure.

By coincidence, all four semi-finalists—India, West Indies, Sri Lanka and Australia—came from Group A. The Australia v. West Indies semi-final at Mohali was full of drama at the end. The Windies were on a high with a victory over World Cup favourites South Africa, and Lara was back in tremendous form with a century. Australia started disastrously, losing 4–15 with the Waugh brothers, Mark Taylor and Ricky Ponting contributing a mere four runs between them. But with Law (72) and Michael Bevan (69) putting on 138 gritty runs for the fifth wicket, Australia reached a moderate total of 207.

Playing confidently, the Windies were 2–165 after 41 overs and needed only 43 runs in the last nine overs. Chanderpaul (80) and captain Richardson were in brilliant form. Just then Glenn McGrath had Chanderpaul caught and it was the beginning of the end. They lost their last eight wickets for 37 runs in the final 50 minutes. Warne bowled a devastating three-over spell in which he took 3–6. But Richardson, who had declared his intention to retire after the World Cup, was still there for the final pulsating over from Damien Fleming. Richardson hit the first ball for a four. Now six runs were needed from five balls with two wickets in hand. Then, in an unwise move, he went for a suicidal single and Ambrose was run out. Came last man Walsh and he was bowled. Incredibly, Australia had won by five runs.

'It was a game we couldn't possibly win, yet we did, and is definitely the best victory I have been involved in one-day cricket,' wrote Mark Waugh in the Foreword of Steve's *World Cup Diary*. Mark Taylor sportingly summed up the thriller by saying the West Indies had won 95 per cent of the match. Panic in the final stages made the Windies lose their cool. For the Australians it was a 'Miracle at Mohali'.

The final between Australia and Sri Lanka at Gadaffi Stadium in Lahore, Pakistan, had all the ingredients of a vendetta movie. The Sri Lankans had the 'we wuz robbed' feeling after the acrimonious Benson & Hedges final in Sydney two months previously. 'We'll teach them a lesson,' vowed their captain Arjuna Rantunga, hinting that their defeats in Australia were due to home umpiring.

Nearly 30,000 turned up to see the World Cup Final, a large majority supporting the Sri Lankans. It was the first day–night match in Pakistan. Sri Lanka won the toss and, as expected, sent Australia in to bat as the Sri Lankans prefer to chase a target. Australia started promisingly and were 1–134 after 25 overs. Taylor and Ponting were in fine touch but the match turned Sri Lanka's way when Aravinda de Silva dismissed both and Australia could total a modest 241. Both the Waughs failed; Mark scored 12 and Steve 13.

Everyone except Taylor and Ponting appeared to have an off day. Maybe there was not enough petrol left in their tank after their Herculean efforts at Madras and Mohali. Not a single four was hit from 19th to 43rd overs. The Sri Lankan spinners bowled superbly and their fielding was outstanding. The Australian total appeared inadequate, given the excellence of Sri Lankan batting form throughout the World Cup and their determination to win. However, they lost two quick wickets, Sanath Jayasuriya being narrowly run out and fellow big-hitter Romesh Kaluwitharana being caught in the deep.

Australia had a chance to break through but their fielding let them down badly. Quite a few catches and half-chances were put down. Heavy evening dew made the ball slippery—especially for their spinners. 'It was a display which reminded me of the Australian side of mid–1980s,' Steve reflected. 'Our intensity was down and we could not get out of neutral.' Aravinda de Silva batted magnificently to score an unbeaten 107 from 124 balls, adding 125 runs with Asanka Gurusinha (65) for the third wicket, and 97 with Ranatunga (47 not out) for the unbroken fourth wicket. Sri Lanka won easily with seven wickets and 22 balls to spare. It was the first time in the 21-year history of World Cup that a side batting second had been victorious.

Even though the Sri Lankans were ecstatic just to receive the Wills World Cup from Pakistan's Prime Minister Benazir Bhutto, defeating Australia was the icing on the cake. In the down-and-out dark corner, the Australians sat in gloom, disappointed with their lacklustre performance. 'What we wanted most was to be able to turn back the clock and start again,' Steve Waugh wrote in his Diary. 'At times such as these, words are of little or no comfort and it's best to let the players work the regrets out of their system.'

The consolations for Australia were entering the final in the first place and Mark Waugh creating two World Cup records by registering three centuries, including two in a row. He scored 484 runs at 80.67; second in aggregate after Tendulkar's 523, and fifth in averages after Ranatunga's 120.50, de Silva's 89.60, Tendulkar's 87.17 and Pakistan's Saeed Anwar's 82.25. Also, in taking 11 wickets (eight caught, three stumped), Australian 'keeper Ian Healy had dismissed most batsmen in this World Cup. More important, the 'Wog' brothers had charmed the subcontinent with their batsmanship and grit—especially after putting on a World Cup record partnership of 207 runs in the first match they played.

⑯ Safrican Safari

The 1996 World Cup left behind one fatality, the axing of coach Bob Simpson. He had nursed, coached, cajoled and converted a lacklustre, sloppily dressed unit of the mid–1980s into a confident, well-oiled and raring-to-go Australian team of early 1990s. He had given them motivation, a pride in themselves and a will to win.

Simmo had worked harmoniously with two captains of different nature—Allan Border labelled by some as 'Captain Grumpy', and Mark Taylor, a gentleman with a mind of his own. Border let Simmo organise off-field events but Taylor wanted his say on and off the field without being an autocrat. Under Taylor (and Simpson), Australia kept winning matches but the loss to Sri Lanka in the World Cup final at Lahore on 17 March 1996 was a bitter pill. Suddenly and surprisingly, Simmo the Supremo became redundant, his use-by date reached.

In his place, Australia had a likeable but unlikely supremo, the fitness fanatic Geoff Marsh who had retired from the first-class scene barely a season before. Marsh and Taylor had formed a formidable opening partnership, the best being their 329-run stand in the Nottingham Test against England in 1989. In mid–1996, they formed a new partnership as manager and captain of the Australian team. Their first Test together was in India in the one-off Test at Delhi in October 1996 played for the inaugural Border–Gavaskar Trophy. It was a chaotic beginning, everything going wrong for the Australians, who lost by seven wickets. The only saving grace for them was Steve Waugh, the sole survivor of the 1986–87 Test series.

The Australian cricketers were under-prepared at Test level. It was nine months since they had played their last Test, and since then there had been a plethora of mind-numbing limited-overs matches. Also, one cannot go to a new country with sharply contrasting pitch conditions (more turn, less bounce) after a solitary rain-interrupted first-class match and expect to win. The air pollution in Delhi and a substandard pitch did not help, but then their Indian counterparts did not wear gas masks, nor did they bat on a different pitch. In other words India, captained for the first time by the 23-year-old batting marvel Sachin Tendulkar, outplayed Australia.

Winning the toss, Australia batted first and was bowled out for 182. India's quickish spinner Anil Kumble was the main destroyer with a 4–63 haul. 'Aussie Kumbled' was the headline in many Indian newspapers the following day. The 'devil' in the pitch must have taken a day off when India batted and totalled 361 for a big lead of 179 runs. Their wicket-keeper Nayan Mongia opened India's innings and scored a polished 152, adding 131 runs for the second wicket with Saurav Ganguly (66).

Australia again started badly and were four down for 78 when rescued by Steve Waugh. One can imagine his state of mind as he went in to bat. He had scored a duck in the first innings, Australia was still over 100 runs in deficit and brother Mark was just given out, cutting Kumble. (Mark is adamant that he had not touched the ball.) Apart from this real crisis, Steve had a few personal problems. In his hurry to pack, he had left behind his good luck charm, a red rag. Also, his normal bat's handle had become loose and he had to take his practice bat along.

Mentally strong and self-analytical, Steve often talks to himself as he goes out to bat and between balls and overs. He later revealed to Greg Baum in *Good Weekend* (the *Sydney Morning Herald*): 'When I got a duck in the first innings, I did think: "Well, I know the reason, I didn't bring the rag." Then I thought: "No, you're being stupid here." If you come to rely on superstition, you're going to be in a bit of trouble, aren't you? It's a bit of a comfort thing. If I've got that rag, I say to myself: "It's nice to have it here." But it's not going to play your shots for you.'

His pulse was racing as he donned his gloves and walked out. A taunt often brings out the best in Steve and he was stung by a remark commentator and former Australian captain Ian Chappell had made two days previously. He had told no. 11 batsman Glenn McGrath that he had played better than Steve in the first innings. Steve was not amused. He was thinking of his reputation and of his country, not of saving the Test but winning it. 'Even when you're walking out, it's one of the most nerve-racking experiences you can ever have. You get a big rush of adrenaline. I'm in, I'm going to play for my country. This could be the most important innings of my life. It could be the last innings of my life.'

As the spinners were bowling, he threw his helmet aside and walked out with his baggy green cap, his priceless possession. To the crowd who clapped him in he looked cool and calm, the 'Ice Man', devoid of emotion. He resembled a bantamweight boxer, not quite ready with a knock-out punch but determined to last 15 rounds and win by points. And defend he did. He played straight to whatever Kumble and Co. hurled at him; sweeping only the loose deliveries—following advice given by Border. 'It sounds corny but I really do concentrate only on the next ball,' he told Baum. 'I don't like to think too far ahead. I don't play for sessions or days. I play the next ball as well as I can.'

In all he played 221 balls, batted for 273 minutes—nine minutes longer than Australia's first innings—and hit only five fours. Steve's iron-clad defence not withstanding, wickets kept tumbling at the other end and Australia was eight wickets down with only a measly 12-run lead. He had not thrown in the towel yet, thinking a lead of 100 would be too hard for the Indian bats to chase on a deteriorating pitch. So, gritting his teeth and tightening his cap on his furrowed brow, Steve took control. He inspired tail-ender Peter McIntyre and added 41 runs for the ninth wicket. Despite Steve's heroic unbeaten 67, Australia was dismissed for 234, setting India a mere 56 runs to win. They lost three quick wickets, including those of first innings centurion Mongia and Tendulkar for ducks, but they reached the target with seven wickets and a day to spare.

Steve in action against Pakistan in a limited-overs international in Hobart in 1996–97. (*Rick Smith*)

Summed up Peter Roebuck: 'Kumble was magnificent but [Steve] Waugh was a match for him, ignoring such deliveries as could be ignored and otherwise resisting with increasing vigilance and immense skill.'

The defeat was disappointing for Australia and heartbreaking for Steve who had fought like a Trojan warrior, just as he had in Kingston the previous year. For the rest it was a painful reminder that they had let their mentor Border down. After all, the Indo-Australian Test series is partly named after him. As Australia had not won a Test in India since 1969, the defeat stung even more. They returned home to face the Windies, who were also thirsting for revenge.

World champions for almost two decades, the West Indies had been humbled by Taylor's men 18 months previously but refused to acknowledge them as their superiors. A change in leadership with the popular Courtney Walsh installed as captain, the universally respected Clive Lloyd as manager and Malcolm Marshall as coach, promised a marvellous series—especially as they had more than capable batsmen in brilliant Brian Lara and Carl Hooper, gutsy grafters like Jimmy Adams and 22-year-old Shivnarine Chanderpaul and a battery of fast bowlers in Curtly Ambrose, Walsh, Ian Bishop, Ken Benjamin, Nixon McLean and Patterson Thomson.

The brief to the six-pronged attack appeared to be: Get the Waughs with head-high bouncers and occasional beamers and the rest will fall into place. It did not quite work out that way. The Waughs had an ordinary series by their high standards; Steve aggregating 188 runs in four Tests at 31.33 and Mark 370 in five Tests at 41.11. Both failed to score a century. Steve's best efforts were 66 at Brisbane and 58 at Melbourne; Mark reached fifties in four of the five Tests, 57 at Brisbane, 67 at Sydney, 82 at Adelaide and 79 at Perth.

Still, Australia retained the Frank Worrell Trophy 3–2, winning at Brisbane (thanks to Ian Healy's unbeaten 161), Sydney and Adelaide, but losing tamely at Melbourne and Perth. Ambrose captured 16 wickets in the two Windies' winning Tests.

The highlights for the series for the Waughs were:

- Steve added 102 with Greg Blewett for fifth wicket in the low-scoring Melbourne Test after Australia was 4–27.

- Mark added 164 for the third wicket with Matthew Hayden in Adelaide, and Australia won by an innings and 183 runs to retain the Frank Worrell Trophy; part-time spinner Michael Bevan grabbing 10 wickets in the match.

- Mark put on 120 runs for the fifth wicket with Bevan in the first innings of the low-scoring Perth Test.

- Mark scored 358 runs at 59.66 in the World Series limited-overs competition, with 102 against the West Indies at Brisbane as his highest.

Their disappointments in the series were:

- Steve developed groin strain when bowling in the Brisbane Test and missed the next Test in Sydney.

- Steve was out to a rank bad ball from Chanderpaul at Adelaide, popping it up to cover; perhaps the most disappointing shot he has played in his career. 'It is unlikely a worse ball has ever dismissed a better batsman in Test cricket,' commented *The Australian*.

- In the second innings of the Sydney Test, Mark and Matthew Elliott were involved in a spectacular mid-pitch collision. In only his second Test, Elliott was moving serenely to his maiden Test ton when he collided with Mark. Mark escaped unscathed as both players cartwheeled through the air but Elliott tore the cartilage in his right knee and was forced to retire hurt in excruciating pain. In a comedy of errors, neither batsman was run-out despite their being sprawled on the ground and out of their crease. This mishap occurred at 2–143 and Mark, the lucky one, was the third batsman out at 209 after scoring 67. The unlucky Elliott missed not only his Test century but also the next three Tests.

- Despite their win in the Test series, Australia failed to make the final of the World Series. (Pakistan beat the West Indies 2–0 in the finals.)

Defeating the West Indies in the Test series did not confirm Australia's status as Test champions. According to a points system devised by *Wisden Cricket Monthly* of January 1997, South Africa was marginally ahead. Thus the series in South Africa was touted as the Championship of Test Cricket.

Since Australia and South Africa had shared the Test series one-all both at home and away in 1993–94, the Safrican Safari of 1997 attracted attention wherever cricket is played. It was also an incentive for Taylor's men to do their best to claim the unofficial crown of world champions. It was an entertaining, seesawing series—especially the all-important second Test at Port Elizabeth which the home team should have won easily but lost thanks to a bowling blitz by young fast bowler Jason Gillespie and a priceless century by Mark Waugh. The Waugh brothers dominated the series. Steve was adjudged Man of the Series (as he was in the previous two series against South Africa), and also joint Man of the Match in the first Test (with Greg Blewett). Mark was Man of the Match in the second Test.

Australia started the series confidently after winning the first seven matches on the tour. The first Test on the Wanderer's ground in Johannesburg is remembered for a brilliant 385-run partnership between Steve (160 runs in 501 minutes off 366 balls with 22 fours) and Blewett (214 runs in 519 minutes from 421 balls with 34 fours).

It was Steve's 12th century in 87 Tests and he passed the Test aggregates of Ian Chappell (5349 runs) and Doug Walters (5357) to become the seventh highest run-scorer among Australians. The Blewett–Steve Waugh partnership was the second highest for the fifth wicket in Test annals, after the 405 between Sid Barnes and Don Bradman in 1946–47, and the 12th highest for any wicket in Tests. It was also the highest stand for any wicket in a Test in South Africa and the fourth highest by Australians in Test cricket.

The only chance offered during this mammoth stand was when Steve, on 45, skied a ball off pace-bowler Lance Kluesner. On the third day after tea, Steve suffered from cramps and let Blewett dominate the partnership. On the third day, 2 March, they became only the tenth pair in Test history to bat through the day, creating records galore and pulverising the home team in the process. Australia declared at 8–628, a lead of 326 runs. It was the first time since the South Africans' return to Test cricket in 1992 that a total in excess of 500 had been made against them. Blewett's 214 was the highest individual score in a Johannesburg Test, the previous highest being England captain Mike Atherton's 185 a year before. *The Australian*'s columnist Mike Coward summed up Blewett's knock as 'breath-taking one day, merely splendid the next'.

With South Africa collapsing for 130 (Warne and Bevan capturing four wickets each and Steve dismissing captain Hansie Cronje), Australia won by an innings and 196 runs. The margin of defeat was their worst against any country since 1949–50. Steve ascribed

Australia's big win to the hard series they had fought against the West Indies a few months before. 'Hard Test matches are good. That's what you want to toughen you up,' he said after the match. 'The first Test is always the key match in the series. It sets up the tone for the series.'

The next Test at Port Elizabeth was a cliffhanger. 'Poor pitches produce poor cricket but great finishes, and it was poetic justice that an unashamed attempt to negate the spinning powers of Shane Warne and Michael Bevan did not stop Australia taking the match and the series, albeit by the narrow margin of two wickets,' Jack Bannister wrote in *Wisden Cricket Monthly*.

It was the grassiest pitch the tourists had encountered and Taylor had no hesitation in sending South Africa in to bat. After being in strife at 4–72, they recovered to total 209. The modest score appeared big when Australia was bundled out for 108. They lost their last eight wickets for 60. South Africa rubbed salt into Australia's wounds when openers Gary Kirsten and Adam Bacher put on 83 runs without loss at stumps on day two, giving the home team a seemingly winning lead of 184 runs with all wickets intact. But incredibly they lost 10 wickets for 85 runs the next morning, Gillespie dismissing three of them to capture eight in the match. Australia was set a daunting task of scoring 270 to win—the highest total of the Test on a wearing pitch with unpredictable bounce.

Cometh the hour, cometh the man. Mark Waugh came in after tea on the third day with the score at 2–30. Elliott had run out Hayden in bizarre circumstances—both batsmen running to the same end, each unaware of the other. It was musical comedy stuff, but funny for neither batsman. The first Test heroes Steve Waugh and Blewett fell cheaply but Mark continued undisturbed, scoring a magnificent 116. He was sixth out at 258; only 12 runs short of the winning target. His 100 had come off 198 balls. In all he stayed for 323 minutes, played 229 deliveries, hit 17 fours, a five (when his shot touched a fielder's helmet) and a six. He later admitted that he had feathered a catch behind the wicket earlier in his innings but no-one had appealed and he stayed.

Support came from left-hander Bevan and the two stylish New South Welshmen added 66 crucial runs. With the score at 5–258 and only a dozen more runs needed for victory, the Test appeared to be over and won. But the topsy-turvy Test took another twist. Mark was bowled by part-time bowler Jacques Kallis. A few balls later Bevan fell to Cronje without addition. Seven runs later Warne was adjudged lbw to Kallis although TV replays showed that it was off a no-ball. Australia had suddenly plummeted from a winning 5–258 to a shaky 8–265.

With five runs needed for victory, no-frills Healy achieved it in style, off one ball. He hit a six off Cronje to win the Test by two wickets and the series 2–0. Healy became the first Australian, and the eleventh player, to win a Test with a six.

Given Australia's poor recent record in chasing victories, it was one of their greatest-ever triumphs. Mark Waugh was ecstatic with his major contribution in converting what appeared a lost Test into a series winner. 'It was the best of my eleven Test hundreds and also my best innings in first-class cricket.' His big thrill was watching a few schoolboys in the crowd holding a placard,

Mark Waugh about to catch Brian Lara in the Brisbane Test of 1996-97. (*Allsport/Shaun Botterill*)

'Mark Waugh is the greatest', when receiving the Man of the Match award. 'I did not pay them to hold that poster,' he quipped.

Mark recalls a hair-raising experience when visiting a game reserve, Shamwari, in Port Elizabeth the next day. Accompanied by brother Steve, skipper Taylor, Andy Bichel, Blewett, Elliott, manager Col Egar and scorer Mike Walsh in two jeeps, they encountered an angry elephant which charged them. 'It was bloody frightening,' he later wrote in Sydney's *Daily Telegraph*. 'His ears were flapping and his trunk was going up and down—he was out to get a piece of us and he nearly did . . . It was a scary moment . . . I didn't want to die the day after making a hundred—mind you, it wouldn't be a bad way to end my career.'

Relaxing before the final Test in South Africa in March 1997. The following month they were ranked numbers one and two batsmen in the world. (*Allsport/Mike Hewett*)

Having already won the series, Australia was struck with the now-familiar FDTDS (final dead Test defeat syndrome) in the next Test at Centurion Park. South Africa won the toss, sent Australia in to bat and eventually won by 8 wickets. Steve shone out in both innings, top-scoring with 67 and an unbeaten 60. Mark Waugh made 42 in the second innings, but fast bowler Allan Donald was the hero with eight scalps in the match. Steve took a battering from Donald. He recalls one particular over. 'It was a quick and fiery over and reminded me of the West Indies in that I got a lot of bruises. I don't think you'll see much better Test cricket than was on the show in that over.'

For the third time in a row against the South Africans, Steve Waugh was adjudged Player of the Series. He had topped batting aggregate and average, scoring 313 runs at 78.25. Mark came third on the list with 209 at 41.80 after Blewett's 271 at 54.20.

Steve retained his number one ranking on the Coopers & Lybrand ratings and Mark jumped over Brian Lara and England's Alec Stewart to be ranked number two. It was a great honour for Australia, as indeed it was for the Waugh family.

Australia also won the exciting seesawing limited-overs series 4–3; winning the second, fourth, fifth and seventh internationals. Hampered by injuries, Mark played only three matches but dominated the second match on his favourite ground, St George's Park in Port Elizabeth, with an unbeaten 115 in 126 balls, clouting eight fours and three sixes. All the sixes came in one over from off-spinner Pat Symcox. With Steve scoring an unbeaten 50 (eight fours and a six), the twins added 107 runs for the unbroken fourth wicket. They thus dominated the limited-overs internationals as well; Steve scoring 301 at 50.16, Mark 118 at 59.00.

It was one of their most satisfying tours and a fine prelude to the Ashes tour due to start less than a month later.

⑰ Good Old Trafford Magic

It is one thing to reach the top, quite another to stay there. After Steve and Mark being ranked as numbers one and two batsmen in the world, many wondered what remained for the Waughs to achieve. Were their recent performances in South Africa the pinnacle of their success? Could the rise and rise of the Waughs continue in England?

They were 32, an age at which Test cricketers think of retirement. Were they running out of incentives? Not quite. Just before the tour to England, Steve was promoted to the vice-captaincy to take his good mate Ian Healy's place. With skipper Mark Taylor's form in a slump there was serious talk of the possibility of Steve taking over the leadership mid-stream in England if Taylor continued to fail. In fact, Steve did captain Australia in the third limited-overs international against England at Lord's.

Mark Waugh had incentives too. Wouldn't it be nice to topple his brother to become the number one batsman in the world? More realistically, he desperately wanted to score a century in the Lord's Test and to have his name on the hallowed list alongside Bradman's, Hammond's, Trumper's, Hobbs' . . . In 1993, he had missed this honour by just one run when bowled by spinner Phil Tufnell. Also, according to Ian Chappell, Mark Waugh was a good candidate as Australia's captain.

Mark Waugh relaxes with a tinnie after his glorious 173 v. Hampshire at Southampton in 1997. (*Alan Crompton*)

'When Allan Border retired I wrote that of all the candidates, including Taylor, I would have chosen Mark Waugh,' Chappell had said. 'He has got a good cricket brain, but the best thing is that he's a gambler. In the field you can see he's always thinking about getting a wicket. That's how he used to bowl. And he's a magnificent batsman . . . The thing about Mark being a captain is that he could lead from the front. If he told the team to go out and attack, you know he'd do it himself. Steve's not that sort of player, nor is Taylor.'

An outspoken person, Mark Waugh criticised England's lack of hunger for success in a pre-tour interview with Jim Maxwell in *ABC Cricket 1997 Ashes Tour* publication. 'Since I've been playing England, we've won easily in every series,' he said. 'I look at the team on paper and think they are good players, but they are not tough enough or hungry enough on the field. They don't play as a team, they worry about themselves. When you are out there, you don't feel that you've got eleven guys against you; they just haven't got the toughness you need to win Test cricket consistently. Man-for-man they are not that far behind us, but they lack hunger.'

Mark must have regretted making that statement. With Taylor strug-

An elegant square-cut by Mark during his 140
in the 1994 Brisbane Test against England.
(Allsport/Ben Radford)

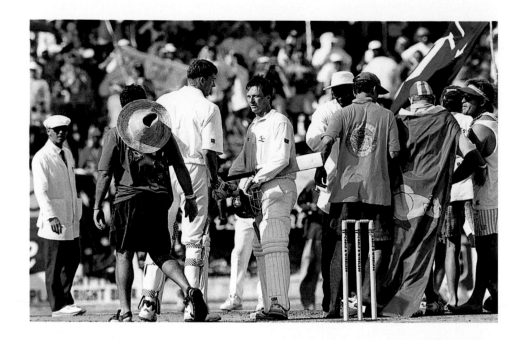

Steve reaches his 200 amid tremendous excitement. An ecstatic moment for him, partner Glenn McGrath and the Aussie supporters who 'invade' the field. *(Allsport/Shaun Botterill)*

Steve with Greg Blewett after their massive 385-run stand in the Johannesburg Test of 1997. *(Allsport/Mike Hewett)*

A magic moment. Steve kisses the Frank Worrell Trophy. *(Allsport/Shaun Botterill)*

Saying it with
Coca-Cola – relaxing
after their Kingston
triumph.
(Allsport/Shaun Botterill)

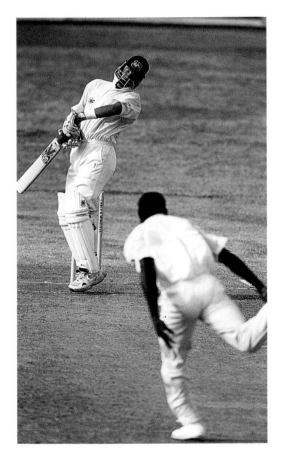

Mark avoids a vicious bouncer
from Winston Benjamin in the
1995 St John's Test.
(Allsport/Clive Mason)

Allan Border congratulates Steve on
bowling Allan Donald in the Cape Town Test of
1994 to finish with his best Test haul of 5-28.
(Allsport/Mike Hewett)

Run brother, don't run! Acting as a runner, Mark is run out, leaving Steve stranded on 99 not out at Perth against England in 1995.
(Allsport/Ben Radford)

A beaming Steve holding the Frank Worrell Trophy with Allan Border and Mark Taylor.
(Allsport/Shaun Botterill)

Man of the Old Trafford
Test, Steve raises a toast.
(Allsport/Clive Mason)

Champers all
round to celebrate
a great victory.
(Allsport/Clive Mason)

Steve takes a
head-over-heels catch
to dismiss Graham
Thorpe off Merv
Hughes in the Trent
Bridge Test of 1993.
(Allsport/Adrian Murrell)

Mark hits a towering
six during the
1998 Sydney Test;
Steve's 100th.
(Allsport/Ben Radford)

A joyous meeting between a promising future and a glorious past when Steve Waugh, 22, has a tête-à-tête with 'Stork' Hunter Hendry, 92, during the Bicentennial Test in Sydney in 1988. Despite their 70-year age difference, the two talked endlessly. Apart from similar styles—both being attractive middle-order batsmen, medium-fast bowlers and safe fielders—they revel in sportsmanship.
(Sydney Morning Herald/White)

'We're 32 today';
v. Derbyshire on
2 June 1997.
(Allsport/Clive Mason)

A ferocious hook—now a rarity—by Steve during his 164 *v*. South Africa in the Adelaide Test of 1994.
(Allsport/Joe Mann)

Give us a hand! Steve and Shane Warne at the tickertape parade in Sydney after the Caribbean conquest.
(Australian Picture Library/Joe Mann)

gling with his batting up to the first Test and knowledgeable critics after his blood, the Australians looked in disarray and the Englishmen resembled—in the first half of the tour at least—a pack of hungry wolves. They won the Texaco trophy 3–0 and the first Test as well.

With few exceptions, the performance of the Waughs fell short of expectations. Steve rewrote records in the third Test on the Old Trafford ground in Manchester and Mark struck a marvellous 95 off 96 balls (with 12 fours) in the third limited-overs international at Lord's. However, Mark's innings, and a total of 269, did not prevent England winning and whitewashing Australia in the one-day series. It was captaincy debut for Steve and he felt that the aggressiveness one associates with Australia was missing so far on the tour.

'In the end we went down with an over to spare but in reality we were dead in the water from around the 20-overs mark,' he wrote candidly in his *1997 Ashes Diary*. 'What is needed in the future is enthusiasm and a ruthless streak, combined with the belief that we have the talent and the courage to express ourselves without fear of reprisals if we fail to come up on top.' He told at a press conference after the match: 'We are missing 5 per cent of an indefinable quality that is at present holding us back.'

Border agreed with Steve. This lack of 'normal Aussie agro' was hard to explain. Perhaps it was non-stop cricket that sapped their zeal and killer instinct. Or was it the poor batting form of Taylor early on the tour and the media making it into a national issue? After all, he had failed to score a fifty in his previous 20 Test innings, which was far from morale-boosting. Dramatically and on cue, Taylor hit a century in the second innings of the first Test at Birmingham. However, the Australian collapse in the first innings, when shot out for a paltry 118, and a 288-run partnership between English batsmen Nasser Hussain (207) and Graham Thorpe (138), could not be neutralised by a rearguard action from Taylor (129) and Greg Blewett (125), and Australia were vanquished by a deliriously happy and hungry England by nine wickets.

During Australia's second innings, there was a scare about Mark Waugh's health. It was suspected that he had appendicitis and was rushed to hospital. Fortunately, it was a misdiagnosis and he came in to bat at no. 6. Unfortunately, he was caught behind for one run off the rampaging Darren Gough who captured six wickets in the Test. This was England's fourth successive win (in three one-dayers and a Test) against old enemies Australia, and the English press went berserk with headlines like: 'They're Coming Home, They're Coming Home, THE ASHES ARE COMING HOME.'

However, the English were in for a rude shock. The gallant century by Taylor in the Birmingham Test had far-reaching effect. A failure in this innings would have meant his demise and Steve Waugh would have gained the captaincy. However, Taylor's success not only saved his career, it also revitalised Australia and the '5 per cent of an indefinable quality' Australia seemed to lack earlier on the tour was regained.

A back strain forced fast bowler Andrew Bichel to return home and he was replaced by the experienced Paul Reiffel. Reiffel's arrival was another factor in the rejuvenation of Australia. His very presence at the other end inspired an erratic Glenn McGrath to regain his accuracy and mean streak. McGrath was simply magnificent on the opening day of the Lord's Test, capturing eight English scalps for 38 runs as England collapsed for 77. Although rain saved England from defeat, Australia had recaptured their ascendancy.

'Ice Man' Steve conquers pain and crises to register his second ton in the Old Trafford Test of 1997. *(Allsport/Clive Mason)*

They levelled the series one-all in the next Test at Old Trafford, the match Steve Waugh considers as among his most satisfying, not so much for the richness of strokes (there were very few of those), nor for the elegance of their execution, but for his staying prowess in extremely difficult batting conditions.

Taylor surprised both friends and foes by deciding to bat after winning the toss on a green pitch—a heaven for English seamers. He explained to his deputy Steve that, although the pitch was grassy and tricky for batting on the opening day, it would get progressively worse and give spinners Warne and Michael Bevan plenty of turn on the final day. Predictably, Australia lost early wickets, being 3–42 before you could say 'I told you so'. Steve started confidently, getting off the mark the first ball. 'There's something significant about seeing runs next to your name and not that big "0",' he said. He played and missed a few times and there were blood-curdling appeals for lbw against him, but he survived. Gradually, he located the middle of his bat though he found the fast bowler Andy Caddick problematic as the sightscreen could not cover the full length of the tall bowler's raised arm.

Injury to his right hand slowed Steve down but he survived as wickets kept falling at the other end. Australia was a depressing 7–160 when Reiffel joined him. At stumps they were still together, having added 66 precious runs despite poor visibility. In fact, the umpires were ready to close the match earlier because of bad light but Steve refused to go. Well-set, he was seeing the ball well and wanted to complete his century that day. With spin bowlers Robert Croft and Mark Ealham operating, he reached his hundred in near darkness by clouting Croft through cover point.

It was his 13th Test ton and was watched by his mother Beverley, wife Lynette, year-old daughter Rosalie and Lynette's parents. It was a proud day for the Waughs but further glory awaited Steve before the Test was finished. Steve was dismissed the next day after scoring 108 runs and adding 70 runs for the eighth wicket. He had stayed for four hours and hit 13 fours. It was more than just statistics, his innings made the difference between winning and losing. 'Gunslinger Waugh Leads the Fightback,' headlined *The Guardian*.

With Warne capturing 6–48, Australia took a vital 73-run lead. Once again Australia started badly, losing 3–39. Once again they were rescued by Steve. He added 92 runs for the fourth wicket with brother Mark who scored 55. At the fall of Mark's wicket, Steve called for an ice-pack to ease the swelling on his thumb. His opening day's injury was further aggravated when on 60. The pain was so intense that he remained strokeless on 67 for 50 minutes. A lesser fighter than Steve would have retired hurt, but Steve carried on gamely.

'The pain gradually worsened to a point where I couldn't force the ball through the field at all,' he wrote in his *1997 Ashes Diary*. 'I was basically defending one-handed, as I tried to minimise the pain that was going through my thumb-joint and the space between thumb and fore-finger.'

At stumps on the third day, he was unbeaten on 82 out of Australia's 6–262. When he pulled off his gloves in the dressing-room, he found the right hand was badly swollen and an unhealthy blue. The following day he became the third Australian after Warren Bardsley (at The Oval in 1909) and Arthur Morris (in Adelaide, 1946–47) to hit centuries in both innings of an Ashes Test. Both Bardsley and Morris were left-handed batsmen, so Steve became the first right-hander to achieve this feat. Steve

In agony but loving it! Steve's right hand has swollen to twice its normal size but who cares after two super tons and a Test win at good Old Trafford? (*Alan Crompton*)

got tensed up in his nervous nineties. 'Going from 97 to 98 to 99 was torturous, especially as I kept recalling how I'd been robbed of three runs earlier in the innings when the umpire had given leg-byes instead of runs,' he recalled.

Without trying to take away anything from his glorious feat, it may be added that when Steve was six, he was lucky to survive an appeal for a catch at short leg which the umpires adjudged to have bounced first. Television replays indicated that it was a catch. However, in view of the handicap of the hand, the innings was a truly a marvellous one. Once again his partner was Reiffel when he reached his second hundred. Australia declared at 8–395, setting England a colossal win-target of 469. They managed only 200 and lost by a huge margin, McGrath grabbing 4–64 and Warne 3–63.

Australia had levelled the series with three Tests to go and the Waugh brothers, Warne and Reiffel had contributed handsomely. Steve was adjudged Man of the Match but his proudest reward was the letter he received from former great Australian batsman Arthur Morris, which he quoted in his *1997 Ashes Diary*: 'Welcome to the A.T.C.C., the Ashes Two Centuries Club. You can be the President and I'll be the C.E.O., as we are the only two left!'

Steve received many more accolades on his dual hundreds. To quote Greg Baum from the *Sydney Morning Herald*: 'To make one century in the face of hazardous batting conditions was brilliant enough. To make another while carrying a legacy from the first was special. To make each of them from a position in which Australia were under dire threat—3–42 in the first innings, 3–39 in the second—was well typical . . . Few batsmen in the world could have made [Steve] Waugh's first innings century, and he alone could have made another in the second innings, with his right hand so badly bruised from the battery of the first that he was still wearing a bandage on it the day after the match. It was the ultimate "Waugh wound".'

For the second time in four days, Old Trafford rose to Steve Waugh, and for the second time the English players joined in. In all he had batted almost ten hours and hit 23 fours. His performance made England's coach David Lloyd exclaim: 'Where can I get a Steve Waugh?' An English columnist suggested that ball bearings, and not blood, flowed through his defiant frame.

'Waugh's first hundred drained the life from his opponents,' Peter Roebuck wrote in the *Sydney Morning Herald*. 'His second buried them. Mark Waugh is the rose to his brother's thorn . . . His [Mark's] innings was critical because Australia had lost crucial wickets to some vibrant bowling from Dean Headley . . . Together these proud Bankstown boys took the match away from England's grasp.'

Both these centuries were scored after Steve had had very little sleep with baby Rosalie waking up three times at night. Lynette volunteered to move into a separate room but Steve would not hear of it.

'I've been witness to many of my brother Stephen's best innings,' Mark wrote in *Inside Edge* magazine. 'Without a doubt, I have to rate his first-up 108 at Old Trafford as a great one. It was outstanding in the difficult conditions with the odds so stacked in favour of the fast bowlers. He needed some luck, but he also had to back himself with positive strokes . . . Concentration and mental toughness have been the stamp of his innings over the past few years. It'll surprise a few people, but get the same Stephen Waugh on the golf course and he's

Flying the victorious Aussie flag after retaining the Ashes in 1997. It's 10 p.m. but Steve Waugh and Justin Langer are still in their baggy green caps. (*Alan Crompton*)

impatient, attempts all the shots and has trouble concentrating. It just shows you how well he has worked to have his batting in perfect focus.'

Added Steve, 'You've got to go through pain to stay in the game and to be successful. As a batsman you've got to cop bruises and bumps if you're scoring runs, so I'm more than happy to take them.'

The next Test at Headingley, Leeds, was a milestone for the Waughs as they became the first brothers to play fifty Tests together. Ian and Greg Chappell played 43 Tests together. Also, Headingley holds fond memories for Steve. It was here in 1989, his 27th Test, that he had scored his maiden Test century, an unbeaten 177, breaking a four-year drought. It was same place, same super success when he had hammered an undefeated 157 in the fourth Test in 1993, adding 332 runs for the unfinished fifth wicket partnership with Border. Thus Steve had amassed 334 runs at Headingley, playing 547 balls and hitting 43 fours without once getting out in eight years. As this Test followed his Old Trafford hundreds a week before, statisticians the world over were rubbing their hands in glee— expecting a double 'hat-trick'—three successive Test hundreds and three consecutive tons on Headingley.

The 1997 Headingley Test was memorable for Australia because they won by an innings to lead the series 2–1, but it was not so memorable for the Waugh twins who made only 12 runs between them in Australia's only innings. Steve's sense of humour was tested by a statistician who consoled him by pointing out that at least he had got an average on the ground. Well, a Test batting average of 338.00 on Headingley is not to be sniffed at!

Gillespie was the hero and the Man of this Test, taking 7–37 and 2–65 as England were bowled out for 172 and 268 in reply to Australia's mammoth total of 501 in 509 minutes—Matthew Elliott (199) and Ricky Ponting (127) adding 268 for the fifth wicket. It is interesting to note how the Waughs usually play their finest innings when Australia is in trouble, and tend to fall cheaply when their team is sailing smoothly. This seems especially true in the case of Steve, the crisis specialist.

Australia went on to win the fifth Test at Trent Bridge, Nottingham, to retain the Ashes 3–1 (with one Test to go) for a record fifth time. The first five Australian batsmen topped 50 runs each, Mark 68—his highest score in the series—and Steve 75 adding 86 runs for the fourth wicket. Australia totalled 427 and with McGrath and Warne taking seven wickets each, and Healy accepting seven catches, Australia won by 264 runs.

Steve cools off with his lucky red rag during the Trent Bridge Test of 1997. (*Allsport/Clive Mason*)

Another feature of the Test was that two sets of brothers played together; Adam and Ben Hollioake—both making their Test debuts for England—and the Waughs playing their 51st Test together. By coincidence, when Steve joined Mark in the first innings, Adam and Ben were bowling in tandem—possibly a Test first.

Australia was again smitten by the final dead Test defeat syndrome in The Oval Test and lost by 19 runs. Recalled to replace the ineffective Croft, left-arm spinner Phil Tufnell proved a match-winner, taking 11 wickets (7–66 and 4–27). The Australians started promisingly by dismissing England for 180 (the menacing McGrath taking 7–76) and led by 40 runs. It was another Aussie quickie, Michael Kasprowicz, who blitzed England out for 163 in the second innings with a 7–36 haul. Set an easy target of 124 to win, the Australians incredibly succumbed to the pace and swing of Caddick (5–42) and the spin of Tufnell to be routed for 104. It was all over in three days with 40 wickets crumbling for only 667 runs, Mark being a Tufnell victim in both innings for 19 and one, and Steve falling to Caddick for 26 and six.

Steve's dual hundreds at Old Trafford excepted, it was a disappointing tour for the Waughs; Steve scoring 390 runs in the six Test series at 39.00 and Mark 209 at 20.90. If Steve's 224 runs in the Old Trafford Test are deleted, he had a poor average of 20.75.

'My tour was one where, along with most batsmen, I didn't really feel as if I got into the series,' Steve concluded in his *Diary*. This could be partially due to splendid bowling but mainly due to poorly prepared and green wickets—made chiefly to blunt free-stroking Australian batsmen with weakness against a ball with lateral movement.

Summed up Greg Baum: 'Australia never had a cricketer like [Steve] Waugh. He spans the ages, from the time when he and Australia were, if not amateurs, amateurish—and it showed in their results—to a time they are polished, professional and the best in the world.'

A Girl Called Rosalie

Steve Waugh's 1997 Tour Diary is a trifecta of sorts, written by Steve, Foreword supplied by wife Lynette, and dedicated to daughter Rosalie in endearing words: 'To my daughter Rosalie, whose smile makes me feel as if I've scored a double hundred every day.'

Lynette ends her Foreword touchingly: 'I was sitting in the front row at Old Trafford clapping as Stephen scored his second hundred, holding Rosalie as, for the first time, she watched her daddy score a hundred. It seemed better still when I thought I could have been at home at 3 a.m., alone with a cup of tea, watching Stephen's achievements on TV and clapping very quietly so as not to wake up the baby.'

Lynette and Rosalie have become part of Steve's cricketing life; helmets and baby clothes mingling marvellously.

'I think sometimes it can take the pressure off your cricket,' he told Malcolm Conn of *The Australian*. 'Family with a new baby is great. It does not affect my cricket at all . . . There's no point in having kids if you're never going to see them. It's good that they are around and they make me feel more relaxed.'

The 'Ice Man' with more steel in him than in the Sydney Harbour Bridge has his softer side too.

Doug Conway on Steve Waugh

Doug Conway is an AAP journalist with a deep understanding of cricket. His assessment:

'The more pressure you put on Steve Waugh the more he concentrates and bats all day. He becomes so totally engrossed in the mental struggles of cricket that there is no room for anything else, including the distraction of pain. It is as if his batting becomes a cocoon from the cares and woes of the world outside.

For a striking example, Australia was in all sorts of trouble when he went in to bat in the Old Trafford Test of 1997; being 3–42 and 3–39. He had painful injuries to both his hands in the later phase of his first innings and an agonising abscess in the tooth. He was also burdened by the worry of a health scare concerning his infant daughter Rosalie which fortunately turned out to be a false alarm. Any mortal would have buckled in under the multiple pressures. Not Steve. He hung in for a total of more than 10 hours and scored magnificent hundreds.

Former England captain Mike Atherton had accused Steve Waugh of being scared of real pace in 1994. But recently he said that if he had to select one batsman to play for his life, Steve would be his man.

In my opinion, Steve would make a brilliant captain at any level. He is very intelligent and it is a pleasure to interview him. He thinks before answering, looks at each question from different angles and anticipates your next question.'

Two Contrasting Tests

Two amazingly contrasting Tests were played in August 1997; one in Colombo in Sri Lanka, the other at The Oval in England. The details are tabulated below:

	Sri Lanka v. India, Colombo	England v. Australia, The Oval
Number of days	5 (2–6 August 1997)	3 (21–23 August 1997)
Result	Drawn	England won by 19 runs
Runs scored	1489	667
Wickets lost	14	40
Runs per wicket	106.36	16.67
Number of centuries	6	0
	(S.T. Jayasuriya 340, R.S. Mahanama 225, S.R. Tendulkar 143, M. Azharuddin 126, P.A. de Silva 126, N.S. Sidhu 111)	(Highest score 62 by G.P. Thorpe)
Century partnerships	5	0
Highest partnership	576 by Jayasuriya & Mahanama	79 by Thorpe & M.R. Ramprakash
Four wickets / innings	0	5
	(Best by Jayasuriya 3–45)	(M.S. Kasprowicz 7–36, P.C.R. Tufnell 7–66 & 4–27, G.D. McGrath 7–76, A.R. Caddick 5–42)

⑱ In the Spotlight

I 997–98 was a season of upheavals and innovation, of bitter off-field confrontations and sweet on-field victories. It created Australian cricket's biggest furore since the Bodyline series of 1932–33 and the painful birth of World Series in 1977. For the Waugh twins it was a season of downs and ups, of fall and rise.

The innovation was the appointment of two captains. Mark Taylor was retained for the Test series against New Zealand and South Africa and Steve Waugh was handed Australian leadership in the Carlton & United limited-overs matches. In between a few disappoint-ments and self-doubt, Steve played his 100th Test on the SCG and nearly scored a century in it, and made nineties in Tests against New Zealand and South Africa to equal an unenviable Test record. After being criticised in the press for his poor batting form and 'indifferent leadership' in the C & U one-dayers, he 'brought home the bacon' by winning the two finals which mattered and lifting the cup.

Mark Waugh's loss of batting form in the first half of the season was a constant source of worry. For Australia to win against the strong South Africans, much depended on Shane Warne and the Waugh brothers. Happily for Australia, Mark regained his form at the right time by scoring splendid centuries in consecutive Test matches in Sydney and Adelaide.

The season started in turmoil and confusion as controversy raged over players' wages and other conditions between the Australian Crick-eters' Association (ACA) and the Australian Cricket Board (ACB). It is beyond the scope of this book to go in detail about this conflict described by some journalists as 'The Great Cricket War'. At the same time one cannot sweep it under the carpet because Steve Waugh, as secretary of the ACA, was involved.

To everybody's relief, the dispute was resolved in early 1998 but it was an unsavoury episode. A Sheffield Shield match between NSW and Victoria at the picturesque North Sydney Oval in October 1997 buzzed with speculation. Whether the players would take strike action, and, if so, when, was the hot topic of conversation in the press box as columnists and reporters talked endlessly to their editors on their

Steve Waugh had to remind the press boys at a media conference at the North Sydney Oval in October 1997 that he had scored an unbeaten century (for NSW v. Victoria). They were more interested in a possible strike action by the players.

mobile phones. Test opener Matthew Elliott's 187 for Victoria and his 303-run stand with newcomer Laurie Harper (160) in 291 minutes were of secondary importance compared with when ACA President Tim May would arrive in Sydney after negotiations with the ACB. Steve Waugh was bombarded with questions before going out to bat, facing a huge Victorian total of 509. It is a credit to his professionalism and his ability to blot out any thoughts except the next ball that he scored an unbeaten 113 that day and went on to amass 202 the next morning when the innings was closed.

ACA v. ACB Clash

A bitter confrontation between the Australian Cricketers' Association (ACA) and the Australian Cricket Board (ACB) dominated the first half of the 1997–98 season. To introduce the key players, the ACB had Denis Rogers as the chairman and Malcolm Speed as the chief executive officer. The ACA, with Tim May as president, was helped by Graham Halbish, a former ACB CEO who was sacked in early 1997 for reasons not revealed, and James Erskine, an entrepreneur with 'negotiating skills and money-raising ideas'.

Basically what the ACA wanted was (a) better pay structure for all first-class cricketers in Australia, not just the Test players, and (b) more say by the players in the way cricket was run in Australia. Contrary to what was believed—and some still believe—the ACA was not trying to run the game, nor were the senior players seeking more money only for themselves. They were asking for a bigger share of a pot they thought was larger than revealed—especially for the non-Test cricket playing Sheffield Shield players. Steve Waugh stated in late 1997 that he was happy with what he was earning but carried on the fight for his underprivileged Shield mates. Also, ACA wanted ACB to consult players in the organisation of fewer overseas tours, better tour itineraries and a tiered contract system.

As to higher pay demands for Shield cricketers who earn from about $30,000 to $50,000 a year, the *Sydney Morning Herald* columnist Malcolm Knox wrote: 'Few people think entertainers who play to near-empty stadia in loss-making matches [ie. Sheffield Shield] should earn double the national wage. If [Shield] cricketers want to be part of the entertainment industry, they should consider themselves lucky that they are not actors, singers, artists or writers.'

Ken Piesse, the editor of *Australian Cricket* magazine, took a different view. 'If extra distribution can be made without affecting the flow of life-preserving dividends to the States, the players should not be denied an extra slice. Improved guarantees at Shield level could enable cricket to win at least some of the battles it is currently losing with multi-gifted teenagers preferring more lucrative games in which to specialise.'

Early on, the public was on the players' side—especially when the ACA had their multi-point proposals all but thrown out by the ACB. However, when the Board revealed the incomes of the top ten cricketers, earning between $275,000 and $475,000 (plus endorsements) per year, the public changed sides. The general view was: How could the cricketers contemplate strike action when five of them earn more than Australia's Prime Minister?

WHAT OUR CRICKETERS ARE PAID

TOP TIER	ACB base offer for 1997/98*	ACB disclosed payments for 1996/97	SECOND TIER	ACB base offer for 1997/98*	ACB disclosed payments for 1996/97
Mark Taylor	$200,000	$485,000	Mark Waugh	$100,000	$275,000
Steve Waugh	$200,000	$440,000	Matthew Elliott	$100,000	$275,000
Ian Healy	$200,000	$440,000	Greg Blewett	$100,000	$275,000
Shane Warne	$200,000	$440,000	Jason Gillespie	$100,000	$275,000
Glenn McGrath	$200,000	$440,000	Paul Reiffel	$100,000	$275,000

Steve Waugh   * Does not include match and bonus payments   Mark Waugh

(Courtesy of the *Sydney Morning Herald*, 11 October 1997)

In terms of PR, further damage was done when, during the Perth Test against New Zealand in November 1997, news leaked out that four important one-day internationals were targeted for strike action the next month. Happily, these strikes were averted. Expecting a possible public backlash, Mark Taylor and Denis Rogers had a fruitful discussion, the ACA called off the industrial action, and the two 'teams' returned to the negotiating table. By March 1998, most of their differences were settled.

'Conjecture and confusion lapped around him but Steve Waugh was the sublime arsonist in the furore yesterday [23 October], joining in the hay burning at the North Sydney Oval,' wrote Phil Wilkins in the *Sydney Morning Herald*.

It was Steve's 46th first-class century and his fourth double hundred as he shared an exhilarating 156-run partnership in 130 twinkling minutes for the third wicket with brother Mark who made 72. Mark peppered the smallish oval with fours and sixes. After sweeping a six into the Doug Walters Hill, he hammered another upon the roof of the Bill O'Reilly Stand. The ball bounced out of the ground into the busy Miller Street, creating momentary traffic chaos. A little later, he holed out to Ian Harvey.

Steve, equally eye-catching but more circumspect, hit 16 fours in his unbeaten 113 that day. His cover-drives were a treat to watch. But at the well-attended press conference, the questions were more about the proposed industrial action than his undefeated ton which made Steve comment tongue-in-cheek: 'I must have played well. It's good to see you all at Shield Cricket. Who said it was dead?' When pointedly asked about the possibility of a strike the next day, he quipped: 'I'll be back, 113 not out on a small ground on a good batting wicket; I'd be silly not to.'

He emphasised that a strike was definitely the last recourse the players desired, but if the ACB 'didn't want to listen to our proposals, I guess it's a last measure'. He returned the next morning to complete a dazzling double century. He could have gone on to hit a triple ton but Taylor declared 102 runs behind to get a result. At another jam-packed press conference, the questions were again all on the impending strike and Steve remarked sarcastically, 'Thanks for asking about the double hundred.' This one-liner, typical of Steve, broke the tension.

In a Mercantile Mutual Cup match the next day, also against Victoria, Mark Waugh struck form with an elegant 57. In another Cup match a fortnight earlier, against South Australia at the North Sydney Oval, the brothers added 141 for the third wicket in only 110 deliveries. Mark hit 76 and Steve 72 as NSW plundered 7–319 in 50 overs, their highest in the competition.

After these early blitzes, Mark's form slipped away and the media put enormous pressure

A classic cover drive by Mark against New Zealand in the Hobart Test of 1997–98. (*Rick Smith*)

on him. He failed in both innings of the first Test against New Zealand at Brisbane. He had failed to score a century in his last 14 Test innings since his peerless hundred at Port Elizabeth eight months before. Since that sublime moment, his Test scores had been 5, 42, 5, 1, 33, 12, 55, 8, 68, 7, 19, 1, 3 and 17; a dismal 276 runs in three continents (South Africa, Europe and Australia) at an average of under 20.

'It's hard to credit but the country's most aristocratic batsman has fallen on hard times,' wrote Mike Coward in *The Australian*. 'He is playing like a pauper. And the fact that he is dropping catches suggests a serious loss of confidence.'

Steve was more positive in assessing Mark's problem. 'I defy anyone to be consistent for a 12-month period or a couple of years in a row,' he told Danny Weidler in the *Sun-Herald*. 'It's just too hard to do. There are going to be times when you are off your game, things aren't 100 per cent with your family, your business, whatever. Mark is just going through a period where he is finding ways to get out. Unusual ways and even a tough call or two. He's just got to believe in himself now because with 11 Test hundreds he knows he has the ability. It's got to come from within, he must believe in himself.'

Mark came out of his slump in the second Test at Perth with a majestic 86. He added 153 runs with Steve (96) and Australia triumphed by an innings to win the series 2–0. This was the Test during which the players' plan—later aborted—to strike in four one-dayers had leaked out. Shortly before his dismissal, Mark lofted a delivery from New Zealand left-arm leg-spinner Daniel Vettori onto the roof of the Lillee–Marsh Stand, approximately 130 metres away and 35 metres high. It was one of the biggest sixes seen in Australia in a decade. The Perth Test was also memorable for Steve, who was not only adjudged Man of the Match but also became the seventh Australian to make 6000 runs in Test cricket. Mark attacked his critics as much as the Kiwi bowlers in the next Test at Hobart, stroking 81 runs. Steve failed with the bat but struck with the ball taking 3–20 (getting close to a hat-trick after claiming Adam Parore and skipper Stephen Fleming off successive balls) and 1–20.

Disappointment awaited Steve after this Test. After an unprecedented two-and-a-half years (from May 1995 to October 1997) as the number one batsman on the Coopers & Lybrand ratings, he was supplanted by Pakistan's Inzamam-ul-Haq. Mark Waugh, who was number two in May 1995, was now out of the top 10 list.

The series with New Zealand was considered as a preparation for tougher times against the efficient, win-oriented South Africans. In the first Test against South Africa, in Melbourne, attended by over 73,000 on Boxing Day, Australia started poorly losing 3-44. Then Steve entered the arena. The fourth wicket fell at 77 and it was once again 'Super Steve' to the rescue. Accompanied by Ricky Ponting, the Tasmanian with Fred Astaire footwork, he regained control and they remained unseparated at stumps on 4–206.

The next morning, Steve, playing his 99th Test, again fell in the nervous nineties (96), after adding 145 runs with Ponting. This was his eighth Test ninety, equalling West Indies batsman Alvin Kallicharran's Test record. Australia took command, with a 123-run first-innings lead, and eventually set the visitors an awesome 379-run target to be scored in about eight hours. The South Africans never went for the run chase but defended well to draw the Test, Jacques Kallis making his maiden Test hundred.

The second Test in Sydney was a landmark for Steve. It was his 100th Test, making him the third Australian after Allan Border and David Boon, and the 16th cricketer, to achieve this honour. In the next Test in Adelaide, Ian Healy joined the elite list. The figures of the 18 players after their 100 Tests are given below:

Test Centurions—Their Figures After 100 Tests

Player	Runs	Aver.	HS	100s	50s	Ct.	St.	Wkts	Aver.	5 W/I	10 W/T
M.C. Cowdrey (Eng.)	7044	46.96	182	21	37	112	0	0	—	0	0
G. Boycott (Eng.)	7518	48.50	246*	20	40	31	0	7	54.57	0	0
C.H. Lloyd (W.I.)	6904	46.33	242*	18	35	76	0	10	62.20	0	0
S.M. Gavaskar (Ind.)	8479	52.34	236*	30	36	88	0	1	177.00	0	0
D.I. Gower (Eng.)	7000	44.02	215	14	35	68	0	1	20.00	0	0
I.V.A. Richards (W.I.)	7336	52.78	291	12	34	101	0	28	50.36	0	0
D.B. Vengsarkar (Ind.)	6356	45.73	166	17	31	68	0	0	—	0	0
A.R. Border (Aus.)	7670	52.18	205	23	35	112	0	16	47.19	0	0
Kapil Dev (Ind.)	4142	31.38	163	6	22	53	0	354	28.88	21	2
Javed Miandad (Pak.)	7694	57.42	280*	22	36	85	1	17	40.12	0	0
C.G. Greenidge (W.I.)	7134	46.02	223	18	34	93	0	0	—	0	0
D.L. Haynes (W.I.)	6486	42.12	184	16	35	58	0	1	8.00	0	0
I.T. Botham (Eng.)	5192	33.93	208	14	22	118	0	383	28.24	27	4
G.A. Gooch (Eng.)	7608	43.47	333	17	41	97	0	22	40.64	0	0
D.C. Boon (Aus.)	7094	44.34	200	20	31	92	0	0	—	0	0
S.R. Waugh (Aus.)	6288	49.51	200	14	37	75	0	85	34.80	3	0
I.A. Healy (Aus.)	3741	28.34	161*	3	20	322	25	0	—	0	0
C.A. Walsh (W.I.)	791	8.89	30*	0	0	21	0	368	25.74	15	2

Abbreviations: HS = Highest score; Ct = Catches; St = Stumpings; * = Not out; 5 W/I = 5 wickets/innings; 10 W/T = 10 wickets/Test.
Note: The rain-abandoned Melbourne Test of 1970–71 not considered as a Test.

At one stage, it appeared that Steve would become the fourth batsman in the group—after Colin Cowdrey, Javed Miandad and Gordon Greenidge—to hit a century in his 100th Test, but was bowled by a superb delivery from the South African speedster Allan Donald for 85. He said philosophically, 'Hundred [runs] would have been nice but at least I didn't get a ninety.'

'Donald not only huffs and puffs but he can bowl the house down; a castle in Stephen [Waugh's] case,' Mike Coward commented in *The Australian*. 'It needed an exceptional bowler to defeat Stephen in this mood and on such a big day.' Earlier, Steve had added 116 runs in 131 minutes with brother Mark (who hit a round 100 with 12 fours) and 98 runs with Ponting (62). This was the fourth time the Waugh twins had added 100 or more runs at Test level.

Runs added	Opponent	Venue	Season
153	England	Birmingham	1993
231	West Indies	Kingston	1994–95
153	New Zealand	Perth	1997–98
116	South Africa	Sydney	1997–98

'It's no nightmare of a wicket,' Mark said after his 12th Test ton. 'It was a good feeling. There's a lot of people here you know, your family. It's special and they're here to see you make a hundred . . . It's always nice to make 100 against South Africa. They're a good side with a good bowling attack.' Especially Donald who had given both the Waughs a terrible working over in one memorable spell—inflicting on them many body blows as they ducked and weaved. Yet they survived and scored.

After leading by 134 runs, Australia shot out their opponents for 113 to win by an innings with a day to spare. The visitors were bamboozled by Warne on a turning pitch. He had followed his first innings haul of 5–75 by capturing 6–34 in the second to take 300 wickets in 63 Tests. He became the second Australian after Dennis Lillee, and the 13th bowler, to reach this landmark.

The Australians were lucky to save the final Test in Adelaide, thanks to the absence of an unfit Donald, disappointing fielding by the tourists (dropping as many as 10 catches) and Mark Waugh's magnificent and tenacious century. The draw enabled Australia to win the series one-nil, confirming their claim as Test champions.

South Africa piled on 517 runs and the home team replied with 350, Taylor carrying his bat for a superb 169 while Shaun Pollock took 7–87. Mark Waugh continued his majestic batting form of Sydney by scoring 63 in the first innings. The visitors declared their second innings at 6–193, challenging Australia to make 361 to win in 107 overs.

They started on the backfoot, being 2–32 at stumps on the fourth day; Mark Waugh unbeaten on 11. He was lucky to be dropped by Adam Bacher off Pat Symcox when only one. The next day wickets kept falling at the other end but Mark stood firm. He added 58 runs with Steve (34) for the fourth wicket and 73 with Ponting for the fifth. It was Mark's day as he survived three more chances, when 96, 107 and 109. In a courageous display of self-denial that one would expect from Border, Boon, Steve or Healy, Mark held up his end for 404 tense minutes, faced 305 deliveries and hit 16 fours. More important, he denied South Africa a victory.

The ending of this fascinating Test was shrouded in controversy by an incident in the final hour. As shown in myriad television replays, Pollock struck Mark above the elbow, the ball looping to Symcox at gully. The stroke was completed and no effort was made to take a run. In pain, Mark, then 107, walked away to nurse his arm and dislodged the bails with his bat. Was it deliberate, accidental or just a reflex action? The on-field umpire referred the matter to the third umpire. The video umpire, Steve Davis, took a long time

Mark's signature tune—an effortless leg flick against the Kiwis. (*Rick Smith*)

and finally resolved the issue in Mark's favour. Skipper Hansie Cronje and his men were outraged by this decision. The match was at a standstill for over five minutes while on-field umpires Steve Randell of Australia and Doug Cowie of New Zealand settled the players.

This is how Mark Waugh explained the weird happening: 'The ball hit me just above the elbow. I completed my shot and thought I was walking away. It must have hit a nerve in my arm because I couldn't control my arm. It went floppy and my bat hit the stumps. I thought I'd completed the shot, and after that it does not matter what happens. I felt like my arm was broken but obviously it wasn't. It was just a nerve. I knew I hit the stumps but I couldn't control where the bat went. But I'd finished the shot.'

Mark bowls in sunnies in the Hobart Test. (*Rick Smith*)

Cronje, however, was not convinced. 'If somebody gets hit on the head, and he's a bit wobbly, and he walks on his stumps, he's out. That's all I want to say.' In anger he threw a stump through the umpires' room after the Test but later wrote a note of apology to the ACB.

By the letter of the Laws of Cricket (Law 35), Mark was not out:

1. Out Hit Wicket.
The striker shall be out *Hit Wicket* if, while the ball is in play:
(a) His wicket is broken with any part of his person, dress, or equipment as a result of any action taken by him in preparing to receive or in receiving a delivery, or in setting off for his first run, immediately after playing, or playing at, the ball.
(b) He hits down his wicket whilst lawfully making a second stroke for the purpose of guarding his wicket with the provisions of Law 34.1 (Out Hit The Ball Twice).
Notes
(a) Not Out Hit Wicket.
A batsman is *not out* under this Law should his wicket be broken in any of the ways referred to in 1(a) above if: (i) It occurs while he is in the act of running, other than in setting off for his first run immediately after playing at the ball, or while he is avoiding being run out or stumped.

Back to the final phase of the Adelaide Test. Three balls after his 'nerve-twitch', Mark clipped the ball into Bacher's midriff at bat-pad. And he dropped it—for the third time in this innings. He was inconsolable because Mark stood between South Africa and victory. Two overs later Mark was given another life. He cut speedster Lance Klusener and Symcox spilled the catch. Somewhere in his youth or childhood, Mark must have done something good! Two balls later Andy Bichel was adjudged lbw and the visitors still had a chance if they could dismiss three tailenders in 33 balls. But Mark and Warne defended and the Test was saved.

'I think it's the longest I've batted in a first-class innings,' Mark said. 'It's good to have another side to my game. I don't think I've done that before—saved a game for Australia. It was the sort of wicket that was hard when you first came in, because it was uneven and sometimes kept low. I don't think we were home and hosed until right at the end.'

For many years a Mark Waugh admirer, Peter Roebuck doubted Mark's status as a Test

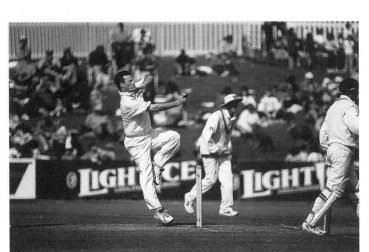

Steve came near a hat-trick in the 1997 Hobart Test, dismissing Adam Parore and Steve Fleming off successive balls. (*Rick Smith*)

great but this Adelaide masterpiece convinced him. He was impressed by the steel in Mark's silk. 'Waugh needed to play a long, defensive innings in tough circumstances to prove to contemporaries and historians that he was no lightweight,' he wrote in the *Sydney Morning Herald*. 'He needed to play an innings out of character to prove he could take command of himself when it was needed . . . He rose above himself, above the situation and seemed immune to the dramas all around . . . Hitherto, Waugh has lacked the will to be a great player. Undoubtedly this was his most wilful innings. Despite moments of fortune, despite its lack of style and glamour, it was the best innings he has ever played.'

Between the Tests in Sydney and Adelaide, the Carlton & United one-day series reached its climax. Steve Waugh was in the hot seat and his initiation as Australian captain in the series was nightmarish. He scored only 12 runs (including three ducks) in the first six matches at a McGrathesque average of 2.00. Even worse, under his captaincy Australia was whitewashed by South Africa in the preliminary rounds.

But Ice Man Steve kept his cool, convinced that Australia would come good at the end. He enjoys tough assignments and challenges and was learning fast. 'Captaining Australia at anything would be great, even marbles,' he told Ken Piesse in *Australian Cricket* magazine. 'It'd be a great honour to have the responsibility to the people out there watching the game who have a high regard for one-day cricket. You shouldn't be treating it with any less importance than Test match cricket.'

Many critics had doubted the wisdom of selecting two different teams under two captains for Tests and one-dayers. The exclusion of warhorse Ian Healy, who had an impressive strike rate, by an inexperienced 'keeper Adam Gilchrist was a subject of national debate. Australia just scraped into the finals by beating New Zealand. In the last preliminary match against the Kiwis, Steve scored an unbeaten 45 after a depressing run of outs; 1, 7, 0, 0, 4, 0. And he was convinced Australia would surprise the South Africans in the finals. He pointed out that the South Africans always do well in preliminary matches but tend to break down under pressure in matches that matter, citing their performance in the 1996 World Cup as evidence. If Steve was playing mind games he was successful.

In an exciting seesawing first final on the MCG—attended by over 44,000—Australia appeared to be on top, being 4–206 at one stage in reply to South Africa's 241. Steve (53) and Michael Bevan (57) added 101 runs, but after them there was the all-too-familiar collapse. The last six wickets tumbled for only 29 runs and Australia lost by six runs.

Mark Waugh lifts his bat after his hundred in the Sydney Test of 1998. (*Allsport/Ben Radford*)

This was Australia's fifth straight loss to South Africa in the one-day series, but Steve opined that the gap between the two teams was narrowing and victories in the last two finals on the SCG were not beyond his new-look team. It was Australia's day on Australia Day when Steve Waugh's team won the second final by seven wickets to level the series. Promotion of left-handed wicket-keeper Gilchrist as an opener was a stroke of genius and he scored a spellbinding 100 off 102 balls.

Now with the series locked one-all, Australia looked in command—especially with trump card Donald ruled unfit. Steve played a superb captain's knock of 71, added 102 runs with the in-form Ricky Ponting (76), and Australia totalled 7–247. South Africa fought to their last man, Paul Adams, who hit 14 runs off Warne's last over, but they lost narrowly.

The little-fancied and heavily criticised Australians surprised most by winning the series. Apart from his 71, Steve had taken a superbly judged catch to dismiss the aggressive big-hitting Lance Klusener and ran out the resilient Brian McMillan at the end to clinch the win. More than his on-field performances, he had contributed to success by his faith in the team and positive thinking.

When he was presented with the Carlton & United trophy, Steve was ecstatic. 'It was a great performance,' he said as he shared the triumphant moment with his squad who had been labelled flops and failures only a week before. 'It was one of the best one-day wins I've been involved in. It was certainly one of the sweetest because we have copped a bit of stick over the past few weeks . . . I rate this win up there with the World Cup semi-final win against the West Indies in Chandigarh [in 1996] for excitement and the guys getting together.'

Failure would have been a shattering blow to Steve, who has always dreamed of leading his country at both limited-over and Test levels. The unexpected success vindicated the selectors' two-team concept and Steve was reappointed to lead Australia's team to New Zealand for a week-long four one-day match tour in February 1998. As Shane Warne was nursing a sore shoulder, he was rested for the tour and Mark Waugh was selected as the vice-captain. For the first time, a country was captained and vice-captained by twins. When asked, 'Are you in any danger of listening to Mark now that he is your deputy?', Steve joked, 'Probably not. Nothing will change. He has never listened to me either.'

Turning serious, he added, 'Mark always has an input as senior players do. A smart captain will always listen to senior players, listen to what they say without necessarily putting it into practice . . . We've probably never been officially captain and vice-captain of a [senior] team before, so it's not a bad place to start—for Australia.'

Under Waugh and Waugh, Australia won the first two one-dayers easily but lost the last two. However, New Zealand was not on their mind. A hard tour of India with their vicious spinners and a baby-faced serial bowler-killer Sachin Tendulkar occupied their horizon.

⑲ Back From the Brink

'**B**abe' Sachin Tendulkar and his 'gang of six'—quicksilver fencers ('Crazy-eyes' Navjot Sidhu, silken Azharuddin, graceful Ganguly, 'Cool Cat' Rahul Dravid) and hissing, swinging 'cobras' (Javagal Srinath and Anil Kumble)—held Australia by the throat in the first two Tests, challenging, if not confiscating, their Test world championship status.

However, in the doom and gloom for the bamboozled Aussies, two men stood firm, refusing to hand over the family jewels or yield to the ransom notes from the attackers. They were Mark and Steve Waugh, who always place a high price on their wickets. Mark scored an elegant 66 (eight fours and a six) in the bewilderingly fluctuating first Test in Chennai (formerly Madras). Steve made 80 and 33 runs in this Test despite a painful groin strain (which slowed him down considerably in the Calcutta Test and forced him to miss the final Test in Bangalore). Mark contributed 153 and 33—both times unbeaten—and richly contributed to Australia's face-saving victory in the final Test.

The Chennai Test was one of the most exciting Tests in recent times, especially for the way it oscillated from one side to the other every session, every day. Openers Sidhu and Nayan Mongia put on 122 runs, but India was shot out for 257, the last five wickets tumbling for only 10 runs. The Australians lost their first five batsmen cheaply for 137 runs, but the last five added 191 and the visitors had a handy first inning lead of 71.

India lost one wicket before wiping out the deficit and the match was in the balance. Then came Tendulkar on the scene and pulverised the opposition—Shane Warne included. He scored a magnificent unbeaten 155 (14 breathtaking fours and six colossal sixes) off only 191 deliveries. It was an innings to cherish and applaud; an innings which would stand comparison with the best that Bradman and Hammond, Compton and Richards could dish out.

Skipper Mohammad Azharuddin declared at 4–418, setting Australia a difficult winning target of 348. They could reach only 168 and lost convincingly although both the Waughs and Ricky Ponting appeared to have received bad decisions. The defeat was only a prelude to worse disasters to hound Australia.

The Australians' recent Test series wins against West Indies, England, New Zealand and South Africa appeared far far away in Calcutta where India trounced them by an innings and plenty with more than a day to spare, and won the series. Some Sunday papers in Australia headlined their stories 'Oh Calcutta' in large type, adding that the Test champs had sunk their crown in the 'Black Hole of Calcutta'. It was Australia's worst defeat in 60 years and the third worst in 121 years involving 580 Tests. Only in 1938,

1891–92 and 1911–12 (all against England) had Australia suffered a more humiliating loss. Against only five wickets lost by India, Australia lost 20, and scored 219 fewer runs.

Steve Waugh was one batsman who refused to be dominated by the home team on the crest of a winning wave and was lustily cheered by a crowd of about 80,000. Challenging the swinging Indian fast bowler (not an oxymoron!) Srinath, the menacingly bouncy leg-spinner Kumble, and an increasingly painful groin strain, Steve Waugh stood like the boy on a burning deck. He came in to bat at 3–15, after Michael Slater (0) and Greg Blewett (0) had fallen in the first over off successive balls from Srinath. Mark Waugh avoided the hat-trick but was adjudged lbw to Srinath. Soon Taylor was caught behind and the visitors were 4–29 and looking at the bottom of the barrel.

Showing no emotion, Steve started with a superb back-foot drive off danger man Srinath. From then on he played the typical Steve Waugh 'nudge-nudge, wink-wink' innings; nudging here, glancing there and interspersing these with majestic cuts and drives which paralysed the fielders. He found a strong ally in Ponting and they started a salvage operation just as they had done in the Boxing Day Test against the South Africans a little over two months previously. They appeared in full command after being engaged in a century partnership, when fate intervened. One minute Steve was moving his feet like a ballerina, the next he was in pain battling a groin strain. This restricted his footwork, the momentum was lost, and so was the concentration of Ponting. The young Tasmanian had hit a confident 60 with seven fours before he was bowled by Kumble.

In the previous match against India A, Steve had hit a century and was determined to record his first Test hundred against India, and also his first in the subcontinent. But the pain escalated to agony and he had to order painkillers and request a runner—Greg Blewett. The move did not work, as Blewett got run out in a three-way tangle, and a devastated Steve returned to the pavilion twenty runs short of the elusive ton. It was a gallant innings reminiscent of his Old Trafford masterpieces of July 1997. Despite physical discomfort and stifling heat, he had battled on for 230 minutes and hit 13 fours. Australia was bowled out for 233 on a good batting pitch.

The next two days were nightmarish for Australia as India plundered 5 for 633 scintillating runs before Azharuddin declared with a mind-boggling lead of 400. After openers Sidhu (97) and Vangipurappu Laxman (95) had put on 191 runs, Dravid (86), Tendulkar (79), Azharuddin (163 not out) and Ganguly (65) ground the attack to dust. Tendulkar played a cameo innings, cutting the first ball he faced for a four and continued to attack Warne who finished with his worst ever Test figures of 0–147.

The pitch was still full of runs but the fall of Michael Slater before stumps on the third day put the visitors in a panic mode. The next day they were bundled out for 181. Steve, still nursing his injury, came in to bat at no. 7 and defended for 173 minutes, scoring 33 four-less runs off 138 deliveries. It was courage in excelsis.

Calcutta, the scene of Australia's great triumph where they had won the World Cup in 1987, became their Waterloo a decade later. But the pugnacious Aussies did not let this reverse upset them. They regrouped and turned the tables on India by winning the final Test at Bangalore by eight wickets. To achieve this with Steve Waugh on the injured list, and with ace speedsters Glenn McGrath and Jason Gillespie recuperating back home, was indeed creditable. Remarkably, this was Australia's first Test win in India since 1969.

There were many heroes for Australia in their stirring fight back; fast bowler Michael Kasprowicz's 5–28 in the second inning which opened the gates for Australia, confident batting by opening batsmen Michael Slater (91 and 42) and Taylor (14 and 102 not out) and Mark Waugh's precious unbeaten 153 (13 fours, four sixes) which enabled Australia to reach 400; only 24 runs behind India. His was the first century by an Australian in the series and his third in five Tests in 1998. Also, his 153 was Mark's highest Test score and his only score of over 150. He had his share of luck, however. During this innings he was 'bowled' when 37 off the bowling of Venkatipathy Raju but the bails did not fall. Also, a few catches were dropped, but he gritted his teeth and carried on despite having gastric problems before and during this innings.

In the second innings he came in at 2–114 with 60 runs needed for a victory. A few quick wickets by India could have swung the match back India's way but the two Marks played sensibly and positively and reached the target with a day to spare; Taylor 102 and Waugh 33. In the Test Mark Waugh had made 186 without getting out and averaged 77.00 in the series. This was the best among the Australians and the third highest overall after Tendulkar's average of 111.50 and Azharuddin's 77.75.

Thus 1998 seems to have heralded a new tougher version of Mark Waugh. The elegance is still there but now he can play all day without losing concentration as his recent efforts in Adelaide and Bangalore indicate. His death-or-glory performance in the above two Test venues led to his being promoted twelve places up to number six ranking as a batsman in the Coopers & Lybrand rating system. With Tendulkar rightfully ranked as number one batsman and Brian Lara as number two, Steve came down one notch to number three.

This ranking system was not on Steve's mind as he prepared to lead Australia against India and Zimbabwe in a Tri-Nation limited-overs international in India. After the Test series, seven members of the squad—including Mark Taylor—were asked to return home, and seven 'one-day specialists' arrived for the series.

Taylor is against Australia's new 'one-country, two-teams, two-captains' policy for Tests and one-dayers. 'We have to look at the set-up of Australian cricket,' he said after the victory in Bangalore. 'I don't think it's a settling process, having two different teams and different captains.' According to him, it unsettles players and results in disappointing performances, for example in Centurion Park, South Africa, in 1997, and more recently in Calcutta. Prior to both these Tests, some players were given their marching orders to make way for one-day specialists.

'I've got to understand where other people are coming from,' Taylor added. 'I don't make all the decisions in Australian cricket. I do less now than I did a year ago, when I was captain of both sides. I think that feeling has gone through the side. There are too many people who are not really sure where they're going at the moment in Australian cricket.'

To minimise the difference between Test and limited-over teams, Taylor hinted immediately after the tour of India that he may resign as Test captain to allow someone else to lead both sides. 'I'm not saying I'd do that but it's something to discuss,' he said.

Two months later he decided to stay as Test captain for the 1998–99 season, but should he decide to relinquish it in the near future, Steve Waugh is most likely to inherit the leadership of both teams, being already the captain of the limited-over side and the vice-captain of the Test team. Although a traditionalist, Steve does not share Taylor's concerns about the two teams for the long and short versions of cricket. He has asked for more time so his one-day side can establish itself before being judged.

'It's the start of a new era,' he said to the press before the first one-dayer in Kochi, India. 'It was never going to be an easy transition. I never expected for one moment that it would be smooth and everyone would be happy about it. I don't think we have given it a fair go as yet. It [the two-team experiment] has been going for only half a season. I'd like to have a look at it after one full year and see where it is going, how the guys are handling it . . . whether it's worked . . . or whether there should be one captain. I'm not prepared at this stage to say whether there should be one captain or two captains. It hasn't had long enough trial period yet.

'I just know from 12 to 13 years' experience that you know when a side comes together and they are making progress, and this one-day side has. I think we're going to be a strong side, we're going to be hard to beat in the 1999 World Cup. We learnt to play a lot tougher cricket [in India and Sharjah]. We were more disciplined in our approach and I think that will be the making of our side.'

He added that Australia could still improve by doing better with both bat and ball in the final five overs of each innings. 'These are the little things that make a good side turn into a really tough side to beat.'

When asked if he would be happy to lead a Test team of which Taylor was a member, Steve diplomatically said, 'That's a long way off, and it's up to the selectors. If I don't get the chance to captain and they [the selectors] think someone else is better for the job, then let them do it. That won't affect me. I'd be happy to take over if the position was available and the selectors wanted me to, but it's not the be-all and end-all for my cricket. You can't pick sides on personalities and friends. If I was captain and Mark [Taylor] was in the side that would be fine, no problems. I wouldn't see that being a problem.'

Although Steve Waugh is the most obvious candidate as Australia's next Test captain, should Taylor stand aside, he is not the only candidate. As Malcolm Knox commented in the *Sydney Morning Herald*, 'Shane Warne has his admirers, particularly among former cricketers who believe his acute cricket mind and popularity among his peers make him a natural leader.' But at the Australian Cricket Board level, Warne faces a few opponents. Some think that he has not matured enough as shown by his occasional on-field confrontations with opponents. Also, some fear that captaincy would affect the performance of Australia's premier bowler.

Mark Waugh's name is also touted as a future Australian captain—especially after his resolute innings in Port Elizabeth in 1997, and at Adelaide and Bangalore in 1998. Although four years older than Warne, Mark has fewer of the health/fitness problems which have affected Steve and Warne in recent years.

'If I was offered the captaincy I'd certainly be able to do it,' he told Michael Koslowski in the *Sun-Herald* after the tour of India and Sharjah in mid–1998. 'I think I've got fairly good cricket knowledge . . . I suppose it's taken until now for people to believe that I've got as much pride as anybody in playing for Australia. I've always had it—I've probably shown it a bit more in the last year or two [1997, 1998] with those innings [at Port Elizabeth, Adelaide, Bangalore]—but I've always had the pride. People just show it in different ways.'

The Australian Cricket Board is looking for a future Australian captain who will be able to reunite the leadership by holding his place in both Test and limited-overs sides, and also be mature in his behaviour on and off the field. That would make it a two-way race between Mark and Steve Waugh. Mark, the seasoned punter, realises that by virtue of his inexperience in leadership even at State level, the selectors would have to gamble to give him the captaincy. 'It's a bit hard to gauge, isn't it?' he mused. 'You don't know how you'd go until you get there. But I've thought to myself that I could do a good job.'

Ian Chappell has always been a strong advocate of Mark Waugh as Australia's captain. He wrote in *Inside Edge* of March 1994 that it is time for Australia to break down the conservative thinking and get a captain with a gambler's flair: 'If I was making the appointment, I'd choose Mark Waugh. Australian cricket needs to take a new direction as far as Test matches are concerned and Mark is the man who can inspire that change with his skilful stroke making, superb fielding and aggressive bowling. In addition, I like the fact that he is a born gambler. The last "punter" who was a successful Australian captain was Richie Benaud. That's good enough for me.'

Chappell concedes that lack of captaincy experience may go against Mark Waugh, but he does not see it as a great problem. According to him, even Allan Border had little captaincy experience before being appointed. An inspiring captain himself in the 1970s, Chappell says: 'Mark Waugh is always plotting the downfall of opponents which suggests that there is a good cricket brain hard at work. His occasional soft dismissals may also be seen as detrimental, but I believe the responsibility might just be the catalyst to take his game to the next plateau.'

Bob Simpson, a successful captain and coach of Australian teams over nearly four decades, considers both Mark and Steve as good captaincy material. 'Steve has the nod at present but I have no doubt that Mark would also make an excellent skipper. He is full of flair, good ideas and good old-fashion nous,' he said recently.

To quote Peter Roebuck from the *Sydney Morning Herald*: 'Steve Waugh has plenty to offer and his captaincy improved notably during this season's [1997–98] one-day series in Australia. His players have faith in him and hold in high regard his determination to win. But [Steve] Waugh's body is creaking and he's a bit long in the tooth—the same can be said of his twin brother. Australia need a captain for the long run—five or six years—and this will count against the Waughs. Shane Warne is my nomination. At 28, he's the right age, has a strong sense of team, showed lots of aggression in his only opportunity to lead an Australian side [v. New Zealand in Sydney in 1997–98] and generally appears capable of holding a group of men together . . . Warne has some disadvantages. In some quarters he is considered uncouth, though this fault lies mostly on the surface. And he's a bowler—Australia hasn't appointed one of this type since Richie Benaud.'

Thus Steve had a lot to prove when he took on a super-confident India and what-do-we-have-to-lose Zimbabweans in a Tri-Nation one-day competition in India which commenced soon after the Bangalore Test. He proved his leadership potential by performing his second Houdini act in three months. Just as he had beaten South Africa in the Carlton & United series finals in Sydney after convincingly losing all four preliminary matches, he turned the tables on India by beating them in the final at Delhi after being trounced in both the preliminaries.

If the third team had been more experienced than Zimbabwe, Australia probably would not have even entered the final, let alone won it. As it turned out, they could just beat the L-plater Zimbabweans by narrow margins of 13 and 16 runs.

In the first preliminary match at Kochi where the temperature was seldom under 40°C, India thrashed the Australian attack to amass 5–309; their one-day specialist batsman Ajay Jadeja scoring an unbeaten 105 and Azharuddin 82. Australia started its reply aggressively, Adam Gilchrist and Mark Waugh putting on 101 for the first wicket in only 11.2 overs—an astonishing run-rate of 9.2. But with the introduction of 'secret weapon' Tendulkar, who took 5–32 in 10 overs, the rest—apart from Michael Bevan—caved in and Australia lost by 41 runs.

'It was exhausting and exhilarating, it was an ordeal and a triumph,' summed up Roebuck. 'It was the noisiest day I've known at the cricket.'

India was even more dominating in their second encounter in Kanpur. After snuffing out Australia for 222, they triumphed by six wickets with 5.3 overs to spare. Tendulkar tore the Aussie bowlers apart by smashing a breathtaking 100 in 88 balls, which included seven spectacular sixes. 'This was the limited-over version of Australia's humbling at Calcutta in the second Test,'w rote Knox.

Australia regained confidence when scoring 3–294 against Zimbabwe. Ponting (145) and Mark Waugh (87) set an Australian record in limited-overs internationals by adding 219 runs in 39.4 overs for the second wicket. Still, their bowling looked sub-standard as Zimbabwe came within 16 runs of their total.

Steve Waugh kept the morale of his team up by saying that it is the final that matters. And sure enough he created a big upset by beating India convincingly in Delhi. According to Knox, Steve Waugh's men committed 'daylight robbery on India, stealing the one-day tournament with a mix of guile and cheek'. Steve himself contributed to this triumph by taking 2–42—his victims being well-set batsmen Azharuddin for 44 and Navjot Sidhu for 38—and scoring 57 runs with three sixes. He came in to bat with the match in the balance, Australia 4–111 in reply to India's 227 and Kumble bowling with venom. With Bevan (75 not out), Steve added 99 vital runs for the fifth wicket. The turning point came in the 41st over when Steve, the captain courageous, clouted spinner Hrishikesh Kanitkar for 19 runs, including two sixes and a four. Until the Waugh assault, the spinner had conceded only 16 runs off six economical overs.

Steve, the inspiring and lucky captain, was rightly judged Man of the Final because of his fine all-round performance. Since his appointment as limited-overs captain, he has won thirteen matches and lost thirteen—including the Coca-Cola Cup in Sharjah in April 1998. In his own words, this is unacceptable. He said that in the matches that mattered, the Australians had played 'with intensity and energy which had been missing. It shows we can win under pressure, which is the big thing at this level. The main objective is to win the big games, which we have done over the past six months.'

Retirement is the furthest thing from Steve's mind at present. 'As long as I'm getting a buzz out of the competitive side of things, like at Eden Gardens in Calcutta or getting the one-day side back to winning the World Cup in 1999, I'm enjoying it. If I'm not enjoying touring or playing at the top level, I won't keep playing. Family will come into it at some stage. At the moment I've still got a fair bit to achieve in my cricket, so I've not put any time frame on it.'

When he does retire Steve wants to help budding Test cricketers do what he has done since 1992— onquer the mental side of the game. Few sportsmen are as mentally tough as Steve Waugh. He can look Ambrose in the eye and make him wilt. 'I guess it is self-belief,' he told Ian Jessup in the *Sun-Herald*.

His advice is often sought by junior members of the side, and he still often seeks advice from others like Allan Border. Steve enjoys batting with tail enders and brings the best out of them. 'I tell them that they are better than they think and I'm not going to hog the strike. If there's a single I'm going to take it and you'll have to fend for yourself. It's amazing what a difference that makes. The key to

Good mates Gavin Robertson and Steve Waugh enjoy a drink during the Bangalore Test. 'Steve is a born leader,' says Gavin. (*Gavin Robertson*)

handling pressure is to enjoy it when you're confronted with it rather than worry about it. I am not overwhelmed by it. I probably was when I was young.'

Neither Steve nor Mark is a fitness fanatic and they both find the modern emphasis on physical side over-rated. 'Cricket is 95 per cent mental and yet you do 95 per cent physical and skill work,' Steve said. 'Everyone says cricket is a mental game yet you can't get any coaching for it . . . I see the mental side as something that really has not been touched upon.'

Inheriting Beverley Waugh's mental toughness, Steve asserts, 'If you believe you can do something, most times you are going to do it.'

Gavin Robertson on the Waughs

Almost the same age as the Waughs, late-bloomer Gavin Robertson made his Test debut in Chennai where Steve played his 102nd and Mark his 76th Test. It was an impressive debut for the off-spinner, who took five wickets and scored 57 runs. He has been playing with the Waughs since 1977. His assessment:

The NSW Under–12 team included myself and the Waugh twins who could do just about everything. It showed foresight on my part to be envious of the best cricketers God has put breath into. At that stage they were considered more as bowlers and batted in the middle order. Mark to me has not changed at all. He has always been a freak at most things and has an immense desire to succeed with a James Dean manner. I remember playing an exhausting tennis match with him in 1994 which was as tense as a Borg v. McEnroe final and which he won 6–3, 4–6, 7–5. 'We should play tennis for three hours instead of that bloody beep test,' he said, referring to the fitness test the team has to do regularly and is not a favourite of Mark's.

As a batsman, Mark is in a class of his own. In a trial match in Bowral between two NSW State squads, Mark hit my first three deliveries for huge sixes and declared his intentions to wicket-keeper Phil Emery that the next three balls would also go for sixes. Without knowing the full capabilities of a chest-high full toss, I accidentally bowled one. Mark skied it to deep mid-wicket and was caught on the boundary line—much to his disgust. When he batted in the second innings, I noticed him being a long way outside the leg stump. So I darted the ball wide outside the off-stump. But lo and behold, he stretched like an acrobat to his right, almost fell over and miraculously hit the ball straight back over my head, through the trees and almost into the neighbouring town of Mittagong. It was a fantastic shot and both Phil and I shook our heads in disbelief.

Any cricket-lover who watched the Mark Waugh v. Shane Warne clash in a Sheffield Shield match on the SCG in 1993–94 will realise that they had witnessed one of the greatest duels between two maestros. Mark scored a magnificent hundred to nullify Warney's menace which to us mortals would have been certain death. Mark is truly one of the world's greatest bats to watch and is capable of turning a match 360 degrees in his team's favour, as he did in the Bangalore Test.

One of the reasons I would have Stephen and Mark Waugh in my World XI is their win-to-loss ratio. They rarely lose and in any sport, they back themselves with every penny they have, and that's why I'd run a marathon to be in their team. Over the years Stephen has had to endure tough times from the press and the selectors but he has always bounced back. He has thus provided a key to success by his inspiring fight backs both as a player and a captain. Anyone who can lift his batting average from mid–30s to nearly 50 in three summers has learnt lessons which should be bottled and sold at a sports store or milk bars!

Off the field Stephen is not that intense. Touring with him can be a hazard because of his practical jokes. I remember a NSW Under–19 trip to Melbourne in 1983–84 when Stephen, Brad McNamara and I spent five nights out of seven at a pinball parlour. As we spent most of our dinner money there, we had to survive on ice-cream. One fateful night we came across a place called Crazy Horse. The lights were flashing and it looked like a pinball parlour so we went inside. It turned out to be a strip joint! We decided to have a quick look at the proceedings but I got bored and fell asleep. A tall bouncer woke me up at 3 a.m., by which time Steve and Brad had long disappeared.

The next morning when I sat down for breakfast the table erupted into a chorus of laughter and I knew it would take a long time to live it down. Stephen had told everyone about my sleepathon. Even now when he introduces me to someone, he uses this story to get a good laugh.

As a photographer Stephen is in the paparazzi class, always ready for an unusual snap. Once a few hours before a one-day match started in Pakistan in 1994, there was a stampede and some spectators were being crushed against a steel fence. I had my camera with me and was clicking away when one of the rescuers accidentally knocked it down and the film got exposed. Ever an opportunist, Stephen rushed to the dressing-room, brought his camera out and took some scoop pictures which were avidly bought by the local press.

Steve is a diverse character who speaks with everyone—be it the Queen of England, a rickshawalla in India or the poor and underprivileged in Pakistan. Recently on the Indian tour, he visited the children of leprosy sufferers near Calcutta and is helping to raise funds for them. He is that type of person, a bloody good bloke.

As bowlers I think both Mark and Stephen would have taken 100 Test wickets each in a different era, when a lesser amount of cricket was played. Workload and injuries have reduced their bowling achievements.

If playing with Sir Donald Bradman was more fun than the Waughs, it would be unimaginable.

Patron of the Destitute

Steve Waugh is more than just a successful Test cricketer with a tough exterior. He is also a man of compassion. When he gloomily returned to his hotel after Australia's humiliating defeat in the Calcutta Test, he found a letter awaiting him. It was from one Mr Shamlu Dudeja, a noted worker and benefactor for the destitute. It read:

'I am glad that you are fighting it out for Australia despite a problem with your leg. And I am sorry the match is not going as all of you may have liked it to go.

But this means that you have a Sunday to spare. Cricket is not the biggest love of my life. So there must be a purpose in God's will that I sat through three days of the current match from the bedside of a patient I was attending to. And I noticed you, when there were a few close-ups of your face—the dashing man with compassion writ large on his face.

'This morning I wake to read your interview in the *Telegraph*. I find that my impression of compassion in your heart is not unfounded. It raised a hope in my heart. Perhaps your charitable heart can help some very deprived children of Calcutta.'

Moved by this letter, the leg-weary and emotionally drained Steve—Australia had lost by an innings and plenty in four days—used the final day allocated to the Test to visit the children of leprosy sufferers at the Udayan Resurrection Home on the outskirts of Barrackpore, 35 kilometres north of Calcutta.

To actually see Steve Waugh in person was a miracle for the 250 boys aged seven to 17. 'Scarcely able to believe Waugh does not live all his life in a television set and is actually among them, the boys follow their god as he inspects the dining hall and classrooms which double as bedrooms,' wrote Mike Coward in *The Australian*. He had accompanied Steve and Dudeja to the Udayan Home and shared a stirring experience.

The stigmatised children not only touched Steve and got photographed with him but actually bowled to their hero. This experience has galvanised him to devote considerable time and effort to raise funds for a building block to accommodate the female children of leprosy victims. According to Coward, the girls carry greater stigma than the boys and are invariably left to fend for themselves in conditions often unfit for human habitation.

Father of a two-year old daughter, Rosalie, Steve is anxious for the girls to have the same opportunities for help and rehabilitation as the boys. In a short time he has raised a good proportion of the US$33,000 needed for a new accommodation block for the girls.

After leaving the smiling, waving boys, Steve asked to be taken to the slums of Calcutta to meet their parents. Here he saw men and women shockingly disfigured by the disease and compelled to live in horrific conditions, shunned by all and surviving by begging in the street. 'Yet for the pain of their lives, they greeted Waugh smilingly,' added Coward.

In recognition of his efforts and in anticipation of a successful fund-raising campaign, Steve has been appointed patron of the girls' wing at the Udayan Home. Dominique Lapierre, renowned worldwide for his many best sellers including *The City of Joy*, is the patron of the boys' wing.

⓴ Oh Brother

The bittersweet tour of India, with its lows and highs, brings us to the last part of a journey for the Waugh twins which started in Canterbury Hospital in 1965 and reached many peaks, most recently in Bangalore and Delhi. It is not the end of their story as they still have a few more seasons of Test and Sheffield Shield cricket left in them, perhaps captaining Australia and, later on, many years of television and media work and possibly cricket administration. For this publication, however, the tour to India in early 1998 was their final frontier.

Having played a total of 181 Tests and having scored 11,699 runs at 46.06 with 28 centuries (plus nine nineties), having taken 131 wickets at 36.96 and 166 catches, how do they compare with other brotherly combinations?

Of the 43 pairs (including three trios) of brothers to have played together at Test level, only six have appeared in tandem in more than 20 Tests. The Waughs are easily in front with 60 Tests together from April 1990 to August 1998. They are followed by another famous Australian brotherhood of Ian and Greg Chappell in 43 Tests from 1970 to 1980, Martin and Jeff Crowe of New Zealand in 36 from 1983 to 1989, Grant and Andy Flower of Zimbabwe in 30 from 1992 until early 1998, Pakistan's Mushtaq and Sadiq Mohammad in 28 from 1969 to 1979, and South Africans Peter and Graeme Pollock in 23 from 1963 to 1970 (when the boycott of their country for its previous apartheid policy curtailed their brilliant Test careers).

The combined Test figures of these six pairs are presented below:

Player	Tests together	Runs	Aver.	HS	100s	Wickets	Catches
Steve Waugh	60	4374	56.81	200	11	40	45
Mark Waugh	60	4052	42.65	140	10	38	65
Total		8426	48.98	200	21	78	110
Ian Chappell	43φ	3509	47.42	196	10	9	57
Greg Chappell	43	3525	57.79	247*	13	30	70
Total		7034	52.10	247*	23	39	127
Martin Crowe	36	2693	47.24	188	8	11	41
Jeff Crowe	36	1533	26.89	128	3	0	40
Total		4226	37.39	188	11	11	81
Grant Flower	30	1991	38.79	201*	5	3	14
Andy Flower	30	1942	42.22	156	5	0	70/5#
Total		3933	40.13	201*	10	3	84/5#
							continued . . .

Player	Tests together	Runs	Aver.	HS	100s	Wickets	Catches
Mushtaq Mohammad	28	1948	41.46	201	7	49	26
Sadiq Mohammad	28	1869	38.14	137	4	0	22
Total		3817	39.76	201	11	49	48
Peter Pollock	23	462	21.00	75*	0	86	7
Graeme Pollock	23	2256	60.97	274	7	4	17
Total		2718	46.07	274	7	90	24

(HS = Highest Score; * = Not Out, # = Stumpings)
φ The rain-abandoned Melbourne Test of 1970–71 is not considered as a Test.

Steve Waugh had appeared in 42 Tests before Mark replaced him in the Adelaide Test against England in January 1991 and marked his belated debut with a splendid ton. The first Test the twins played together was against the West Indies at Port-of-Spain in April 1991 and they celebrated it without any fanfare by adding 58 runs for the sixth wicket. The table below gives their statistics when *not* playing together.

Player	Tests	Runs	Aver.	HS	100s	Wickets	Catches
Steve	43	2106	37.60	177*	3	46	33
Mark	18	1167	44.88	153*	4	7	24
Total	61	3273	39.91	177*	7	53	57

From these data, it is discerned that Steve's batting average is significantly higher when batting with Mark (56.81) than when batting without him (37.60). On the other hand, Mark's average is similar when batting with Steve (42.65) or without him (44.88). There could be another explanation. Steve tightened his technique and attitude after being dropped from the Australian team in 1991. However, a combined batting average of 48.98 when they have played together and of 39.91 when they have not is of some statistical significance.

It is surprising that despite appearing in tandem in 60 Tests, the Waughs have been engaged in only four century partnerships (see Chapter 18) and registered centuries in the same Test only once. This was in the memorable Kingston Test in April–May 1995 when Steve (200) and Mark (126) added 231 runs which enabled Australia to beat the Windies. The century partnerships by the Waugh brothers are listed on the next page.

Before them, three pairs of brothers had hit hundreds in the same Test. The Chappells achieved it three times in their magnificent Test careers; against England at The Oval in 1972 when Ian scored 118 and Greg 113, and against New Zealand in both innings at Wellington in 1973–74. In this Test, the Chappells totalled an incredible 646 runs at 215.33; Ian 145 and 121, Greg 247 not out and 133; putting on 264 and 86 runs for the third wicket.

The other two pairs to hit centuries in the same Test are Sadiq (103 not out) and Mushtaq Mohammad (101) against New Zealand at Hyderabad in 1976–77; and Zimbabwe's Grant Flower (201 not out) and Andy Flower (156) adding 269 runs—a fraternal record—against Pakistan at Harare in 1994–95. The Flower power enabled Zimbabwe to record their first Test win in 11 Tests. The contrasting Pollock brothers demonstrated their all-round excellence in the Trent Bridge Test in Nottingham in 1965. Graeme stroked a majestic 125 and 59 and Peter took 5–53 and 5–34 to rout England.

In a Sheffield Shield match for NSW v. Western Australia at Perth in December 1990, the Waugh twins were engaged in a world record fifth wicket partnership of 464 runs, both hitting unbeaten double centuries (Mark 229, Steve 216). This remains the only instance of both brothers scoring double centuries in the same innings of a first-class match.

In the six months from May 1995 to January 1996, the Waughs established an impressive but obscure Test record. Between them, they scored seven centuries in seven successive Tests, as detailed in Chapter 14. This bettered a record set by Ian and Greg Chappell in 1975–76. After Ian's 192 in the final Test against England at The Oval, Greg hit hundreds in both innings (123 and an unbeaten 109) in Australia's next Test, v. the West Indies in Brisbane. In the following Test at Perth, Ian said 'My turn' and scored 156. After a ton-less Test for them in Melbourne, Greg stroked a silken, unbeaten 112 in Sydney. This gave the Chappells five hundreds in five Tests.

The best the four Mohammad brothers (Wazir, Hanif, Mushtaq and Sadiq) could achieve was four centuries in four Tests, despite their 29 hundreds in 173 Tests—66 of these in various fraternal combinations—from 1952 to 1981. The Mohammads provide the third instance of three brothers playing together in the same Test. In the Karachi Test of 1969–70 against New Zealand, Hanif, Mushtaq and Sadiq appeared together.

Test Century Partnerships by Steve Waugh

Batting partner	Runs	Wkt	v.	Series	Venue
Blewett, G.S.	385	5th	S.A.	1996–97	Johannesburg
Border, A.R.	332*	5th	Eng.	1993	Headingley
Jones, D.M.	260*	6th	S.L.	1989–90	Hobart
Waugh, M.E.	231	4th	W.I.	1994–95	Kingston
Border, A.R.	208	5th	S.A.	1993–94	Adelaide
Blewett, G.S.	203	6th	Eng.	1994–95	Perth
Wood, G.M.	200	5th	W.I.	1988–89	Perth
Healy, I.A.	180*	6th	Eng.	1993	Old Trafford
Border, A.R.	177	6th	N.Z.	1985–86	Christchurch
Border, A.R.	159	5th	N.Z.	1993–94	Brisbane
Waugh, M.E.	153	5th	Eng.	1993	Edgbaston
Waugh, M.E.	153	4th	N.Z.	1997–98	Perth
Taylor, M.A.	149	4th	S.L.	1989–90	Brisbane
Hughes, M.G.	147	7th	Eng.	1989	Headingley
Matthews, G.R.J.	146*	6th	Eng.	1986–87	Adelaide
Ponting, R.T.	145	5th	S.A.	1997–98	Melbourne
Warne, S.K.	142*	7th	N.Z.	1993–94	Brisbane
Healy, I.A.	142	6th	W.I.	1996–97	Brisbane
Jones, D.M.	138	5th	Eng.	1989	Headingley
Blewett, G.S.	135	5th	Pak.	1995–96	Brisbane
Lawson, G.F.	130	9th	Eng.	1989	Lord's
Healy, I.A.	130	6th	S.L.	1995–96	Adelaide
Bevan, M.G.	121	5th	Pak.	1994–95	Karachi
Boon, D.C.	118	2nd	W.I.	1992–93	Sydney
Reiffel, P.R.	117	7th	S.L.	1995–96	Adelaide
Waugh, M.E.	116	4th	S.A.	1997–98	Sydney
Border, A.R.	116	4th	N.Z.	1987–88	Adelaide
Ponting, R.T.	115	5th	S.L.	1995–96	Melbourne
Blewett, G.S.	113	5th	W.I.	1994–95	Kingston
Ponting, R.T.	112	5th	Ind.	1997–98	Calcutta
Healy, I.A.	109	6th	Pak.	1994–95	Rawalpindi
Healy, I.A.	108	6th	S.A.	1993–94	Cape Town
Blewett, G.S.	102	5th	W.I.	1996–97	Melbourne

Test Century Partnerships by Mark Waugh

Batting partner	Runs	Wkt	v.	Series	Venue
Waugh, S.R.	231	4th	W.I.	1994–95	Kingston
Border, A.R.	204	5th	W.I.	1992–93	Melbourne
Jones, D.M.	186	5th	W.I.	1990–91	St John's
Slater, M.J.	183	3rd	Eng.	1994–95	Perth
Slater, M.J.	182	3rd	Eng.	1994–95	Brisbane
Boon, D.C.	175	3rd	Eng.	1993	Lord's
Matthews, G.R.J.	171	6th	Eng.	1990–91	Adelaide
Taylor, M.A.	169	4th	S.A.	1993–94	Melbourne
Hayden, M.L.	164	3rd	W.I	1996–97	Adelaide
Slater, M.J.	156	3rd	S.L.	1995–96	Perth
Waugh, S.R.	153	5th	Eng.	1993	Edgbaston
Waugh, S.R.	153	4th	N.Z.	1997–98	Perth
Border, A.R.	150	4th	N.Z.	1993–94	Hobart
Border, A.R.	140*	5th	S.A.	1993–94	Durban
Taylor, M.A.	126	3rd	S.A.	1997–98	Adelaide
Bevan, M.G.	125	4th	Pak.	1994–95	Rawalpindi
Boon, D.C.	125	3rd	N.Z.	1993–94	Brisbane
Boon, D.C.	123	3rd	Eng.	1993	Trent Bridge
Emery, P.A.	122	4th	Pak.	1994–95	Lahore
Boon, D.C.	122	3rd	Pak.	1994–95	Karachi
Bevan, M.G.	120	5th	W.I.	1996–97	Perth
Waugh, S.R.	116	4th	S.A.	1997–98	Sydney
Boon, D.C.	109	3rd	Eng.	1993	Old Trafford
Boon, D.C.	108*	3rd	Eng.	1993	Edgbaston
Boon, D.C.	106	3rd	W.I.	1994–95	St John's
Boon, D.C.	106	3rd	Eng.	1993	Headingley
Boon, D.C.	106	3rd	W.I.	1992–93	Brisbane
Boon, D.C.	103	3rd	S.L.	1995–96	Melbourne
Healy, I.A.	101	7th	W.I.	1990–91	Georgetown
Boon, D.C.	101	5th	W.I.	1990–91	Kingston

The other Test trios were E.M., W.G. and G.F. Grace for England v. Australia at The Oval in 1880, and Alec and George Hearne for England v. South Africa and a third brother Frank Hearne (for South Africa) in the same Cape Town Test of 1891–92. Trevor Chappell, the youngest brother of Ian and Greg, also played three Tests for Australia in 1981 but these were without either brother.

In the 1995–96 season, Dean Waugh became the third member of the Waugh brotherhood to represent NSW in Sheffield Shield, a reward for his 5000-plus run aggregate for Bankstown Club in Sydney's first-grade. The spotlight is focused so strongly on Steve and Mark that younger brothers Dean and Danny have been left in a darkish background.

Now 29, Dean is a delightful striker of the ball. He is his own man and does not try to copy either of his illustrious brothers. According to father Rodger, Dean is ideally suited for limited-overs matches and should be a regular for NSW in Mercantile Mutual Cup matches. 'Although a big hitter, more so than even Steve and Mark, he is a nervous starter. I can't watch him as he goes in. Steve is also like that but to a lesser extent. Young Danny is the easiest to watch, I don't know why.'

Dean blazed 1019 runs at 56.61 for Bankstown in 1995–96, including a blockbuster innings of 210 against Mosman on the North Sydney Oval. This performance elevated Bankstown to second place on the premiership table and the right to meet Hurstville in the grand final. It also promoted Dean to a place in the NSW team against Allan Border-led Queenslanders in the Sheffield Shield on the Sydney Cricket Ground the following month. Sadly, this remains his only Shield appearance. Going in at no. 5, he scored 19 and 3, did not bowl but caught Border. As this was Border's final innings on the SCG, Dean remembers this catch with immense pride.

He considers his selection in the Shield match as his most memorable moment. 'It felt great to finally get there. I'd been trying for years for this honour, being in the NSW practice squad in 1990. It was a marvellous feeling playing first-class cricket on the hallowed SCG turf against players like Allan Border.'

It was equally satisfying for him to captain the Bankstown Club in the first-grade final the next month. Among the players he led were Steve, Mark and Danny. 'Pity we lost and did not perform that well, but it was a moment to cherish; all four brothers in the same team in a grand final,' he recalled. Dean opened and made 22 and a top score of 59, Steve at no. 3 scored 23 and 14, Mark at no. 4 three and 13, and Danny at no. 7 four and 23.

All four of them playing together reminded Dean of the backyard contests of his childhood. 'We had major battles; even then Steve played the hardest,' he told Ray Kershler in the *Daily Telegraph*. 'I did a lot of fielding, younger brothers always do that. I was the one who had to recover the ball from some cranky neighbours through the side of the fence. As I was skinny, I always had to squeeze through the fence to retrieve the balls. I was glad when Danny came along as he was younger and skinnier! There were always broken windows, ours and neighbours.'

Dean remembers Steve's sudden rise to the top. 'He took everybody by surprise. It seemed that one minute he was playing in the driveway with us, then grade cricket for Bankstown and chosen for NSW and Australia! It was pretty meteoric, progressing so quickly. At that stage I was concentrating on my own game more than his. On the day of his [Test] debut in 1985, I was playing Poidevin-Gray Shield for Bankstown and I heard at lunch that he was batting.'

Educated at Panania Primary School and East Hills Boys High, Dean Parma Waugh first played with Panania RSL Under–10s team when seven before progressing to Milperra Vikings, and was selected for NSW Under–16s. Although overlooked for NSW Under–17s, Under–19s and the State Colts team, he was selected in a few NSW Second XI matches. He kept trying and when 21 made the NSW state squad in 1990. He also played league cricket in England for four seasons from 1988 to 1991 and in 1996 represented NSW in the Super–8 tournament in Cairns, Townsville and Brisbane, scoring 233 runs at 58.25 in seven matches, hitting three fifties and taking three wickets and three catches. He was voted the joint Man of the Series with Adam Gilchrist.

Apart from his single Sheffield Shield appearance in 1996, Dean was picked in three Mercantile Mutual matches that year without achieving much success. He scored 47 runs at 15.67, with 28 as his highest score. Married to Joanne Waters in May 1998, he sells sports memorabilia and rare photographs. 'My whole family—especially Mum and Dad—have been the greatest influence in my life as they brought us up in a sporting environment. Mum has been simply great; rushing from ground to ground to watch us play on the same day—a huge task!'

The youngest brother, Danny James Waugh is 21 and not overawed by his elder brothers' reputations. Unlike them, he is blond and a left-hander and smiles a lot. He smiled more during our half an hour conversation than I have seen Steve and Mark smile in 12 years. He was selected for NSW Under–16s and, currently a first-grader for Bankstown, he has made a few centuries in Poidevin-Gray Shield and in grade matches for Bankstown. In November 1997 against Mosman at the Allan Border Oval, the 'other' Waugh brothers made headlines in local papers, Danny scoring an unbeaten 105 and Dean 60.

Danny Waugh, the youngest in the famous brotherhood, is the only left-hander.

'As a left-arm spinner, I have taken a few 5-fors,' Danny said, his ear-to-ear smile indicating that taking wickets was more satisfying to him than making runs. Did he receive any coaching from his famous brothers? 'They occasionally gave tips but I try to iron out faults myself. Alan Campbell from my club took special interest in my development. I also learnt a lot when playing Yorkshire league in 1994.' Danny's earlier role model was Allan Border. 'I bat left-handed like him and bowl left-arm orthodox spin as well. But my favourite cricketer is Viv Richards. He made cricket buzz with excitement.'

When chatting with Danny, one had the feeling that his favourite person is Steve. They seem to have a common bond and enjoy each other's company. Danny is not sure whether it is a help or a hindrance to be a kid brother of famous names like Steve and Mark. 'All I know is that it's a thrill to watch them on the field. Earlier on I used to get nervous when they went out to bat in an important match—even watching them on TV. Not so now. Besides cricket I enjoy playing golf but don't get too much time to practise what with my lawn-mowing job and playing cricket.'

According to Bev, Danny is a gifted golfer but 'did not spend enough time at it. He had enormous talent in golf but did not develop it. He is now embarking on a career in graphic design and also some cricket coaching.'

'It was very hard for Danny to get into first-grade with his brothers so successful,' Rodger said. 'If he had another surname, he would probably have played earlier and more regularly in the first-grade.'

However, far from being jealous of their brothers' eminence and high world rankings, Dean and Danny are enormously proud of them. When asked who he considered the better cricketer—Steve or Mark—Dean pondered for a while and replied, 'Well, they are different players of equal value to Australia. Mark appears more carefree in the field and Stephen more serious but it's not quite as simple as that. Off the field Stephen is more of a joker even though when playing he doesn't like to give too much away.'

According to Dean, Mark is 'what you see is what you get', but Steve is more complex. 'They've been together a long time and the important thing is that they respect each other and would stick up for one another when it was needed.'

Does he ever feel envious of his brothers' superstar status? 'Well, I'm happy playing first-grade cricket but I've not ruled out the possibility of going higher,' Dean said philosophically. 'Once you get a chance you've got to cash in.

Alan Crompton with Steve, Lynette, baby Rosalie and Sir Paul Getty in England 1997. (*Alan Crompton*)

But not everyone can play for Australia. They pick only 12 players and when two of the places are taken by your brothers, there are not too many positions left.'

Alan Crompton on the Waughs

The former Chairman of the Australian Cricket Board, Alan Crompton, managed Australian cricket tours overseas including to India in 1987 when Australia won the World Cup, and to England in 1997. His assessment:

Stephen and Mark Waugh are usually discussed in that order. Mark has not acquired his nickname of Junior for nothing—it's all due, apparently, to four minutes difference in age! Let's have a look at them in reverse order for a change.

Mark's superb natural ability, grace, the appearance of being so relaxed at the crease and the appearance of having so much time in his stroke play are bywords. That's not to say that Stephen in any way lacks natural ability, as at this level everything is relative. Mark's relaxed and apparently happy-go-lucky attitude to life belies the determination he has to perform well for the Australian team and to see it prevail. The absence of these qualities would not have allowed Mark to deliver the match-winning or match-saving centuries for Australia at Port Elizabeth in March 1997, Adelaide in 1998 (both against South Africa) and Bangalore in 1998—not to mention his century in Australia's win over South Africa in Sydney in 1998. Only a player committed to the cause produces performances like that—and I was in the privileged position as manager of the 1997 Ashes tour to note Mark's concern at his performances which by his lofty standards were disappointing, despite illness during the Edgbaston Test and strong hands in the Old Trafford and Trent Bridge Tests. Mark's nature sometimes hides his determination to do well for Australia, sometimes unfairly and to his cost.

Stephen makes no effort to hide his total dedication to the cause of the Australian cricket team and his fierce determination to see it play to its ability—and nor is there any reason for him to hide these qualities. Like so many Australian cricketers, he wears his heart on his sleeve. Again, as manager of the 1987 World Cup team to India and Pakistan, I was fortunate and privileged to have an early insight into young Stephen's qualities. He earned the nickname 'The Ice Man' in that tournament, particularly for his clear thinking and apparently nerveless bowling late in the innings and for some superb cameo innings in the crunch, performances which contributed so much to Australia's World Cup win. These performances did not represent a false dawn, and Stephen's dedication to and pride in the Australian team and Australian cricket are well documented.

To me, he possesses all the '-ION's'—all those words ending in '-ION' so evident on the field in his concentration, application and determination, and similarly so evident off the field in his organisation, preparation and dedication. To see Stephen's preparation for a big match, at training and in the dressing-room, is to gain some insight into the reasons for his success. His organisational quality happily spills into his personal life, evident in his detailed organisation—on the run, with wife Lynette—of Rosalie's first birthday party at Taunton, Somerset, during the 1997 Ashes Tour, a party to which I was privileged to be invited.

On tour, Mark and Stephen do not seek each other out any more than they do any other team member, and to find them in the same conversation or in the same group of players in a restaurant or elsewhere is a matter of coincidence rather than planning. They are two extraordinary and different cricketers despite being twins. But clearly, their success lies partly (but only partly) in their genes, and for this the cricket world says a big thank you to Rodger and Bev!

㉑ Twin Trivia

Greek and Roman mythologies are replete with famous twins; Hercules and Iphicles, Apollo and Diana, Romulus and Remus, Castor and Pollux. In primitive cultures twins were linked to Gods and were believed to control thunder, lightning and typhoons. In rugby union and rugby league, Australia produced well-known twins Glen and Mark Ella and Chris and Paul Dawson amongst others. In cricket, apart from the Waughs, the only well-known twins are Alec and Eric Bedser of Surrey, England. The Bedsers are almost identical in looks but not so in cricketing ability. Alec played 51 Tests for England as a fast-medium bowler and took 236 wickets at 24.89. Eric, a useful batsman and an off-spinner for Surrey, did not play a Test. The only twins in Australian first-class cricket before the Waughs were the Nagels in the 1930s. Lisle Nagel played a solitary Test in 1932, scoring 0 and 21 not out and capturing important wickets of Wally Hammond and the senior Nawab of Pataudi. Lisle played for Victoria, five years before his twin brother Vernon. Lisle was 6 feet 6 inches (195 cm) tall and swung the ball disconcertingly, his best being 8–32 for an Australian XI against MCC in Melbourne in 1932–33. This led to his being picked in the first Test of the Bodyline series. He toured India with Frank Tarrant's side in 1934–35 and performed creditably. Twin brother Vernon played four matches for Victoria.

* X-rays have revealed that both Steve and Mark have a mysterious gap in their spinal vertebrae which accounts for their back spasms and stress fractures, reported Phil Wilkins in *Cricketer* (Australia) magazine of November 1990. Whether they were born with the defect or this was caused by constant bowling in their developing years is unclear. The spasms hinder them only when they bowl and not when they bat, or play golf or tennis.

* Steve's daughter Rosalie shares her birthday with two all-time great female sporting stars, tennis ace Evonne Goolagong-Cawley and squash queen Heather McKay.

* Batting at no. 5, Steve scored 200 runs in the final Test against the West Indies at Kingston in May 1995. By an eerie coincidence, the number of his hotel room during that Test was 5–200.

* In the above Test, Steve and Mark added 231 runs, scoring centuries in the same Test for the first time. Both reached their eighth Test hundred in exactly the same time: 231 minutes. Interestingly, the Australian score at stumps on the second day read 4–231.

The Bedser twins, Alec and Eric, flanked by former Australian Test cricketers David Sincock and Brian Booth. (*Ronald Cardwell*)

* In Steve's 100th Test appearance (against South Africa in Sydney in January 1998), Mark scored exactly 100.

* Steve and Mark have registered 14 Test centuries each. However, while Steve has fallen in the nervous nineties eight times—a record he shares with the West Indies batsman Alvin Kallicharran—Mark has only one such disappointment; 99 v. England at Lord's in 1993.

* In limited-overs internationals, Mark has recorded 11 centuries in 158 matches while Steve has hit only one in 245.

* In two of the three Perth Tests since 1995, three Australians have been dismissed on 96; Mark Taylor and Ricky Ponting (on debut) v. Sri Lanka in 1995–96 and Steve Waugh v. New Zealand in 1997–98.

* Mark Waugh's Sheffield Shield debut (against Tasmania at Hobart in October 1985) coincided with Steve's first first-class century in the same match.

* The Waughs scored a century each in three consecutive Sheffield Shield matches for NSW v. Western Australia on the WACA ground in Perth. In December 1990, they added a world record fifth wicket partnership of 464 runs and became the only brothers to score double centuries in the same innings of a first-class match (Mark 229 not out, Steve 216 not out). In November 1991, Steve (115) and Mark (136) added 98 for the third wicket and in the Sheffield Shield final in March 1992, Steve (113) and Mark (163) added 204 runs also for the third wicket.

* On 15 October 1991, Steve (126) and Mark (112) were associated in a 240-run breathtaking partnership for NSW v. Victoria at the North Sydney Oval in a FAI Cup one-dayer. And on 5 October 1997, on the same ground, the twins added 141 for the third wicket off only 110 deliveries (Mark 76, Steve 72) as NSW plundered 7–319 in 50 overs, their highest in the competition.

* In August 1989, the twins hit a century each in the same match in Chelmsford, England, when they played against each other. For the touring Australians, Steve made an unbeaten 100 in the second innings and Mark 100 not out and 57 for Essex.

* The 464 run partnership between Mark and Steve Waugh in December 1990 reminded old-timers of other fraternal stands. In the final of the Pentangular Tournament in Bombay (now Mumbai) in 1943–44, Test batsman Vijay Hazare (309) and younger brother Vivek (21) added 300 runs for the sixth wicket. Yet their team, Rest, lost to the Hindus by an innings.

For Worcestershire v. Hampshire at Worcester in July 1899, the Foster brothers hit a century each in both innings. Opener W.L. Foster scored 140 and 172 not out and Test cricketer R.E. Foster 134 and 101. Similarly, Chappell brothers Ian and Greg hit centuries in both innings of the March 1974 Wellington Test against New Zealand, as detailed in the previous chapter.

In the 1966 Ranji Trophy final against Bombay in Bombay, Rajasthan's Hanumant

Singh, an elegant Test batsman, scored 109 and 213 not out. His brother Suryaveer made 79 and 132. They added 176 and 213 runs for the third wicket but their team lost.

The Mohammad brothers Wazir, Raees and Hanif provide the only instance of three brothers hitting a century in one innings. This was for Karachi v. Services in 1954–55.

A twin duo—the Waughs behind the Bedser twins. (*Mark Ray*)

* It was big centuries or nothing for the Waugh twins against Tasmania in the 1989–90 Sheffield Shield season. On Australia Day in Hobart, Steve struck 196 and Mark made a duck. In the return match in Sydney two months later, Mark hit an unbeaten 198 when Steve was away on Test duties in New Zealand.

* Steve shares a few similarities with Bill Alley, the hard-hitting, no-frills Australian who played professional cricket in England in the 1950s and 1960s. Both were honoured as *Wisden*'s Cricketers of the Year for their performances in county cricket for Somerset—Alley in 1962, Steve in 1989.

* In the 1987–88 Sheffield Shield season, NSW fielded three Steves (Small, Smith and Waugh) and three Marks (Taylor, O'Neill and Waugh). All three Marks shone against Tasmania at Devonport in December 1987. Mark Taylor (72) and Steve Smith (84) added 113 runs for the opening wicket, Taylor and Trevor Bayliss 75 for the second, Taylor and Mark O'Neill (130 not out) 52 for the third, O'Neill and Greg Matthews 40 for the fourth and O'Neill and Mark Waugh (101 not out) had an unbroken stand of 187 for the fifth as NSW declared at 4–467; a Mark (or two) in the middle throughout the innings!

* When Steve Waugh joined brother Mark at the batting crease in the Nottingham Test of 1997, England's debutant brothers Adam and Ben Hollioke were bowling in tandem.

* During a Mercantile Mutual Cup match between NSW and Western Australia at the WACA in Perth on 22 October 1995, Steve skied a six off Tom Moody which hit the Mercantile Mutual sign. This earned him $140,000 which he shared with his teammates after donating a portion to the Children's Hospital fund in Sydney. Steve is so far the only batsman to hit a MM sign in the history of the competition. Mark Waugh has hit many spectacular sixes in his career; his towering six off New Zealand's left-arm leg-spinner Daniel Vettori in the Perth Test of 1997–98 being one of the biggest seen in Australia. He has so far hit 31 sixes in Test Cricket, a record among the Australians, next best being Allan Border with 28. In limited-over internationals, Dean Jones has hit most sixes among Australians, 60; followed by Border and Mark Waugh, with 44 each and Steve Waugh with 43.

* Steve was behind Australia's two hair-raising one-run victories over India in separate World Cup matches. In Bombay in 1987, he bowled the final over with India needing six runs to win. He conceded four runs before bowling Maninder Singh, the last man, and Australia won by a wafer-thin margin of one run.

Five years later in another cliffhanger against India in the 1992 World Cup match in Brisbane, Australia once again won by the narrowest possible margin. Needing four runs for a stirring victory, Javagal Srinath swung lustily. Fielding on the boundary line, Steve dropped the catch but picked it up and threw it back in one dazzling action to acting wicket-keeper David Boon. Batsman Venkatipathy Raju was beaten returning for the third run which would have tied the match.

* Mark, born four minutes after Steve, is nicknamed Junior. It would have been more apt to nickname Steve 'Senior' because of his initials (S.R.). During the Bangalore Test in India in March 1998, ABC commentator and *The Australian*'s columnist Mike Coward described Steve as 'an old 32' and Mark as 'a young 32', as the latter has played Test cricket for only eight years compared with Steve's 14.

* In 78 Tests, Mark has figured in 30 century partnerships. Of these 11 were with David Boon. Out of his 14 Test tons, eight were scored while Boon was the sheet anchor at no. 3. From Boon's retirement until the end of 1997, Mark made only one Test hundred, (v. South Africa at Port Elizabeth in 1997) in 19 Tests. However, since January 1998 he has realised that there can be life after Boon as he notched three hundreds (at Sydney, Adelaide and Bangalore) in five Tests. In 103 Tests, Steve has been a partner in 33 century stands, five times each with Allan Border, Greg Blewett and Ian Healy, and four times with brother Mark.

* Power of five: Mark Waugh scored 550 runs in the Test series in England in 1993. David Boon, with whom he shared five century partnerships in the first five Tests, totalled five more runs in the series; 555. Also, Boon and Steve Waugh accepted five catches each in the series.

* After the tour of England in 1993, both Steve and Mark were averaging 39 with the bat; Steve 39.45 in 58 Tests, Mark 39.34 in 27 with a highest score of 139. At that time Mark averaged 39.06 with the ball and had accepted 39 catches.

* Another figure curiosity. Allan Border closed Australia's innings at 601 with Steve unbeaten on 177 in the Headingley Test of 1989. Geoff Lawson declared NSW's innings also at 601 with Steve unbeaten on 216, v. Western Australia at Perth in 1990.

* Little wonder they call Sri Lanka a 'war-torn' country. In the Youth test series between Australia and Sri Lanka in 1983–84 Mark Waugh had scored 123 in the second Test in Adelaide and Steve 187 in the third and final Test in Melbourne. In the official 1995–96 Test series against Sri Lanka, Mark hit 111 in the first Test at Perth, Steve 131 not out in the second Test in Melbourne and 170 in the third and final Test in Adelaide.

* Steve's favourite all-time Australian cricketers are Stan McCabe and Doug Walters. The current batsmen he enjoys to watch the most are Sachin Tendulkar ('the best since Bradman') and Brian Lara. The vintage cricketer he would most like to have played with is Sir Donald Bradman, 'just to find out how good he really was'. The best bowlers he faced were Curtly Ambrose, 'his first ball as quick as his last', and Allan Donald. His favourite room-mates: Tim May and Ian Healy. Favourite song: 'Khe Sahn' by Cold Chisel; and his favourite animal: Merv Hughes! The greatest influence in cricket: Bob Simpson and Alan Davidson. Greatest thrill: winning the World Cup in Calcutta in 1987 and meeting the Don. Favourite drink: Southern Comfort and Coke.

* Steve's favourite ground has to be Headingley, Leeds, where he has a Test batting average of 338.00. He has averaged more than 100 with the bat at five more venues: 200.00

at Kingston, 186.00 at Lord's, 127.00 at Centurion (in South Africa), 106.00 at Delhi and 102.50 at Johannesburg. He has a 'nervous ninety' batting average at Old Trafford, Manchester (99.25) and at Rawalpindi (98.00). Mark Waugh has a 'century' batting average on only one ground, Durban (156.00). Next best for him is Kingston (82.50).

* The most nerve-racking moment in Mark Waugh's life in the 1996–97 season was when he and Steve were impromptu stars in the filming of *Waughs—This Is Your Life* segment. In his book *A Year to Remember*, he describes it as more daunting an assignment 'than facing Curtly Ambrose on a fast track with cracks all through it'.

* Mark is not too happy with brother Steve's claim that he gets premonitions about his dismissals. It happened a ball before Mark was bowled by Phil Tufnell for 99 in the 1993 Lord's Test, a ball before he was caught off Mark Ilott in the Birmingham Test two months later and a ball before he was caught off Ambrose in the Bridgetown Test in 1995. More remarkably, when Steve was in America in 1992, he had a nightmare that Mark would make a pair of ducks against Sri Lanka in the Colombo Test. And he did! 'Why wouldn't Stephen dream me up a double century now and again?' Mark commented in his *A Year to Remember*.

Statistics

(Figures accurate to 1 August 1998)

(Compiled with the help of Ross Dundas)

Stephen Rodger WAUGH

(Born 2 June 1965 at 8.14 p.m.,

Canterbury Hospital, Canterbury, NSW)

	M	Runs	HS	100	Avrge	Ct	Wkt	Avrge	Best
Sheffield Shield	66	5087	216*	15	51.38	71	82	30.65	6–51
Test cricket	103	6480	200	14	48.72	77	86	35.30	5–28
Other first-class	82	4980	161	18	57.91	65	72	28.49	4–71
Total first-class	**251**	**16547**	**216***	**47**	**52.03**	**213**	**240**	**31.67**	**6–51**
International limited-overs	245	5639	102*	1	31.68	84	184	34.17	4–33
Domestic limited-overs	31	1158	131	2	44.54	13	34	24.85	4–32

Mark Edward WAUGH

(Born 2 June 1965 at 8.18 p.m.,

Canterbury Hospital, Canterbury, NSW)

	M	Runs	HS	100	Avrge	Ct	Wkt	Avrge	Best
Sheffield shield	68	5474	229*	20	54.20	83	50	36.00	4–130
Test cricket	78	5219	153*	14	43.13	89	45	40.13	5–40
Other first-class	131	10232	219*	33	62.01	139	95	40.46	6–68
Total first-class	**277**	**20925**	**229***	**67**	**54.07**	**311**	**190**	**39.21**	**6–68**
International limited-overs	158	5385	130	11	38.19	59	79	30.67	5–24
Domestic limited-overs	34	1101	112	1	36.70	18	18	31.61	3–23

Dean Parma WAUGH

(Born 3 February 1969, Campsie, NSW)

	M	Runs	HS	100	Avrge	Ct	Wkt	Avrge	Best
First-class	1	22	19	—	11.00	1	—	—	—
Domestic limited-overs	3	47	28	—	15.67	—	—	—	—

Abbreviations: M = Matches; Inn = Innings; NO or * = Not out; HS = Highest score; Ct = Caught; Stk/Rt = Strike rate; 5 = 5 wickets/innings; 10 = 10 wickets/match; Bwd = Bowled; C&B = Caught & Bowled; Stp = Stumped; HW = Hit wicket; R/O = Runs/Overs; Best = Best bowling figures.

S.R. Waugh

(Right-hand batsman, right-arm medium bowler)

BATTING AND FIELDING
First-Class Career

Debut: 1984–85 New South Wales v. Queensland, Brisbane

Season	Country	M	Inn	NO	Runs	HS	0s	50	100	Avrge	Ct
1984–85	Australia	5	7	—	223	94	1	2	—	31.86	8
1985–86	Zimbabwe	1	1	—	30	30	—	—	—	30.00	—
1985–86	Australia	7	12	2	378	119*	1	—	2	37.80	4
1985–86	New Zealand	5	8	—	124	74	2	1	—	15.50	4
1986–87	India	6	7	3	227	82	—	2	—	56.75	4
1986–87	Australia	13	21	2	741	89	3	6	—	39.00	24
1987	England	4	6	3	340	137*	—	1	2	113.33	4

Season	Country	M	Inn	NO	Runs	HS	0s	50	100	Avrge	Ct
1987–88	Australia	10	15	1	517	170	—	3	1	36.93	12
1988	England	15	24	6	1314	161	1	4	6	73.00	20
1988–89	Pakistan	6	9	—	160	59	1	1	—	17.78	4
1988–89	Australia	14	24	1	711	118	1	3	1	30.91	12
1989	England	16	24	8	1030	177*	2	3	4	64.38	6
1989–90	Australia	12	19	3	704	196	—	3	2	44.00	5
1989–90	New Zealand	1	2	—	50	25	—	—	—	25.00	—
1990–91	Australia	8	11	1	598	216*	—	4	1	59.80	3
1990–91	West Indies	6	7	2	229	96*	—	2	—	45.80	1
1991–92	Zimbabwe	2	2	—	130	119	—	—	1	65.00	3
1991–92	Australia	8	11	—	472	115	—	2	2	42.91	9
1992–93	Australia	9	16	1	523	100*	2	1	2	34.87	11
1992–93	New Zealand	4	6	1	250	75	1	2	—	50.00	2
1993	England	16	21	8	875	157*	1	2	3	67.31	7
1993–94	Australia	9	15	4	976	190*	—	2	4	88.73	5
1993–94	South Africa	5	7	1	400	102	1	3	1	66.67	7
1994–95	Pakistan	3	4	1	224	98	1	3	—	74.67	4
1994–95	Australia	9	17	4	849	206	2	6	1	65.31	9
1994–95	West Indies	6	8	3	510	200	—	4	1	102.00	7
1995–96	Australia	10	18	3	952	170	2	3	4	63.47	5
1996–97	India	2	3	1	94	67*	1	1	—	47.00	—
1996–97	Australia	7	12	1	609	186*	1	3	2	55.36	8
1996–97	South Africa	5	7	1	404	160	—	3	1	67.33	5
1997	England	13	17	—	924	154	1	4	4	54.35	9
1997–98	Australia	10	17	4	720	202*	—	5	1	55.38	9
1997–98	India	4	5	—	259	107	—	1	1	51.80	2
Total		**251**	**383**	**65**	**16547**	**216***	**25**	**80**	**47**	**52.03**	**213**

Country	M	Inn	NO	Runs	HS	0s	50	100	Avrge	Ct
Australia	131	215	27	8973	216*	13	43	23	47.73	124
England	64	92	25	4483	177*	5	14	19	66.91	46
India	12	15	4	580	107	1	4	1	52.73	6
New Zealand	10	16	1	424	75	3	3	—	28.27	6
Pakistan	9	13	1	384	98	2	4	—	32.00	8
South Africa	10	14	2	804	160	1	6	2	67.00	12
West Indies	12	15	5	739	200	—	6	1	73.90	8
Zimbabwe	3	3	—	160	119	—	—	1	53.33	3

Batting position	Inn	NO	Runs	HS	0s	50	100	Avrge
1/2	1	—	15	15	—	—	—	15.00
3	74	8	3518	206	4	13	12	53.30
4	79	12	3407	196	4	14	12	50.85
5	99	17	5008	200	4	31	14	61.07
6	99	22	3755	216*	11	18	7	48.77
7	22	4	700	134*	—	3	2	38.89
8	8	2	113	71	2	1	—	18.83
9	1	—	31	31	—	—	—	31.00

Team	M	Inn	NO	Runs	HS	0s	50	100	Avrge	Ct
AUSTRALIA	103	162	29	6480	200	15	38	14	48.72	77
Australian XI	54	66	13	2959	154	3	14	10	55.83	31
New South Wales	74	124	14	5424	216*	6	23	15	49.31	81
Somerset	19	30	9	1654	161	1	5	8	78.76	24
Young Australians	1	1	—	30	30	—	—	—	30.00	—

How dismissed:	Inns	NO	Bwd	Ct	LBW	Stp	RO	HW
	383	65	67	200	37	5	9	—

Centuries

Highest score: 216* New South Wales *v.* Western Australia, Perth, 1990–91

Score	Team	Opponent	Venue	Season
107*	New South Wales	Tasmania	Hobart	1985–86
119*	New South Wales	South Australia	Sydney	1985–86
111*	Somerset	Surrey	The Oval	1987
137*	Somerset	Gloucestershire	Bristol	1987
170	New South Wales	Victoria	Sydney	1987–88

Score	Team	Opponent	Venue	Season
115*	Somerset	Hampshire	Southampton	1988
103*	Somerset	Warwickshire	Bath	1988
137	Somerset	Sussex	Bath	1988
101*	Somerset	Glamorgan	Taunton	1988
161	Somerset	Kent	Canterbury	1988
112*	Somerset	Middlesex	Uxbridge	1988
118	New South Wales	Queensland	Brisbane	1988–89
177*	AUSTRALIA	ENGLAND	Leeds	1989
152*	AUSTRALIA	ENGLAND	Lord's	1989
112	Australian XI	Hampshire	Southampton	1989
100*	Australian XI	Essex	Chelmsford	1989
134*	AUSTRALIA	SRI LANKA	Hobart	1989–90
196	New South Wales	Tasmania	Hobart	1989–90
216*	New South Wales	Western Australia	Perth	1990–91
119	Australian XI	Zimbabweans	Bulawayo	1991–92
115	New South Wales	Western Australia	Perth	1991–92
113	New South Wales	Western Australia	Perth	1991–92
100*	Australian XI	West Indians	Hobart	1992–93
100	AUSTRALIA	WEST INDIES	Sydney	1992–93
124	Australian XI	Sussex	Hove	1993
157*	AUSTRALIA	ENGLAND	Leeds	1993
123	Australian XI	Kent	Canterbury	1993
122	New South Wales	Victoria	Melbourne	1993–94
147*	AUSTRALIA	NEW ZEALAND	Brisbane	1993–94
190*	New South Wales	Tasmania	Hobart	1993–94
164	AUSTRALIA	SOUTH AFRICA	Adelaide	1993–94
102	Australian XI	Orange Free State	Bloemfontein	1993–94
206	New South Wales	Tasmania	Hobart	1994–95
200	AUSTRALIA	WEST INDIES	Kingston	1994–95
107	New South Wales	Tasmania	Sydney	1995–96
112*	AUSTRALIA	PAKISTAN	Brisbane	1995–96
131*	AUSTRALIA	SRI LANKA	Melbourne	1995–96
170	AUSTRALIA	SRI LANKA	Adelaide	1995–96
106	New South Wales	Queensland	Bankstown	1996–97
186*	New South Wales	Queensland	Brisbane	1996–97
160	AUSTRALIA	SOUTH AFRICA	Johannesburg	1996–97
115	Australian XI	Nottinghamshire	Nottingham	1997
108	AUSTRALIA	ENGLAND	Manchester	1997
116	AUSTRALIA	ENGLAND	Manchester	1997
154	Australian XI	Kent	Canterbury	1997
202*	New South Wales	Victoria	Sydney	1997–98
107	Australian XI	India 'A'	Jamshedpur	1997–98

Test Career

Debut: 1985–86 Australia *v.* India, Melbourne

Season	Opponent	Venue	M	Inn	NO	Runs	HS	0s	50	100	Avrge	Ct
1985–86	India	Australia	2	4	—	26	13	1	—	—	6.50	—
1985–86	New Zealand	New Zealand	3	5	—	87	74	1	1	—	17.40	2
1986–87	India	India	3	4	3	59	39*	—	—	—	59.00	2
1986–87	England	Australia	5	8	1	310	79*	2	3	—	44.29	8
1987–88	New Zealand	Australia	3	4	—	147	61	—	2	—	36.75	3
1987–88	England	Australia	1	1	—	27	27	—	—	—	27.00	—
1987–88	Sri Lanka	Australia	1	1	—	20	20	—	—	—	20.00	3
1988–89	Pakistan	Pakistan	3	5	—	92	59	1	1	—	18.40	2
1988–89	West Indies	Australia	5	9	1	331	91	—	3	—	41.38	3
1989	England	England	6	8	4	506	177*	1	1	2	126.50	4
1989–90	New Zealand	Australia	1	1	—	17	17	—	—	—	17.00	—
1989–90	Sri Lanka	Australia	2	4	1	267	134*	—	2	1	89.00	2
1989–90	Pakistan	Australia	3	4	—	44	20	—	—	—	11.00	1
1989–90	New Zealand	New Zealand	1	2	—	50	25	—	—	—	25.00	—
1990–91	England	Australia	3	4	—	82	48	—	—	—	20.50	1
1990–91	West Indies	West Indies	2	3	1	32	26	—	—	—	16.00	1
1992–93	West Indies	Australia	5	9	—	228	100	1	—	1	25.33	5
1992–93	New Zealand	New Zealand	3	4	—	178	75	1	2	—	44.50	1
1993	England	England	6	9	4	416	157*	—	2	1	83.20	5

Season	Opponent	Venue	M	Inn	NO	Runs	HS	0s	50	100	Avrge	Ct
1993–94	New Zealand	Australia	3	3	2	216	147*	—	—	1	216.00	1
1993–94	South Africa	Australia	1	2	—	165	164	—	—	1	82.50	1
1993–94	South Africa	South Africa	3	4	1	195	86	1	2	—	65.00	3
1994–95	Pakistan	Pakistan	2	3	—	171	98	1	2	—	57.00	2
1994–95	England	Australia	5	10	3	345	99*	2	3	—	49.29	3
1994–95	West Indies	West Indies	4	6	2	429	200	—	3	1	107.25	6
1995–96	Pakistan	Australia	3	5	1	200	112*	—	—	1	50.00	1
1995–96	Sri Lanka	Australia	2	3	2	362	170	—	1	2	362.00	1
1996–97	India	India	1	2	1	67	67*	1	1	—	67.00	—
1996–97	West Indies	Australia	4	6	—	188	66	1	2	—	31.33	2
1996–97	South Africa	South Africa	3	5	1	313	160	—	2	1	78.25	3
1997	England	England	6	10	—	390	116	1	1	2	39.00	4
1997–98	New Zealand	Australia	3	5	1	130	96	—	1	—	32.50	4
1997–98	South Africa	Australia	3	5	—	238	96	—	2	—	47.60	1
1997–98	India	India	2	4	—	152	80	—	1	—	38.00	2
Total			**103**	**162**	**29**	**6480**	**200**	**15**	**38**	**14**	**48.72**	**77**

Opponents			M	Inn	NO	Runs	HS	0s	50	100	Avrge	Ct
ENGLAND			32	50	12	2076	177*	6	10	5	54.63	25
INDIA			8	14	4	304	80	2	2	—	30.40	4
NEW ZEALAND			17	24	3	825	147*	2	6	1	39.29	11
PAKISTAN			11	17	1	507	112*	2	3	1	31.69	6
SRI LANKA			5	8	3	649	170	—	3	3	129.80	6
SOUTH AFRICA			10	16	2	911	164	1	6	2	65.07	8
WEST INDIES			20	33	4	1208	200	2	8	2	41.66	17

Innings	Inn	NO	Runs	HS	0s	50	100	Avrge	Ct
First	61	12	2973	177*	3	17	8	60.67	24
Second	41	4	1944	200	3	12	4	52.54	24
Third	42	10	1300	134*	6	9	2	40.63	10
Fourth	18	3	263	47*	3	—	—	17.53	19

Batting at Each Venue

Venue	M	Inn	NO	Runs	HS	0s	50	100	Avrge	Ct
in Australia										
Adelaide	10	17	2	708	170	1	3	2	47.20	10
Brisbane	11	17	2	667	147*	1	4	2	44.47	8
Hobart	4	7	3	220	134*	—	—	1	55.00	1
Melbourne	11	20	3	727	131*	—	4	1	42.76	3
Perth	9	13	1	558	99*	2	5	—	46.50	14
Sydney	10	14	1	463	100	3	3	1	35.62	4
in England										
Birmingham	3	4	—	147	59	—	1	—	36.75	3
Leeds	3	3	2	338	177*	—	—	2	338.00	1
Lord's	3	4	3	186	152*	1	—	1	186.00	—
Manchester	3	5	1	397	116	—	2	2	99.25	1
Nottingham	3	5	1	149	75	1	1	—	37.25	4
The Oval	3	6	1	95	26	—	—	—	19.00	4
in India										
Calcutta	1	2	—	113	80	—	1	—	56.50	—
Chennai	2	4	2	53	27	—	—	—	26.50	4
Delhi	2	3	2	106	67*	1	1	—	106.00	—
Mumbai	1	1	—	6	6	—	—	—	6.00	—
in New Zealand										
Auckland	2	4	—	42	41	2	—	—	10.50	1
Christchurch	2	3	—	137	74	—	2	—	45.67	1
Wellington	3	4	—	136	75	—	1	—	34.00	1
in Pakistan										
Faisalabad	1	2	—	20	19	—	—	—	10.00	1
Karachi	2	4	—	86	73	2	1	—	21.50	—
Lahore	1	1	—	59	59	—	1	—	59.00	1
Rawalpindi	1	1	—	98	98	—	1	—	98.00	2
in South Africa										
Cape Town	1	1	—	86	86	—	1	—	86.00	1
Centurion	1	2	1	127	67	—	2	—	127.00	1
Durban	1	1	—	64	64	—	1	—	64.00	1

Venue	M	Inn	NO	Runs	HS	0s	50	100	Avrge	Ct
Johannesburg	2	3	1	205	160	1	—	1	102.50	2
Port Elizabeth	1	2	—	26	18	—	—	—	13.00	1
in West Indies										
Bridgetown	2	3	1	71	65	—	1	—	35.50	4
Kingston	1	1	—	200	200	—	—	1	200.00	1
Port-of-Spain	2	3	1	110	63*	—	1	—	55.00	1
St John's	1	2	1	80	65*	—	1	—	80.00	1

Country	M	Inn	NO	Runs	HS	0s	50	100	Avrge	Ct
Australia	55	88	12	3343	170	7	19	7	43.99	40
England	18	27	8	1312	177*	2	4	5	69.05	13
India	6	10	4	278	80	1	2	—	46.33	4
New Zealand	7	11	—	315	75	2	3	—	28.64	3
Pakistan	5	8	—	263	98	2	3	—	32.88	4
South Africa	6	9	2	508	160	1	4	1	72.57	6
West Indies	6	9	3	461	200	—	3	1	76.83	7

Batting position	Inn	NO	Runs	HS	0s	50	100	Avrge
3	7	—	252	100	1	1	1	36.00
4	8	2	196	90	1	1	—	32.67
5	60	8	2874	200	4	19	7	55.27
6	64	14	2606	177*	7	14	5	52.12
7	18	3	535	134*	—	3	1	35.67
8	5	2	17	12*	2	—	—	5.67

How dismissed:	Inn	NO	Bwd	Ct	LBW	Stp	RO	HW
	162	29	27	86	15	3	2	—

Centuries
Highest score: 200 Australia *v.* West Indies, Kingston, 1994–95

Score	Team	Opponent	Venue	Season
177*	Australia	England	Leeds	1989
152*	Australia	England	Lord's	1989
134*	Australia	Sri Lanka	Hobart	1989–90
100	Australia	West Indies	Sydney	1992–93
157*	Australia	England	Leeds	1993
147*	Australia	New Zealand	Brisbane	1993–94
164	Australia	South Africa	Adelaide	1993–94
200	Australia	West Indies	Kingston	1994–95
112*	Australia	Pakistan	Brisbane	1995–96
131*	Australia	Sri Lanka	Melbourne	1995–96
170	Australia	Sri Lanka	Adelaide	1995–96
160	Australia	South Africa	Johannesburg	1996–97
108	Australia	England	Manchester	1997
116	Australia	England	Manchester	1997

Nineties

Score	Team	Opponent	Venue	Season
90	Australia	West Indies	Brisbane	1988–89
91	Australia	West Indies	Perth	1988–89
92	Australia	England	Manchester	1989
98	Australia	Pakistan	Rawalpindi	1994–95
94*	Australia	England	Melbourne	1994–95
99*	Australia	England	Perth	1994–95
96	Australia	New Zealand	Perth	1997–98
96	Australia	South Africa	Melbourne	1997–98

Sheffield Shield Career
Debut: 1984–85 New South Wales *v.* Queensland, Brisbane

Season	M	Inn	NO	Runs	HS	0s	50	100	Avrge	Ct
1984–85	5	7	—	223	94	1	2	—	31.86	8
1985–86	4	6	2	325	119*	—	—	2	81.25	3
1986–87	7	12	1	384	89	1	3	—	34.91	14
1987–88	5	9	1	323	170	—	1	1	40.38	6
1988–89	8	14	—	359	118	1	—	1	25.64	7

Season	M	Inn	NO	Runs	HS	0s	50	100	Avrge	Ct
1989–90	5	8	1	308	196	—	—	1	44.00	1
1990–91	5	7	1	516	216*	—	4	1	86.00	2
1991–92	6	9	—	448	115	—	2	2	49.78	7
1992–93	2	4	—	78	38	1	—	—	19.50	2
1993–94	4	8	2	503	190*	—	1	2	83.83	3
1994–95	4	7	1	504	206	—	3	1	84.00	6
1995–96	4	8	—	343	107	1	2	1	42.88	2
1996–97	3	6	1	421	186*	—	1	2	84.20	6
1997–98	4	7	3	352	202*	—	2	1	88.00	4
Total	**66**	**112**	**13**	**5087**	**216***	**5**	**21**	**15**	**51.38**	**71**

Opponents	M	Inn	NO	Runs	HS	0s	50	100	Avrge	Ct
Queensland	17	30	4	1035	186*	1	4	3	39.81	14
South Australia	12	19	1	639	119*	—	2	1	35.50	12
Tasmania	12	20	4	1344	206	—	6	5	84.00	11
Victoria	16	29	3	1323	202*	2	7	3	50.88	25
Western Australia	9	14	1	746	216*	2	2	3	57.38	9

Innings		Inn	NO	Runs	HS	0s	50	100	Avrge	Ct
First		35	2	2160	216*	1	5	9	65.45	21
Second		31	2	1416	202*	3	8	4	48.83	20
Third		28	5	988	186*	1	4	2	42.96	12
Fourth		18	4	523	89	—	4	—	37.36	18

Batting at Each Venue

Venue	M	Inn	NO	Runs	HS	0s	50	100	Avrge	Ct
Adelaide	5	8	—	270	73	—	1	—	33.75	5
Bankstown	1	2	—	141	106	—	—	1	70.50	—
Brisbane	7	13	3	532	186*	—	1	2	53.20	7
Devonport	1	1	—	39	39	—	—	—	39.00	1
Hobart (Bel)	3	6	3	703	206	—	1	3	234.33	2
Hobart (TCA)	2	2	—	172	107	—	1	1	86.00	4
Melbourne	5	10	1	317	122	—	1	1	35.22	5
Newcastle	5	10	1	130	53	—	1	—	14.44	3
North Sydney	1	2	2	262	202*	—	1	1	—	2
Perth	6	10	1	629	216*	2	1	3	69.89	7
St Kilda	2	4	—	160	59	—	2	—	40.00	2
Sydney	28	44	2	732	170	3	11	3	41.24	33

Batting position	Inn	NO	Runs	HS	0s	50	100	Avrge
3	51	6	2782	206	1	10	10	61.82
4	33	3	1099	196	2	5	2	36.63
5	9	2	452	119*	—	3	1	64.57
6	14	2	626	216*	2	2	2	52.17
7	1	—	1	1	—	—	—	1.00
8	3	—	96	71	—	1	—	32.00
9	1	—	31	31	—	—	—	31.00

How dismissed:	Inn	NO	Bwd	Ct	LBW	Stp	RO	HW
	112	13	22	63	7	1	6	—

Centuries

Highest score: 216* New South Wales *v.* Western Australia, Perth, 1990–91

Score	Team	Opponent	Venue	Season
107*	New South Wales	Tasmania	Hobart	1985–86
119*	New South Wales	South Australia	Sydney	1985–86
170	New South Wales	Victoria	Sydney	1987–88
118	New South Wales	Queensland	Brisbane	1988–89
196	New South Wales	Tasmania	Hobart	1989–90
216*	New South Wales	Western Australia	Perth	1990–91
115	New South Wales	Western Australia	Perth	1991–92
113	New South Wales	Western Australia	Perth	1991–92
122	New South Wales	Victoria	Melbourne	1993–94
190*	New South Wales	Tasmania	Hobart	1993–94
206	New South Wales	Tasmania	Hobart	1994–95

Score	Team	Opponent	Venue	Season
107	New South Wales	Tasmania	Sydney	1995–96
106	New South Wales	Queensland	Bankstown	1996–97
186*	New South Wales	Queensland	Brisbane	1996–97
202*	New South Wales	Victoria	Sydney	1997–98

International Limited-Overs Career
Debut: 1985–86 Australia *v.* New Zealand, Melbourne

Season	Tournament	Venue	M	Inn	NO	Runs	HS	0s	50	100	Avrge	Stk/Rt	Ct
1985–86	World Series Cup	AUS	12	10	3	266	81	—	2	—	38.00	65.04	2
1985–86	Rothman's Cup	NZ	4	4	—	111	71	—	1	—	27.75	78.17	2
1985–86	Austral-Asia Cup	UAE	1	1	—	26	26	—	—	—	26.00	70.27	—
1986–87	India v. Australia	IND	6	4	2	111	57*	—	1	—	55.50	86.05	—
1986–87	Challenge Cup	AUS	3	3	—	127	82	—	1	—	42.33	73.41	—
1986–87	World Series Cup	AUS	10	10	3	245	83*	—	1	—	35.00	65.68	3
1986–87	Sharjah Cup	UAE	3	3	—	42	20	—	—	—	14.00	47.19	1
1987–88	World Cup	I/P	8	8	5	167	45	—	—	—	55.67	97.66	3
1987–88	World Series Cup	AUS	10	8	2	199	68	2	1	—	33.17	83.26	3
1987–88	Australia v. England	AUS	1	1	—	27	27	—	—	—	27.00	108.00	—
1988–89	Pakistan v. Australia	PAK	1	1	—	7	7	—	—	—	7.00	77.78	—
1988–89	World Series Cup	AUS	11	10	3	270	54	1	1	—	38.57	86.54	4
1989	England v. Australia	ENG	3	3	—	113	43	—	—	—	37.67	67.26	—
1989–90	Nehru Cup	IND	5	4	1	83	53*	1	1	—	27.67	112.16	3
1989–90	World Series	AUS	9	8	2	104	31*	1	—	—	17.33	50.98	4
1989–90	Rothman's Series	NZ	5	4	—	72	36	—	—	—	18.00	53.73	3
1989–90	Austral-Asia Cup	UAE	4	2	—	98	64	—	1	—	49.00	74.81	1
1990–91	World Series	AUS	10	9	5	141	65*	—	1	—	35.25	68.45	4
1990–91	West Indies v. Australia	WI	5	5	2	86	26*	—	—	—	28.67	84.31	3
1991–92	World Series	AUS	10	7	2	60	34	—	—	—	12.00	57.69	9
1991–92	World Cup	ANZ	8	7	—	187	55	—	1	—	26.71	78.24	2
1992–93	World Series	AUS	10	10	1	213	64	—	1	—	23.67	59.66	4
1992–93	New Zealand v. Australia	NZ	5	5	1	120	39	—	—	—	30.00	68.97	3
1993	England v. Australia	ENG	3	3	1	41	27	—	—	—	20.50	97.62	—
1993–94	World Series	AUS	9	8	2	141	33	—	—	—	23.50	66.20	2
1993–94	South Africa v. Australia	SAF	8	8	2	291	86	—	2	—	48.50	90.37	2
1993–94	Austral-Asia Cup	UAE	3	1	—	53	53	—	1	—	53.00	73.61	—
1994–95	Singer World Series	SL	3	3	—	53	30	—	—	—	17.67	63.10	—
1994–95	Wills Triangular Series	PAK	5	5	1	153	59*	—	2	—	38.25	75.37	2
1994–95	World Series	AUS	1	1	—	0	0	1	—	—	0.00	0.00	1
1994–95	New Zealand Centenary	NZ	4	4	1	81	44*	—	—	—	27.00	52.94	1
1994–95	West Indies v. Australia	WI	5	5	—	164	58	—	1	—	32.80	90.61	—
1995–96	World Series	AUS	4	4	1	128	102*	—	—	1	42.67	73.99	2
1995–96	World Cup	IPS	7	7	2	226	82	—	3	—	45.20	76.87	3
1996–97	Singer World Series	SL	4	4	—	214	82	—	3	—	53.50	89.17	3
1996–97	Titan Cup	IND	5	5	—	152	41	—	—	—	30.40	64.14	1
1996–97	CUB Series	AUS	6	6	—	159	57	—	1	—	26.50	67.37	3
1996–97	South Africa v. Australia	SAF	7	7	1	301	91	1	4	—	50.17	88.27	3
1997	England v. Australia	ENG	3	3	—	60	24	—	—	—	20.00	62.50	2
1997–98	CUB Series	AUS	10	9	1	181	71	3	2	—	22.63	73.88	2
1997–98	New Zealand v. Australia	NZ	4	3	—	112	47	—	—	—	37.33	81.16	1
1997–98	Triangular Cup	IND	5	4	—	131	57	1	1	—	32.75	98.50	2
1997–98	Coca-Cola Cup	UAE	5	5	—	123	70	—	1	—	24.60	82.55	—
Total			**245**	**222**	**44**	**5639**	**102***	**11**	**34**	**1**	**31.68**	**74.63**	**84**

Opponents	M	Inn	NO	Runs	HS	0s	50	100	Avrge	Stk/Rt	Ct
Bangladesh	1	—	—	—	—	—	—	—	—	—	—
England	26	25	8	576	83*	1	2	—	33.88	73.10	7
India	39	34	7	906	81	1	7	—	33.56	72.36	12
Kenya	1	1	—	82	82	—	1	—	82.00	89.13	—
New Zealand	49	41	9	875	71	3	3	—	27.34	72.19	16
Pakistan	29	28	5	655	82	2	5	—	28.48	70.13	10
Sri Lanka	20	16	4	352	102*	1	1	1	29.33	78.40	5
South Africa	35	34	4	1065	91	3	9	—	35.50	75.32	11
West Indies	38	37	5	883	58	—	4	—	27.59	73.28	18
Zimbabwe	7	6	2	245	82	—	2	—	61.25	112.39	5

Innings		Inn	NO	Runs	HS	0s	50	100	Avrge	Stk/Rt	Ct
First		137	26	3403	102*	5	19	1	30.66	77.17	48
Second		85	18	2236	91	6	15	—	33.37	71.07	36

Batting at Each Venue

Venue	M	Inn	NO	Runs	HS	0s	50	100	Avrge	Stk/Rt	Ct
in Australia											
Adelaide	14	11	6	293	83*	—	3	—	58.60	75.71	1
Brisbane	11	11	3	214	45	—	—	—	26.75	66.05	7
Hobart	5	4	—	102	55	—	1	—	25.50	88.70	5
Melbourne	41	36	9	903	102*	5	5	1	33.44	70.22	13
Perth	16	15	2	288	82	2	1	—	22.15	64.43	2
Sydney	36	33	5	610	71	1	2	—	21.79	66.45	17
in England											
Birmingham	1	1	1	6	6*	—	—	—	—	200.00	—
Leeds	1	1	—	19	19	—	—	—	19.00	45.24	—
Lord's	3	3	—	60	35	—	—	—	20.00	100.00	1
Manchester	2	2	—	62	35	—	—	—	31.00	59.05	—
Nottingham	1	1	—	43	43	—	—	—	43.00	70.49	—
The Oval	1	1	—	24	24	—	—	—	24.00	68.57	1
in India											
Ahmedabad	2	2	—	57	48	—	—	—	28.50	85.07	—
Bangalore	2	2	—	69	41	—	—	—	34.50	81.18	1
Calcutta	1	1	1	5	5*	—	—	—	—	125.00	—
Chandigarh (MS)	2	2	—	36	33	—	—	—	18.00	61.02	—
Chandigarh (SS)	1	1	—	1	1	—	—	—	1.00	14.29	—
Chennai (Chpk)	3	3	2	117	53*	—	1	—	117.00	114.71	—
Chennai (Corp)	1	1	1	59	59*	—	1	—	—	83.10	1
Cuttack	1	1	1	10	10*	—	—	—	—	71.43	2
Delhi	4	3	1	156	57*	—	2	—	78.00	98.11	3
Faridabad	1	1	—	40	40	—	—	—	40.00	66.67	1
Guwahati	1	1	—	37	37	—	—	—	37.00	55.22	—
Hyderabad	2	1	1	25	25*	—	—	—	—	73.53	—
Indore	2	2	1	14	13*	—	—	—	14.00	82.35	—
Jaipur	2	1	—	57	57	—	1	—	57.00	87.69	—
Kanpur	1	1	—	0	0	1	—	—	0.00	0.00	—
Kochi	1	1	—	26	26	—	—	—	26.00	78.79	—
Margoa	1	1	—	2	2	—	—	—	2.00	50.00	1
Mumbai	2	2	—	7	7	1	—	—	3.50	41.18	1
Nagpur	1	1	1	5	5*	—	—	—	—	71.43	2
Rajkot	1	—	—	—	—	—	—	—	—	—	—
Srinagar	1	1	—	20	20	—	—	—	20.00	105.26	—
Visakhapatnam	1	1	—	82	82	—	1	—	82.00	89.13	—
in New Zealand											
Auckland	8	7	—	151	39	—	—	—	21.57	65.65	1
Christchurch	5	4	—	53	30	—	—	—	13.25	47.75	5
Dunedin	3	3	1	75	29	—	—	—	37.50	86.21	1
Hamilton	2	2	—	42	23	—	—	—	21.00	79.25	—
Napier	1	1	—	42	42	—	—	—	42.00	87.50	—
Wellington	4	4	1	171	71	—	1	—	57.00	69.51	3
in Pakistan											
Faisalabad	1	1	—	23	23	—	—	—	23.00	62.16	1
Lahore	5	5	1	109	56	—	1	—	27.25	76.76	1
Multan	1	1	1	59	59*	—	1	—	—	83.10	—
Rawalpindi	1	1	—	14	14	—	—	—	14.00	93.33	—
in Sri Lanka											
Colombo (PIS)	3	3	—	126	82	—	1	—	42.00	85.71	—
Colombo (PSS)	1	1	—	30	30	—	—	—	30.00	90.91	—
Colombo (SSC)	3	3	—	111	55	—	2	—	37.00	77.08	3
in South Africa											
Bloemfontein	2	2	—	133	91	—	1	—	66.50	100.76	1
Cape Town	2	2	—	23	23	1	—	—	11.50	100.00	—
Centurion	1	1	—	89	89	—	1	—	89.00	85.58	—
Durban	2	2	—	3	2	—	—	—	1.50	12.50	1
East London	2	2	1	117	67*	—	2	—	117.00	96.69	—
Johannesburg	2	2	1	66	46*	—	—	—	66.00	80.49	2

Venue	M	Inn	NO	Runs	HS	0s	50	100	Avrge	Stk/Rt	Ct
Port Elizabeth	3	3	1	75	50*	—	1	—	37.50	87.21	—
Verwoerdburg	1	1	—	86	86	—	1	—	86.00	94.51	1
in United Arab Emirates											
Sharjah	16	12	—	342	70	—	3	—	28.50	71.55	2
in West Indies											
Kingstown	1	1	—	25	25	—	—	—	25.00	86.21	—
Bridgetown	2	2	—	31	26	—	—	—	15.50	79.49	1
Georgetown	2	2	1	37	26*	—	—	—	37.00	71.15	—
Kingston	1	1	1	6	6*	—	—	—	—	85.71	1
Port-of-Spain	4	4	—	151	58	—	1	—	37.75	96.79	1

Country	M	Inn	NO	Runs	HS	0s	50	100	Avrge	Stk/Rt	Ct
Australia	123	110	25	2410	102*	8	12	1	28.35	69.31	45
England	9	9	1	214	43	—	—	—	26.75	69.93	2
India	34	30	9	825	82	2	6	—	39.29	83.76	12
New Zealand	23	21	2	534	71	—	1	—	28.11	68.90	10
Pakistan	8	8	2	205	59*	—	2	—	34.17	77.36	2
Sri Lanka	7	7	—	267	82	—	3	—	38.14	82.41	3
South Africa	15	15	3	592	91	1	6	—	49.33	89.29	5
Sharjah	16	12	—	342	70	—	3	—	28.50	71.55	2
West Indies	10	10	2	250	58	—	1	—	31.25	88.34	3

Batting position	Inn	NO	Runs	HS	0s	50	100	Avrge	Stk/Rt
3	10	—	191	37	1	—	—	19.10	59.13
4	51	5	1411	102*	3	11	1	30.67	70.59
5	89	16	2604	91	5	16	—	35.67	76.41
6	57	17	1186	73*	2	6	—	29.65	77.31
7	15	6	247	57*	—	1	—	27.44	84.59

How dismissed:	Inn	NO	Bwd	Ct	LBW	Stp	RO	HW
	222	44	48	86	11	8	24	1

Highest score: 102* Australia *v.* Sri Lanka, Melbourne, 1995–96

Domestic Limited-Overs Career
Debut: 1984–85 New South Wales *v.* Victoria, Melbourne

Season	M	Inn	NO	Runs	HS	0s	50	100	Avrge	Stk/Rt	Ct
1984–85	1	—	—	—	—	—	—	—	—	—	1
1985–86	1	1	—	47	47	—	—	—	47.00	66.20	—
1986–87	2	2	—	2	2	1	—	—	1.00	33.33	1
1987–88	4	4	—	101	56	—	1	—	25.25	78.91	—
1988–89	3	3	1	82	81*	1	1	—	41.00	109.33	1
1989–90	—	—	—	—	—	—	—	—	—	—	—
1990–91	4	4	2	88	66*	—	1	—	44.00	60.69	1
1991–92	4	4	—	239	126	—	1	1	59.75	86.28	—
1992–93	4	4	1	269	131	—	1	1	89.67	85.13	1
1993–94	2	2	—	94	59	—	1	—	47.00	97.92	2
1994–95	—	—	—	—	—	—	—	—	—	—	—
1995–96	3	3	—	140	90	—	1	—	46.67	73.68	2
1996–97	—	—	—	—	—	—	—	—	—	—	—
1997–98	3	3	—	96	72	—	1	—	32.00	90.57	4
Total	**31**	**30**	**4**	**1158**	**131**	**2**	**8**	**2**	**44.54**	**82.13**	**13**

Opponents	M	Inn	NO	Runs	HS	0s	50	100	Avrge	Stk/Rt	Ct
Queensland	7	7	—	390	131	—	3	1	55.71	90.28	1
South Australia	4	4	1	227	85*	—	2	—	75.67	81.07	3
Tasmania	5	5	2	207	81*	—	2	—	69.00	94.09	3
Victoria	9	8	1	208	126	2	—	1	29.71	69.10	3
Western Australia	6	6	—	126	90	—	1	—	21.00	71.19	3

Innings	Inn	NO	Runs	HS	0s	50	100	Avrge	Stk/Rt	Ct
First	18	2	813	131	—	5	2	50.81	88.27	8
Second	12	2	345	90	2	3	—	34.50	70.55	5

Batting at Each Venue

Venue	M	Inn	NO	Runs	HS	0s	50	100	Avrge	Stk/Rt	Ct
Adelaide	1	1	1	85	85*	—	1	—	—	89.47	1

Venue	M	Inn	NO	Runs	HS	0s	50	100	Avrge	Stk/Rt	Ct
Brisbane	6	6	—	341	131	—	3	I	56.83	90.69	I
Melbourne	3	2	—	I	I	I	—	—	0.50	6.67	2
North Sydney	6	6	—	309	126	—	I	I	51.50	88.79	5
Perth	6	6	—	126	90	—	I	—	21.00	71.19	3
Sydney	9	9	3	296	81*	I	2	—	49.33	74.19	I

Batting position	Inn	NO	Runs	HS	0s	50	100	Avrge	Stk/Rt
3	23	2	1067	131	I	7	2	50.81	85.29
4	I	—	I	I	—	—	—	1.00	12.50
5	6	2	90	66*	I	I	—	22.50	59.60

How dismissed:	Inn	NO	Bwd	Ct	LBW	Stp	RO	HW
	30	4	3	18	2	—	3	—

Centuries

Highest score: 131 New South Wales *v.* Queensland, Brisbane, 1992–93

Score	Team	Opponent	Venue	Season
126	New South Wales	Victoria	North Sydney	1991–92
131	New South Wales	Queensland	Brisbane	1992–93

BOWLING
First-Class Career

Debut: 1984–85 New South Wales *v.* Queensland, Brisbane

Season	Country	M	Balls	Mdns	Runs	Wkts	Avrge	5	10	Best
1984–85	Australia	5	432	25	156	3	52.00	—	—	1–15
1985–86	Zimbabwe	I	125	2	85	2	42.50	—	—	2–57
1985–86	Australia	7	408	18	190	4	47.50	—	—	2–36
1985–86	New Zealand	5	318	12	151	7	21.57	—	—	4–56
1986–87	India	6	582	15	367	10	36.70	—	—	4–71
1986–87	Australia	13	1551	49	772	25	30.88	I	—	5–69
1987	England	4	672	22	348	11	31.64	—	—	3–48
1987–88	Australia	10	1311	59	499	23	21.70	I	—	5–50
1988	England	15	138	5	60	3	20.00	—	—	2–33
1988–89	Pakistan	6	756	33	362	4	90.50	—	—	1–15
1988–89	Australia	14	2190	68	1114	36	30.94	2	—	6–51
1989	England	16	1057	39	571	23	24.83	—	—	3–10
1989–90	Australia	12	54	3	19	I	19.00	—	—	1–13
1989–90	New Zealand	I	—	—	—	—	—	—	—	—
1990–91	Australia	8	642	26	319	4	79.75	—	—	1–7
1990–91	West Indies	6	468	16	234	3	78.00	—	—	3–76
1991–92	Zimbabwe	2	162	14	21	2	10.50	—	—	2–2
1991–92	Australia	8	750	35	342	12	28.50	—	—	3–23
1992–93	Australia	9	780	34	389	7	55.57	—	—	3–90
1992–93	New Zealand	4	330	21	108	5	21.60	—	—	2–21
1993	England	16	439	19	229	7	32.71	—	—	2–9
1993–94	Australia	9	480	22	190	7	27.14	—	—	4–26
1993–94	South Africa	5	539	31	157	11	14.27	I	—	5–28
1994–95	Pakistan	3	228	8	90	I	90.00	—	—	1–28
1994–95	Australia	9	—	—	—	—	—	—	—	—
1994–95	West Indies	6	222	8	100	8	12.50	—	—	2–14
1995–96	Australia	10	486	21	200	10	20.00	—	—	4–4
1996–97	India	2	78	5	25	I	25.00	—	—	1–25
1996–97	Australia	7	283	15	116	I	116.00	—	—	1–15
1996–97	South Africa	5	165	3	94	2	47.00	—	—	1–4
1997	England	13	156	5	97	I	97.00	—	—	1–13
1997–98	Australia	10	330	17	151	6	25.17	—	—	3–20
1997–98	India	4	102	2	44	—	—	—	—	—
Total		**251**	**16234**	**652**	**7600**	**240**	**31.67**	**5**	**—**	**6–51**

Country	M	Balls	Mdns	Runs	Wkts	Avrge	5	10	Best
Australia	131	9697	392	4457	139	32.06	4	—	6–51
England	64	2462	90	1305	45	29.00	—	—	3–10
India	12	762	22	436	11	39.64	—	—	4–71
New Zealand	10	648	33	259	12	21.58	—	—	4–56
Pakistan	9	984	41	452	5	90.40	—	—	1–15

Country	M	Balls	Mdns	Runs	Wkts	Avrge	5	10	Best
South Africa	10	704	34	251	13	19.31	1	—	5–28
West Indies	12	690	24	334	11	30.36	—	—	3–76
Zimbabwe	3	287	16	106	4	26.50	—	—	2–2

Team	M	Balls	Mdns	Runs	Wkts	Avrge	5	10	Best
AUSTRALIA	103	6863	298	3036	86	35.30	3	—	5–28
Australian XI	54	2768	109	1431	54	26.50	—	—	4–71
New South Wales	74	5668	216	2640	84	31.43	2	—	6–51
Somerset	19	810	27	408	14	29.14	—	—	3–48
Young Australians	1	125	2	85	2	42.50	—	—	2–57

Wickets taken:	Wkts	Bwd	Ct	C&B	LBW	Stp	HW
	240	44	148	7	39	2	—

Batsmen dismissed:	Wkts	1/2	3	4	5	6	7	8	9	10	11
	240	47	29	30	37	31	15	18	16	10	7

Five Wickets in an Innings
Best bowling: 6–51 New South Wales v. Queensland, Sydney, 1988–89

Wkts	Team	Opponent	Venue	Season
5–69	Australia	England	Perth	1986–87
5–50	New South Wales	Tasmania	Sydney	1987–88
5–92	Australia	West Indies	Melbourne	1988–89
6–51	New South Wales	Queensland	Sydney	1988–89
5–28	Australia	South Africa	Cape Town	1993–94

Test Career
Debut: 1985–86 Australia v. India, Melbourne

Season	Opponent	Venue	M	Balls	Mdns	Runs	Wkts	Avrge	5	10	Best
1985–86	India	Australia	2	108	5	69	2	34.50	—	—	2–36
1985–86	New Zealand	New Zealand	3	216	9	83	5	16.60	—	—	4–56
1986–87	India	India	3	210	5	130	2	65.00	—	—	1–29
1986–87	England	Australia	5	651	26	336	10	33.60	1	—	5–69
1987–88	New Zealand	Australia	3	450	26	169	2	84.50	—	—	1–2
1987–88	England	Australia	1	137	5	51	3	17.00	—	—	3–51
1987–88	Sri Lanka	Australia	1	168	11	47	4	11.75	—	—	4–33
1988–89	Pakistan	Pakistan	3	468	17	216	2	108.00	—	—	1–44
1988–89	West Indies	Australia	5	834	17	472	10	47.20	1	—	5–92
1989	England	England	6	342	15	208	2	104.00	—	—	1–38
1989–90	New Zealand	Australia	1	—	—	—	—	—	—	—	—
1989–90	Sri Lanka	Australia	2	36	3	6			—	—	
1989–90	Pakistan	Australia	3	18	—	13	1	13.00	—	—	1–13
1989–90	New Zealand	New Zealand	1	—	—	—	—	—	—	—	—
1990–91	England	Australia	3	228	15	90	1	90.00	—	—	1–7
1990–91	West Indies	West Indies	2	210	6	90	—	—	—	—	—
1992–93	West Indies	Australia	5	348	14	162	3	54.00	—	—	1–14
1992–93	New Zealand	New Zealand	3	246	18	71	2	35.50	—	—	1–15
1993	England	England	6	192	9	82	2	41.00	—	—	2–45
1993–94	New Zealand	Australia	3	108	3	41	1	41.00	—	—	1–10
1993–94	South Africa	Australia	1	144	10	30	4	7.50	—	—	4–26
1993–94	South Africa	South Africa	3	467	29	130	10	13.00	1	—	5–28
1994–95	Pakistan	Pakistan	2	180	5	78	1	78.00	—	—	1–28
1994–95	England	Australia	5	—	—	—	—	—	—	—	—
1994–95	West Indies	West Indies	4	144	7	62	5	12.40	—	—	2–14
1995–96	Pakistan	Australia	3	96	2	40	1	40.00	—	—	1–18
1995–96	Sri Lanka	Australia	2	114	8	34	4	8.50	—	—	4–34
1996–97	India	India	1	78	5	25	1	25.00	—	—	1–25
1996–97	West Indies	Australia	4	151	7	63	1	63.00	—	—	1–15
1996–97	South Africa	South Africa	3	51	1	20	1	20.00	—	—	1–4
1997	England	England	6	120	3	76	—	—	—	—	—
1997–98	New Zealand	Australia	3	90	6	30	4	7.50	—	—	3–20
1997–98	South Africa	Australia	3	186	10	74	2	37.00	—	—	1–12
1997–98	India	India	2	72	1	38			—	—	
Total			103	6863	298	3036	86	35.30	3	—	5–28

Opponents	M	Balls	Mdns	Runs	Wkts	Avrge	5	10	Best
ENGLAND	32	1670	73	843	18	46.83	1	—	5–69
INDIA	8	468	16	262	5	52.40	—	—	2–36
NEW ZEALAND	17	1110	62	394	14	28.14	—	—	4–56
PAKISTAN	11	762	24	347	5	69.40	—	—	1–13
SRI LANKA	5	318	22	87	8	10.88	—	—	4–33
SOUTH AFRICA	10	848	50	254	17	14.94	1	—	5–28
WEST INDIES	20	1687	51	849	19	44.68	1	—	5–92

Innings		Balls	Mdns	Runs	Wkts	Avrge	5	10	Best
First		2463	111	1066	36	29.61	—	—	4–26
Second		2189	90	1064	19	56.00	—	—	3–51
Third		714	35	239	11	21.73	—	—	4–34
Fourth		1497	62	667	20	33.35	3	—	5–28

Bowling at Each Venue

Venue	M	Balls	Mdns	Runs	Wkts	Avrge	5	10	Best
in Australia									
Adelaide	10	900	50	343	11	31.18	—	—	4–26
Brisbane	11	673	25	298	10	29.80	—	—	3–76
Hobart	4	234	11	81	5	16.20	—	—	3–20
Melbourne	11	678	34	361	13	27.77	1	—	5–92
Perth	9	891	29	420	10	42.00	1	—	5–69
Sydney	10	491	19	224	4	56.00	—	—	3–51
in England									
Birmingham	3	168	7	87	1	87.00	—	—	1–38
Leeds	3	60	3	38	—	—	—	—	—
Lord's	3	156	6	107	1	107.00	—	—	1–49
Manchester	3	60	1	40	—	—	—	—	—
Nottingham	3	120	8	38	—	—	—	—	—
The Oval	3	90	2	56	2	28.00	—	—	2–45
in India									
Calcutta	1	—	—	—	—	—	—	—	—
Chennai	2	162	4	98	1	98.00	—	—	1–44
Delhi	2	114	5	54	2	27.00	—	—	1–25
Mumbai	1	84	2	41	—	—	—	—	—
in New Zealand									
Auckland	2	174	9	52	3	17.33	—	—	1–14
Christchurch	2	174	10	65	4	16.25	—	—	4–56
Wellington	3	114	8	37	—	—	—	—	—
in Pakistan									
Faisalabad	1	174	9	80	1	80.00	—	—	1–44
Karachi	2	258	6	131	2	65.50	—	—	1–28
Lahore	1	138	5	42	—	—	—	—	—
Rawalpindi	1	78	2	41	—	—	—	—	—
in South Africa									
Cape Town	1	189	12	48	5	9.60	1	—	5–28
Centurion	1	—	—	—	—	—	—	—	—
Durban	1	164	12	40	3	13.33	—	—	3–40
Johannesburg	2	138	6	46	3	15.33	—	—	1–4
Port Elizabeth	1	27	—	16	—	—	—	—	—
in West Indies									
Bridgetown	2	180	6	80	—	—	—	—	—
Kingston	1	90	5	23	2	11.50	—	—	2–14
Port-of-Spain	2	48	1	29	1	29.00	—	—	1–19
St John's	1	36	1	20	2	10.00	—	—	2–20

Country	M	Balls	Mdns	Runs	Wkts	Avrge	5	10	Best
Australia	55	3867	168	1727	53	32.58	2	—	5–69
England	18	654	27	366	4	91.50	—	—	2–45
India	6	360	11	193	3	64.33	—	—	1–25
New Zealand	7	462	27	154	7	22.00	—	—	4–56
Pakistan	5	648	22	294	3	98.00	—	—	1–28
South Africa	6	518	30	150	11	13.64	1	—	5–28
West Indies	6	354	13	152	5	30.40	—	—	2–14

Wickets taken:	Wkts	Bwd	Ct	C&B	LBW	Stp	HW				
	86	12	48	5	21	—	—				

Batsmen dismissed:	Wkts	1/2	3	4	5	6	7	8	9	10	11
	86	12	9	8	16	12	5	9	6	5	4

Five Wickets in an Innings

Best bowling: 5–28 Australia *v.* South Africa, Cape Town, 1993–94

Wkts	Team	Opponent	Venue	Season
5–69	Australia	England	Perth	1986–87
5–92	Australia	West Indies	Melbourne	1988–89
5–28	Australia	South Africa	Cape Town	1993–94

Sheffield Shield Career

Debut: 1984–85 New South Wales *v.* Queensland, Brisbane

Season	M	Balls	Mdns	Runs	Wkts	Avrge	5	10	Best
1984–85	5	432	25	156	3	52.00	—	—	1–15
1985–86	4	300	13	121	2	60.50	—	—	1–15
1986–87	7	870	23	424	15	28.27	—	—	3–33
1987–88	5	556	17	232	14	16.57	1	—	5–50
1988–89	8	1296	49	620	26	23.85	1	—	6–51
1989–90	5	—	—	—	—	—	—	—	—
1990–91	5	414	11	229	3	76.33	—	—	1–33
1991–92	6	564	25	261	9	29.00	—	—	3–23
1992–93	2	246	12	131	3	43.67	—	—	3–90
1993–94	4	198	8	113	2	56.50	—	—	1–15
1994–95	4	—	—	—	—	—	—	—	—
1995–96	4	276	11	126	5	25.20	—	—	2–25
1996–97	3	132	8	53	—	—	—	—	—
1997–98	4	54	1	47	—	—	—	—	—
Total	**66**	**5338**	**203**	**2513**	**82**	**30.65**	**2**	**—**	**6–51**

Opponents	M	Balls	Mdns	Runs	Wkts	Avrge	5	10	Best
Queensland	17	1419	60	672	26	25.85	1	—	6–51
South Australia	12	738	32	327	7	46.71	—	—	1–15
Tasmania	12	868	25	415	16	25.94	1	—	5–50
Victoria	16	1401	56	612	15	40.80	—	—	3–23
Western Australia	9	912	30	487	18	27.06	—	—	4–30

Innings		Balls	Mdns	Runs	Wkts	Avrge	5	10	Best
First		1860	75	834	23	36.26	—	—	3–23
Second		1753	74	723	25	28.92	1	—	5–50
Third		783	26	441	22	20.05	1	—	6–51
Fourth		942	28	515	12	42.92	—	—	2–25

Bowling at Each Venue

Venue	M	Balls	Mdns	Runs	Wkts	Avrge	5	10	Best
Adelaide	5	102	6	53	—	—	—	—	—
Bankstown	1	60	5	16	—	—	—	—	—
Brisbane	7	891	39	416	13	32.00	—	—	3–33
Devonport	1	174	7	68	2	34.00	—	—	2–68
Hobart (Bel)	3	36	—	38	—	—	—	—	—
Hobart (TCA)	2	204	4	106	4	26.50	—	—	2–36
Melbourne	5	354	16	124	4	31.00	—	—	3–23
Newcastle	5	372	12	183	5	36.60	—	—	3–38
North Sydney	1	—	—	—	—	—	—	—	—
Perth	6	750	23	416	13	32.00	—	—	3–49
St Kilda	2	303	9	151	3	50.33	—	—	2–39
Sydney	28	2092	82	942	38	24.79	2	—	6–51

Wickets taken:	Wkts	Bwd	Ct	C&B	LBW	Stp	HW				
	82	15	56	2	7	2	—				

Batsmen dismissed:	Wkts	1/2	3	4	5	6	7	8	9	10	11
	82	19	10	10	11	11	3	4	9	3	2

Five Wickets in an Innings

Best bowling: 6–51 New South Wales *v.* Queensland, Sydney, 1988–89

Wkts	Team	Opponent	Venue	Season
5–50	New South Wales	Tasmania	Sydney	1987–88
6–51	New South Wales	Queensland	Sydney	1988–89

International Limited-Overs Career

Debut: 1985–86 Australia *v.* New Zealand, Melbourne

Season	Tournament	Venue	M	Balls	Mdns	Runs	Wkts	Avrge	5	Best	Stk/Rt	RPO
1985–86	World Series Cup	AUS	12	318	4	231	7	33.00	—	2–28	45.43	4.36
1985–86	Rothman's Cup	NZ	4	210	1	159	4	39.75	—	1–31	52.50	4.54
1985–86	Austral-Asia Cup	UAE	1	36	1	25	—	—	—	—	—	4.17
1986–87	India v. Australia	IND	6	276	1	229	7	32.71	—	2–44	39.43	4.98
1986–87	Challenge Cup	AUS	3	149	—	113	6	18.83	—	4–48	24.83	4.55
1986–87	World Series Cup	AUS	10	510	4	345	15	23.00	—	3–26	34.00	4.06
1986–87	Sharjah Cup	UAE	3	144	1	116	2	58.00	—	1–33	72.00	4.83
1987–88	World Cup	I/P	8	381	4	288	11	26.18	—	2–36	34.64	4.54
1987–88	World Series Cup	AUS	10	539	3	381	17	22.41	—	4–33	31.71	4.24
1987–88	Australia v. England	AUS	1	60	—	42	1	42.00	—	1–42	60.00	4.20
1988–89	Pakistan v. Australia	PAK	1	48	—	42	1	42.00	—	1–42	48.00	5.25
1988–89	World Series Cup	AUS	11	468	—	373	8	46.63	—	3–57	58.50	4.78
1989	England v. Australia	ENG	3	198	2	162	3	54.00	—	2–45	66.00	4.91
1989–90	Nehru Cup	IND	5	—	—	—	—	—	—	—	—	—
1989–90	World Series	AUS	9	96	—	77	2	38.50	—	1–26	48.00	4.81
1989–90	Rothman's Series	NZ	5	—	—	—	—	—	—	—	—	—
1989–90	Austral-Asia Cup	UAE	4	174	2	112	4	28.00	—	2–22	43.50	3.86
1990–91	World Series	AUS	10	456	5	346	7	49.43	—	2–39	65.14	4.55
1990–91	West Indies v. Australia	WI	5	192	1	153	5	30.60	—	2–25	38.40	4.78
1991–92	World Series	AUS	10	483	5	304	16	19.00	—	3–31	30.19	3.78
1991–92	World Cup	ANZ	8	364	1	277	8	34.63	—	3–36	45.50	4.57
1992–93	World Series	AUS	10	495	4	353	9	39.22	—	2–25	55.00	4.28
1992–93	New Zealand v. Australia	NZ	5	214	—	173	3	57.67	—	2–27	71.33	4.85
1993	England v. Australia	ENG	3	174	—	151	5	30.20	—	3–53	34.80	5.21
1993–94	World Series	AUS	9	366	2	218	4	54.50	—	2–20	91.50	3.57
1993–94	South Africa v. Australia	SAF	8	336	2	282	5	56.40	—	2–48	67.20	5.04
1993–94	Austral-Asia Cup	UAE	3	144	1	117	2	58.50	—	2–17	72.00	4.88
1994–95	Singer World Series	SL	3	144	1	81	5	16.20	—	3–16	28.80	3.38
1994–95	Wills Triangular Series	PAK	5	222	2	144	2	72.00	—	2–35	111.00	3.89
1994–95	World Series	AUS	1	—	—	—	—	—	—	—	—	—
1994–95	New Zealand Centenary	NZ	4	—	—	—	—	—	—	—	—	—
1994–95	West Indies v. Australia	WI	5	135	1	123	3	41.00	—	2–61	45.00	5.47
1995–96	World Series	AUS	4	24	—	28	—	—	—	—	—	7.00
1995–96	World Cup	IPS	7	186	2	157	5	31.40	—	2–22	37.20	5.06
1996–97	Singer World Series	SL	4	150	3	111	3	37.00	—	1–20	50.00	4.44
1996–97	Titan Cup	IND	5	78	—	76	2	38.00	—	2–52	39.00	5.85
1996–97	CUB Series	AUS	6	18	—	24	—	—	—	—	—	8.00
1996–97	South Africa v. Australia	SAF	7	30	—	25	—	—	—	—	—	5.00
1997	England v. Australia	ENG	3	42	—	42	—	—	—	—	—	6.00
1997–98	CUB Series	AUS	10	24	—	14	1	14.00	—	1–14	24.00	3.50
1997–98	New Zealand v. Australia	NZ	4	177	1	126	3	42.00	—	2–46	59.00	4.27
1997–98	Triangular Cup	IND	5	102	—	97	3	32.33	—	2–42	34.00	5.71
1997–98	Coca-Cola Cup	UAE	5	168	—	171	5	34.20	—	4–40	33.60	6.11
Total			**245**	**8331**	**54**	**6288**	**184**	**34.17**	**—**	**4–33**	**45.28**	**4.52**

Opponents	M	Balls	Mdns	Runs	Wkts	Avrge	5	Best	Stk/Rt	R/O
Bangladesh	1	60	2	22	2	11.00	—	2–22	30.00	2.20
England	26	1128	7	870	26	33.46	—	3–26	43.38	4.63
India	39	1419	5	1160	37	31.35	—	4–40	38.35	4.90
Kenya	1	42	—	43	—	—	—	—	—	6.14
New Zealand	49	1708	10	1307	31	42.16	—	2–23	55.10	4.59
Pakistan	29	861	4	640	19	33.68	—	4–48	45.32	4.46
Sri Lanka	20	582	3	437	15	29.13	—	4–33	38.80	4.51
South Africa	35	822	6	602	12	50.17	—	2–20	68.50	4.39
West Indies	38	1463	10	1062	35	30.34	—	3–31	41.80	4.36
Zimbabwe	7	246	7	145	7	20.71	—	2–22	35.14	3.54

Innings		Balls	Mdns	Runs	Wkts	Avrge	5	Best	Stk/Rt	R/O
First		4696	27	3523	103	34.20	—	4–40	45.59	4.50
Second		3635	27	2765	81	34.14	—	4–33	44.88	4.56

Bowling at Each Venue

Venue	M	Balls	Mdns	Runs	Wkts	Avrge	5	Best	Stk/Rt	R/O
in Australia										
Adelaide	14	496	2	337	8	42.13	—	2–30	62.00	4.08
Brisbane	11	444	4	329	12	27.42	—	3–31	37.00	4.45
Hobart	5	174	1	133	4	33.25	—	2–28	43.50	4.59
Melbourne	41	1354	4	910	25	36.40	—	3–26	54.16	4.03
Perth	16	719	9	528	22	24.00	—	4–48	32.68	4.41
Sydney	36	1123	8	829	30	27.63	—	4–33	37.43	4.43
in England										
Birmingham	1	48	—	55	1	55.00	—	1–55	48.00	6.88
Leeds	1	—	—	—	—	—	—	—	—	—
Lord's	3	156	—	135	1	135.00	—	1–43	156.00	5.19
Manchester	2	126	1	98	5	19.60	—	3–53	25.20	4.67
Nottingham	1	66	1	47	1	47.00	—	1–47	66.00	4.27
The Oval	1	18	—	20	—	—	—	—	—	6.67
in India										
Ahmedabad	2	60	—	46	1	46.00	—	1–46	60.00	4.60
Bangalore	2	54	—	52	2	26.00	—	2–52	27.00	5.78
Calcutta	1	54	—	37	2	18.50	—	2–37	27.00	4.11
Chandigarh (MS)	2	42	—	30	1	30.00	—	1–30	42.00	4.29
Chandigarh (SS)	1	58	—	37	2	18.50	—	2–37	29.00	3.83
Chennai (Chpk)	3	95	3	59	2	29.50	—	2–52	47.50	3.73
Chennai (Corp)	1	24	—	25	—	—	—	—	—	6.25
Cuttack	1	24	—	9	1	9.00	—	1–9	24.00	2.25
Delhi	4	222	—	204	6	34.00	—	2–42	37.00	5.51
Faridabad	1	—	—	—	—	—	—	—	—	—
Guwahati	1	24	—	24	—	—	—	—	—	6.00
Hyderabad	2	—	—	—	—	—	—	—	—	—
Indore	2	36	—	36	2	18.00	—	2–36	18.00	6.00
Jaipur	2	42	—	42	—	—	—	—	—	6.00
Kanpur	1	—	—	—	—	—	—	—	—	—
Kochi	1	—	—	—	—	—	—	—	—	—
Margoa	1	—	—	—	—	—	—	—	—	—
Mumbai	2	18	—	22	2	11.00	—	2–22	9.00	7.33
Nagpur	1	42	2	22	2	11.00	—	2–22	21.00	3.14
Rajkot	1	60	1	49	2	24.50	—	2–49	30.00	4.90
Srinagar	1	54	—	44	2	22.00	—	2–44	27.00	4.89
Visakhapatnam	1	42	—	43	—	—	—	—	—	6.14
in New Zealand										
Auckland	8	162	1	132	3	44.00	—	2–27	54.00	4.89
Christchurch	5	150	1	106	3	35.33	—	1–24	50.00	4.24
Dunedin	3	102	—	51	1	51.00	—	1–36	102.00	3.00
Hamilton	2	46	—	59	—	—	—	—	—	7.70
Napier	1	60	—	56	—	—	—	—	—	5.60
Wellington	4	141	—	114	3	38.00	—	2–46	47.00	4.85
in Pakistan										
Faisalabad	1	60	1	40	—	—	—	—	—	4.00
Lahore	5	192	1	149	4	37.25	—	2–35	48.00	4.66
Multan	1	60	1	37	—	—	—	—	—	3.70
Rawalpindi	1	30	—	26	—	—	—	—	—	5.20
in Sri Lanka										
Colombo (PIS)	3	120	3	93	3	31.00	—	1–24	40.00	4.65
Colombo (PSS)	1	36	—	32	1	32.00	—	1–32	36.00	5.33
Colombo (SSC)	3	138	1	67	4	16.75	—	3–16	34.50	2.91
in South Africa										
Bloemfontein	2	60	—	48	2	24.00	—	2–48	30.00	4.80
Cape Town	2	24	—	22	—	—	—	—	—	5.50
Centurion	1	—	—	—	—	—	—	—	—	—
Durban	2	54	—	49	—	—	—	—	—	5.44
East London	2	54	1	25	1	25.00	—	1–25	54.00	2.78
Johannesburg	2	60	—	54	—	—	—	—	—	5.40

Venue	M	Balls	Mdns	Runs	Wkts	Avrge	5	Best	Stk/Rt	R/O
Port Elizabeth	3	84	1	81	2	40.50	—	1–33	42.00	5.79
Verwoerdburg	1	30	—	28	—	—	—	—	—	5.60
in United Arab Emirates										
Sharjah	16	666	5	541	13	41.62	—	4–40	51.23	4.87
in West Indies										
Kingstown	1	—	—	—	—	—	—	—	—	—
Bridgetown	2	42	—	25	2	12.50	—	2–25	21.00	3.57
Georgetown	2	72	—	80	1	80.00	—	1–47	72.00	6.67
Kingston	1	42	1	32	2	16.00	—	2–32	21.00	4.57
Port-of-Spain	4	171	1	139	3	46.33	—	2–61	57.00	4.88

Country	M	Balls	Mdns	Runs	Wkts	Avrge	5	Best	Stk/Rt	R/O
Australia	123	4310	28	3066	101	30.36	—	4–33	42.67	4.27
England	9	414	2	355	8	44.38	—	3–53	51.75	5.14
India	34	951	6	781	27	28.93	—	2–22	35.22	4.93
New Zealand	23	661	2	518	10	51.80	—	2–27	66.10	4.70
Pakistan	8	342	3	252	4	63.00	—	2–35	85.50	4.42
Sri Lanka	7	294	4	192	8	24.00	—	3–16	36.75	3.92
South Africa	15	366	2	307	5	61.40	—	2–48	73.20	5.03
Sharjah	16	666	5	541	13	41.62	—	4–40	51.23	4.87
West Indies	10	327	2	276	8	34.50	—	2–25	40.88	5.06

Wickets taken:	Wkts	Bwd	Ct	C&B	LBW	Stp	HW				
	184	44	113	6	21	—	—				

Batsmen dismissed:	Wkts	1/2	3	4	5	6	7	8	9	10	11
	184	36	23	21	34	15	12	17	11	10	5

Best bowling: 4–33 Australia *v.* Sri Lanka, Sydney, 1987–88

Domestic Limited-Overs Career
Debut: 1984–85 New South Wales *v.* Victoria, Melbourne

Season	M	Balls	Mdns	Runs	Wkts	Avrge	5	Best	Stk/Rt	RPO
1984–85	1	60	4	47	—	—	—	—	—	4.70
1985–86	1	60	2	37	3	12.33	—	3–37	20.00	3.70
1986–87	2	102	2	102	2	51.00	—	1–50	51.00	6.00
1987–88	4	202	3	132	5	26.40	—	2–21	40.40	3.92
1988–89	3	120	2	97	5	19.40	—	3–29	24.00	4.85
1989–90	—	—	—	—	—	—	—	—	—	—
1990–91	4	170	2	116	5	23.20	—	4–32	34.00	4.09
1991–92	4	174	3	127	7	18.14	—	3–25	24.86	4.38
1992–93	4	138	—	122	5	24.40	—	3–50	27.60	5.30
1993–94	2	30	—	34	1	34.00	—	1–34	30.00	6.80
1994–95	—	—	—	—	—	—	—	—	—	—
1995–96	3	24	—	19	—	—	—	—	—	4.75
1996–97	—	—	—	—	—	—	—	—	—	—
1997–98	3	12	—	12	1	12.00	—	1–12	12.00	6.00
Total	**31**	**1092**	**18**	**845**	**34**	**24.85**	**—**	**4–32**	**32.12**	**4.64**

Opponents	M	Balls	Mdns	Runs	Wkts	Avrge	5	Best	Stk/Rt	R/O
Queensland	7	186	4	145	8	18.13	—	3–25	23.25	4.68
South Australia	4	168	4	104	8	13.00	—	3–37	21.00	3.71
Tasmania	5	214	—	163	7	23.29	—	2–21	30.57	4.57
Victoria	9	278	8	230	7	32.86	—	4–32	39.71	4.96
Western Australia	6	246	2	203	4	50.75	—	3–29	61.50	4.95

Innings		Balls	Mdns	Runs	Wkts	Avrge	5	Best	Stk/Rt	R/O
First		612	6	496	18	27.56	—	3–29	34.00	4.86
Second		480	12	349	16	21.81	—	4–32	30.00	4.36

Bowling at Each Venue

Venue	M	Balls	Mdns	Runs	Wkts	Avrge	5	Best	Stk/Rt	R/O
Adelaide	1	36	—	18	2	9.00	—	2–18	18.00	3.00
Brisbane	6	186	4	145	8	18.13	—	3–25	23.25	4.68
Melbourne	3	90	4	78	—	—	—	—	—	5.20
North Sydney	6	138	1	123	6	20.50	—	2–30	23.00	5.35

Venue	M	Balls	Mdns	Runs	Wkts	Avrge	5	Best	Stk/Rt	R/O
Perth	6	246	2	203	4	50.75	—	3–29	61.50	4.95
Sydney	9	396	7	278	14	19.86	—	4–32	28.29	4.21

Wickets taken:	Wkts	Bwd	Ct	C&B	LBW	Stp	HW
	34	9	24	—	1	—	—

Batsmen dismissed	Wkts	1/2	3	4	5	6	7	8	9	10	11
	34	6	5	4	3	4	4	3	3	2	—

Best bowling: 4–32 New South Wales *v.* Victoria, Sydney, 1990–91

M.E. Waugh

(Right-hand batsman, right-arm medium/off-spin bowler)

BATTING AND FIELDING
First-Class Career
Debut: 1984–85 New South Wales *v.* Queensland, Brisbane

Season	Country	M	Inn	NO	Runs	HS	0s	50	100	Avrge	Ct
1985–86	Australia	7	11	—	167	41	2	—	—	15.18	6
1985–86	Zimbabwe	2	4	2	176	83	—	2	—	88.00	4
1986–87	Australia	1	2	—	26	26	1	—	—	13.00	—
1987–88	Zimbabwe	2	3	1	123	61	—	1	—	61.50	1
1987–88	Australia	10	16	3	833	116	1	4	4	64.08	18
1988	England	3	4	—	178	86	—	1	—	44.50	2
1988–89	Australia	11	21	3	727	103*	4	4	2	40.39	9
1989	England	24	39	4	1537	165	2	8	4	43.91	31
1989–90	Australia	12	17	4	1009	198*	1	2	5	77.62	18
1990	England	22	33	6	2072	207*	4	8	8	76.74	18
1990–91	Australia	8	13	1	840	229*	2	3	3	70.00	9
1990–91	West Indies	9	12	2	522	139*	1	2	2	52.20	13
1991–92	Australia	12	18	—	924	163	2	4	3	51.33	19
1992	England	16	24	7	1314	219*	2	6	4	77.29	27
1992–93	Sri Lanka	5	9	—	291	118	4	2	1	32.33	5
1992–93	Australia	9	16	2	883	200*	1	3	3	63.07	8
1992–93	New Zealand	3	3	—	25	13	1	—	—	8.33	2
1993	England	16	25	6	1361	178	—	9	4	71.63	18
1993–94	Australia	10	16	—	765	119	—	6	2	47.81	10
1993–94	South Africa	6	10	2	573	154	—	—	3	71.63	3
1994–95	Pakistan	4	5	—	277	71	—	4	—	55.40	3
1994–95	Australia	9	17	—	827	140	1	4	3	48.65	13
1994–95	West Indies	7	9	1	418	126	—	3	1	52.25	6
1995	England	16	29	2	1392	173	—	6	5	51.56	19
1995–96	Australia	11	19	2	805	116	1	5	2	47.35	11
1996–97	India	2	4	1	76	26	—	—	—	25.33	3
1996–97	Australia	7	13	—	564	159	2	4	1	43.38	12
1996–97	South Africa	5	7	—	395	124	—	1	2	56.43	5
1997	England	13	20	3	746	173	—	3	2	43.88	11
1997–98	Australia	11	17	2	747	115*	1	5	2	49.80	6
1997–98	India	4	7	2	332	153*	1	2	1	66.40	1
Total		**277**	**443**	**56**	**20925**	**229***	**34**	**102**	**67**	**54.07**	**311**

Country	M	Inn	NO	Runs	HS	0s	50	100	Avrge	Ct
Australia	118	196	17	9117	229*	19	44	30	50.93	139
England	110	174	28	8600	219*	8	41	27	58.90	126
India	6	11	3	408	153*	1	2	1	51.00	4
New Zealand	3	3	—	25	13	1	—	—	8.33	2
Pakistan	4	5	—	277	71	—	4	—	55.40	3
Sri Lanka	5	9	—	291	118	4	2	1	32.33	5
South Africa	11	17	2	968	154	—	1	5	64.53	8
West Indies	16	21	3	940	139*	1	5	3	52.22	19
Zimbabwe	4	7	3	299	83	—	3	—	74.75	5

Batting position	Inn	NO	Runs	HS	0s	50	100	Avrge
1/2	10	—	293	132	2	1	1	29.30
3	56	10	2437	219*	5	11	7	52.98
4	264	23	13650	207*	17	69	45	56.64

Batting position	Inn	NO	Runs	HS	0s	50	100	Avrge
5	68	11	3004	229*	6	15	9	52.70
6	34	7	1292	139*	3	5	5	47.85
7	8	3	237	88	1	1	—	47.40
8	2	2	3	2*	—	—	—	—
9	1	—	9	9	—	—	—	9.00

Team	M	Inn	NO	Runs	HS	0s	50	100	Avrge	Ct
AUSTRALIA	78	128	7	5219	153*	10	32	14	43.13	89
Australian XI	36	49	11	2600	178	1	11	10	68.42	30
Essex	80	128	19	6448	219*	8	29	21	59.16	97
New South Wales	83	138	19	6658	229*	15	30	22	55.95	95

How dismissed:	Inn	NO	Bwd	Ct	LBW	Stp	RO	HW
	443	56	67	251	45	7	17	—

Centuries

Highest score: 229* New South Wales *v.* Western Australia, Perth, 1990–91

Score	Team	Opponent	Venue	Season
101*	New South Wales	Tasmania	Devonport	1987–88
114*	New South Wales	Victoria	Sydney	1987–88
100*	New South Wales	Victoria	Melbourne	1987–88
116	New South Wales	Tasmania	Sydney	1987–88
103*	New South Wales	West Indians	Sydney	1988–89
100*	New South Wales	Tasmania	Devonport	1988–89
109	Essex	Hampshire	Ilford	1989
110	Essex	Middlesex	Uxbridge	1989
100*	Essex	Australian XI	Chelmsford	1989
165	Essex	Leicestershire	Leicester	1989
172	New South Wales	South Australia	Adelaide	1989–90
100*	New South Wales	Victoria	Albury	1989–90
100*	New South Wales	Victoria	Melbourne	1989–90
137	New South Wales	South Australia	Sydney	1989–90
198*	New South Wales	Tasmania	Sydney	1989–90
166*	Essex	Worcestershire	Worcester	1990
125	Essex	Hampshire	Southampton	1990
204	Essex	Gloucestershire	Ilford	1990
103	Essex	Warwickshire	Birmingham	1990
126	Essex	Derbyshire	Colchester	1990
103*	Essex	Sussex	Chelmsford	1990
207*	Essex	Yorkshire	Middlesbrough	1990
169	Essex	Kent	Chelmsford	1990
229*	New South Wales	Western Australia	Perth	1990–91
112	New South Wales	South Australia	Sydney	1990–91
138	AUSTRALIA	ENGLAND	Adelaide	1990–91
108	Australian XI	Jamaica	Kingston	1990–91
139*	AUSTRALIA	WEST INDIES	St John's	1990–91
136	New South Wales	Western Australia	Perth	1991–92
158	New South Wales	South Australia	Sydney	1991–92
163	New South Wales	Western Australia	Perth	1991–92
120	Essex	Kent	Chelmsford	1992
219*	Essex	Lancashire	Ilford	1992
125*	Essex	Gloucestershire	Southend	1992
138*	Essex	Worcestershire	Kidderminster	1992
118	Australian XI	Sri Lankan Board XI	Matara	1992–93
200*	New South Wales	West Indians	Sydney	1992–93
164	New South Wales	South Australia	Adelaide	1992–93
112	AUSTRALIA	WEST INDIES	Melbourne	1992–93
178	Australian XI	Surrey	The Oval	1993
152*	Australian XI	Glamorgan	Neath	1993
137	AUSTRALIA	ENGLAND	Birmingham	1993
108	Australian XI	Essex	Chelmsford	1993
111	AUSTRALIA	NEW ZEALAND	Hobart	1993–94
119	New South Wales	Victoria	Sydney	1993–94
134	Australian XI	Northern Transvaal	Verwoerdburg	1993–94

Score	Team	Opponent	Venue	Season
154	Australian XI	Orange Free State	Bloemfontein	1993–94
113*	AUSTRALIA	SOUTH AFRICA	Durban	1993–94
113	New South Wales	Queensland	Sydney	1994–95
140	AUSTRALIA	ENGLAND	Brisbane	1994–95
132	New South Wales	Tasmania	Hobart	1994–95
126	AUSTRALIA	WEST INDIES	Kingston	1994–95
126	Essex	Surrey	The Oval	1995
173	Essex	Somerset	Southend	1995
136	Essex	Hampshire	Colchester	1995
121*	Essex	Derbyshire	Chelmsford	1995
121	Essex	Derbyshire	Chelmsford	1995
116	AUSTRALIA	PAKISTAN	Sydney	1995–96
111	AUSTRALIA	SRI LANKA	Perth	1995–96
159	New South Wales	Queensland	Brisbane	1996–97
124	Australian XI	Natal	Durban	1996–97
116	AUSTRALIA	SOUTH AFRICA	Port Elizabeth	1996–97
173	Australian XI	Hampshire	Southampton	1997
142*	Australian XI	Middlesex	Lord's	1997
100	AUSTRALIA	SOUTH AFRICA	Sydney	1997–98
115*	AUSTRALIA	SOUTH AFRICA	Adelaide	1997–98
153*	AUSTRALIA	INDIA	Bangalore	1997–98

Test Career

Debut: 1990–91 Australia *v.* England, Adelaide

Season	Opponent	Venue	M	Inn	NO	Runs	HS	0s	50	100	Avrge	Ct
1990–91	England	Australia	2	3	—	187	138	—	—	1	62.33	1
1990–91	West Indies	West Indies	5	8	2	367	139*	1	2	1	61.17	10
1991–92	India	Australia	4	6	—	83	34	1	—	—	13.83	10
1992–93	Sri Lanka	Sri Lanka	3	6	—	61	56	4	1	—	10.17	3
1992–93	West Indies	Australia	5	9	—	340	112	1	2	1	37.78	6
1992–93	New Zealand	New Zealand	2	2	—	25	13	—	—	—	12.50	—
1993	England	England	6	10	1	550	137	—	5	1	61.11	9
1993–94	New Zealand	Australia	3	3	—	215	111	—	1	1	71.67	3
1993–94	South Africa	Australia	3	5	—	116	84	—	1	—	23.20	4
1993–94	South Africa	South Africa	3	5	1	233	113*	—	—	1	58.25	2
1994–95	Pakistan	Pakistan	3	4	—	220	71	—	3	—	55.00	3
1994–95	England	Australia	5	10	—	435	140	—	2	1	43.50	8
1994–95	West Indies	West Indies	4	6	—	240	126	—	1	1	40.00	3
1995–96	Pakistan	Australia	3	5	—	300	116	—	2	1	60.00	4
1995–96	Sri Lanka	Australia	3	4	—	255	111	—	2	1	63.75	2
1996–97	India	India	1	2	—	49	26	—	—	—	24.50	2
1996–97	West Indies	Australia	5	9	—	370	82	1	4	—	41.11	8
1996–97	South Africa	South Africa	3	5	—	209	116	—	—	1	41.80	3
1997	England	England	6	10	—	209	68	—	2	—	20.90	6
1997–98	New Zealand	Australia	3	5	—	196	86	—	2	—	39.20	1
1997–98	South Africa	Australia	3	5	1	279	115*	1	1	2	69.75	—
1997–98	India	India	3	6	2	280	153*	1	1	1	70.00	1
Total			**78**	**128**	**7**	**5219**	**153***	**10**	**32**	**14**	**43.13**	**89**

Opponents			M	Inn	NO	Runs	HS	0s	50	100	Avrge	Ct
ENGLAND			19	33	1	1381	140	—	9	3	43.16	24
INDIA			8	14	2	412	153*	2	1	1	34.33	13
NEW ZEALAND			8	10	—	436	111	—	3	1	43.60	4
PAKISTAN			6	9	—	520	116	—	5	1	57.78	7
SRI LANKA			6	10	—	316	111	4	3	1	31.60	5
SOUTH AFRICA			12	20	2	837	116	1	2	4	46.50	9
WEST INDIES			19	32	2	1317	139*	3	9	3	43.90	27

Innings	Inn	NO	Runs	HS	0s	50	100	Avrge	Ct
First	46	1	2118	140	4	16	5	47.07	31
Second	32	2	1645	153*	1	7	6	54.83	28
Third	35	1	910	113*	5	8	1	26.76	12
Fourth	15	3	546	116	—	1	2	45.50	18

Batting at Each Venue

Venue	M	Inn	NO	Runs	HS	0s	50	100	Avrge	Ct
in Australia										
Adelaide	8	15	1	622	138	2	3	2	44.43	13
Brisbane	7	11	—	507	140	—	4	1	46.09	8
Hobart	3	5	—	292	111	—	2	1	58.40	4
Melbourne	7	11	—	427	112	2	3	1	38.82	7
Perth	7	10	—	466	111	—	3	1	46.60	5
Sydney	7	12	—	462	116	—	2	2	38.50	10
in England										
Birmingham	2	4	1	205	137	—	1	1	68.33	1
Leeds	2	2	—	60	52	—	1	—	30.00	5
Lord's	2	2	—	132	99	—	1	—	66.00	1
Manchester	2	4	—	137	64	—	2	—	34.25	1
Nottingham	2	4	—	146	70	—	2	—	36.50	4
The Oval	2	4	—	79	49	—	—	—	19.75	3
in India										
Bangalore	1	2	2	186	153*	—	—	1	—	1
Calcutta	1	2	—	10	10	1	—	—	5.00	—
Chennai	1	2	—	84	66	—	1	—	42.00	—
Delhi	1	2	—	49	26	—	—	—	24.50	2
in New Zealand										
Christchurch	1	1	—	13	13	—	—	—	13.00	—
Wellington	1	1	—	12	12	—	—	—	12.00	—
in Pakistan										
Karachi	1	2	—	81	61	—	1	—	40.50	1
Lahore	1	1	—	71	71	—	1	—	71.00	2
Rawalpindi	1	1	—	68	68	—	1	—	68.00	—
in Sri Lanka										
Colombo (PIS)	1	2	—	0	0	2	—	—	0.00	—
Colombo (SSC)	1	2	—	61	56	—	1	—	30.50	2
Moratuwa	1	2	—	0	0	2	—	—	0.00	1
in South Africa										
Cape Town	1	1	—	7	7	—	—	—	7.00	1
Centurion	1	2	—	47	42	—	—	—	23.50	—
Durban	1	2	1	156	113*	—	—	1	156.00	—
Johannesburg	2	3	—	96	42	—	—	—	32.00	3
Port Elizabeth	1	2	—	136	116	—	—	1	68.00	1
in West Indies										
Bridgetown	2	3	1	63	40	—	—	—	31.50	4
Georgetown	1	2	—	102	71	—	1	—	51.00	2
Kingston	2	2	—	165	126	—	—	1	82.50	2
Port-of-Spain	2	3	—	73	64	—	1	—	24.33	4
St John's	2	4	1	204	139*	1	1	1	68.00	1

Country	M	Inn	NO	Runs	HS	0s	50	100	Avrge	Ct
Australia	39	64	1	2776	140	4	17	8	44.06	47
England	12	20	1	759	137	—	7	1	39.95	15
India	4	8	2	329	153*	1	1	1	54.83	3
New Zealand	2	2	—	25	13	—	—	—	12.50	—
Pakistan	3	4	—	220	71	—	3	—	55.00	3
Sri Lanka	3	6	—	61	56	4	1	—	10.17	3
South Africa	6	10	1	442	116	—	—	2	49.11	5
West Indies	9	14	2	607	139*	1	3	2	50.58	13

Batting position	Inn	NO	Runs	HS	0s	50	100	Avrge
1/2	1	—	9	9	—	—	—	9.00
3	1	—	66	66	—	1	—	66.00
4	96	4	4137	153*	4	26	11	44.97
5	15	1	415	113*	4	3	1	29.64
6	13	2	589	139*	1	2	2	53.55
7	2	—	3	3	1	—	—	1.50

How dismissed:	Inns	NO	Bwd	Ct	LBW	Stp	RO	HW
	128	7	19	80	20	—	2	—

Centuries

Highest score: 153* Australia *v.* India, Bangalore, 1997–98

Score	Team	Opponent	Venue	Season
138*	Australia	England	Adelaide	1990–91
139*	Australia	West Indies	St John's	1990–91
112	Australia	West Indies	Melbourne	1992–93
137	Australia	England	Birmingham	1993
111	Australia	New Zealand	Hobart	1993–94
113*	Australia	South Africa	Durban	1993–94
140	Australia	England	Brisbane	1994–95
126	Australia	West Indies	Kingston	1994–95
116	Australia	Pakistan	Sydney	1995–96
111	Australia	Sri Lanka	Perth	1995–96
116	Australia	South Africa	Port Elizabeth	1996–97
100	Australia	South Africa	Sydney	1997–98
115*	Australia	South Africa	Adelaide	1997–98
153*	Australia	India	Bangalore	1997–98

Nineties

Score	Team	Opponent	Venue	Season
99	Australia	England	Lord's	1993

Sheffield Shield Career

Debut: 1985–86 New South Wales *v.* Tasmania, Hobart

Season	M	Inn	NO	Runs	HS	0s	50	100	Avrge	Ct
1985–86	6	9	—	150	41	1	—	—	16.67	6
1986–87	1	2	—	26	26	1	—	—	13.00	—
1987–88	10	16	3	833	116	1	4	4	64.08	18
1988–89	9	17	1	552	100*	3	3	1	34.50	7
1989–90	11	16	4	967	198*	1	2	5	80.58	18
1990–91	4	6	1	487	229*	2	1	2	97.40	6
1991–92	7	11	—	762	163	1	3	3	69.27	9
1992–93	3	6	1	343	164	—	1	1	68.60	2
1993–94	3	6	—	370	119	—	3	1	61.67	2
1994–95	3	5	—	312	132	—	1	2	62.40	2
1995–96	5	10	2	250	57	1	1	—	31.25	5
1996–97	2	4	—	194	159	1	—	1	48.50	4
1997–98	4	6	1	228	72	—	2	—	45.60	4
Total	**68**	**114**	**13**	**5474**	**229***	**12**	**21**	**20**	**54.20**	**83**

Opponents	M	Inn	NO	Runs	HS	0s	50	100	Avrge	Ct
Queensland	18	32	2	1209	159	5	9	2	40.30	20
South Australia	12	18	1	1215	172	1	4	5	71.47	9
Tasmania	12	18	4	922	198*	3	1	5	65.86	18
Victoria	14	25	5	1056	119	2	5	5	52.80	18
Western Australia	12	21	1	1072	229*	1	2	3	53.60	18

Innings		Inn	NO	Runs	HS	0s	50	100	Avrge	Ct
First		34	3	1658	229*	6	6	6	53.48	33
Second		33	2	2019	198*	2	6	9	65.13	21
Third		27	6	1173	159	2	6	4	55.86	7
Fourth		20	2	624	100*	2	3	1	34.67	22

Batting at Each Venue

Venue	M	Inn	NO	Runs	HS	0s	50	100	Avrge	Ct
Adelaide	6	9	1	643	172	—	3	2	80.38	3
Albury	1	2	1	104	100*	—	—	1	104.00	2
Bankstown	1	2	—	4	4	1	—	—	2.00	2
Brisbane	9	17	1	766	159	3	7	1	47.88	10
Devonport	2	3	2	201	101*	1	—	2	201.00	3
Hobart (Bel)	3	5	—	151	132	2	—	1	30.20	3
Hobart (TCA)	1	2	—	41	28	—	—	—	20.50	1
Melbourne	6	11	3	463	100*	—	3	2	57.88	8
Newcastle	5	9	—	205	69	2	1	—	22.78	6

Venue	M	Inn	NO	Runs	HS	0s	50	100	Avrge	Ct
North Sydney	1	2	—	74	72	—	1	—	37.00	1
Perth	8	14	1	811	229*	—	—	3	62.38	12
Sydney	25	38	4	2011	198*	3	6	8	59.15	32

Batting position	Inn	NO	Runs	HS	0s	50	100	Avrge
1/2	7	—	267	132	1	1	1	38.14
3	11	1	392	100*	2	1	1	39.20
4	50	4	2723	164	6	13	10	59.20
5	32	5	1635	229*	2	5	6	60.56
6	11	2	320	114*	1	—	2	35.56
7	3	1	137	88	—	1	—	68.50

How dismissed:	Inn	NO	Bwd	Ct	LBW	Stp	RO	HW
	114	13	13	74	6	2	6	—

Centuries

Highest score: 229* New South Wales *v.* Western Australia, Perth, 1990–91

Score	Team	Opponent	Venue	Season
101*	New South Wales	Tasmania	Devonport	1987–88
114*	New South Wales	Victoria	Sydney	1987–88
100*	New South Wales	Victoria	Melbourne	1987–88
116	New South Wales	Tasmania	Sydney	1987–88
100*	New South Wales	Tasmania	Devonport	1988–89
172	New South Wales	South Australia	Adelaide	1989–90
100*	New South Wales	Victoria	Albury	1989–90
100*	New South Wales	Victoria	Melbourne	1989–90
137	New South Wales	South Australia	Sydney	1989–90
198*	New South Wales	Tasmania	Sydney	1989–90
229*	New South Wales	Western Australia	Perth	1990–91
112	New South Wales	South Australia	Sydney	1990–91
136	New South Wales	Western Australia	Perth	1991–92
158	New South Wales	South Australia	Sydney	1991–92
163	New South Wales	Western Australia	Perth	1991–92
164	New South Wales	South Australia	Adelaide	1992–93
119	New South Wales	Victoria	Sydney	1993–94
113	New South Wales	Queensland	Sydney	1994–95
132	New South Wales	Tasmania	Hobart	1994–95
159	New South Wales	Queensland	Brisbane	1996–97

International Limited-Overs Career

Debut: 1988–89 Australia *v.* Pakistan, Adelaide

Season	Tournament	Venue	M	Inn	NO	Runs	HS	0s	50	100	Avrge	Stk/Rt	Ct
1988–89	World Series Cup	AUS	7	6	—	131	42	—	—	—	21.83	85.62	3
1989–90	World Series	AUS	1	1	—	14	14	—	—	—	14.00	100.00	—
1990–91	World Series	AUS	10	10	2	176	62	2	1	—	22.00	74.89	6
1990–91	West Indies *v.* Australia	WI	5	5	—	156	67	—	1	—	31.20	100.65	2
1991–92	World Series	AUS	5	3	—	20	17	1	—	—	6.67	57.14	1
1991–92	World Cup	ANZ	5	5	1	145	66*	—	1	—	36.25	101.40	4
1992–93	Sri Lanka *v.* Australia	SL	3	3	—	93	52	—	1	—	31.00	83.04	2
1992–93	World Series	AUS	10	9	—	259	57	—	3	—	28.78	66.07	6
1992–93	New Zealand *v.* Australia	NZ	5	5	—	308	108	1	3	1	61.60	82.80	3
1993	England *v.* Australia	ENG	3	3	—	183	113	—	1	1	61.00	87.98	2
1993–94	World Series	AUS	11	11	1	405	107	—	2	1	40.50	74.59	2
1993–94	South Africa *v.* Australia	SAF	8	8	1	199	71	1	2	—	28.43	66.33	4
1993–94	Austral-Asia Cup	UAE	2	2	1	80	64*	—	1	—	80.00	73.39	—
1994–95	Singer World Series	SL	3	3	—	108	61	—	1	—	36.00	69.68	—
1994–95	Wills Triangular Series	PAK	6	6	1	243	121*	1	1	1	48.60	78.90	—
1994–95	World Series	AUS	4	4	1	63	41	—	—	—	21.00	53.85	—
1994–95	New Zealand Centenary	NZ	4	4	—	179	74	—	1	—	44.75	89.95	1
1994–95	West Indies *v.* Australia	WI	4	4	—	125	70	1	1	—	31.25	96.15	3
1995–96	World Series	AUS	10	10	—	357	130	1	3	1	35.70	73.46	4
1995–96	World Cup	IPS	7	7	1	484	130	1	1	3	80.67	85.51	1
1996–97	Singer World Series	SL	4	4	—	100	50	—	1	—	25.00	80.65	2

Season	Tournament	Venue	M	Inn	NO	Runs	HS	0s	50	100	Avrge	Stk/Rt	Ct
1996–97	Titan Cup	IND	4	4	—	107	50	—	1	—	26.75	65.24	1
1996–97	CUB Series	AUS	7	7	1	358	102	—	2	1	59.67	71.60	3
1996–97	South Africa v. Australia	SAF	4	3	1	118	115*	1	—	1	59.00	82.52	2
1997	England v. Australia	ENG	3	3	—	131	95	—	1	—	43.67	81.88	—
1997–98	CUB Series	AUS	9	9	—	320	104	—	—	1	35.56	73.90	2
1997–98	New Zealand v. Australia	NZ	4	4	—	196	85	—	2	—	49.00	76.86	1
1997–98	Triangular Cup	IND	5	5	—	178	87	—	1	—	35.60	77.06	1
1997–98	Coca-Cola Cup	UAE	5	5	1	149	81	—	1	—	37.25	82.78	3
Total			**158**	**153**	**12**	**5385**	**130**	**10**	**32**	**11**	**38.19**	**77.80**	**59**

Opponents	M	Inn	NO	Runs	HS	0s	50	100	Avrge	Stk/Rt	Ct
England	12	12	—	462	113	1	3	1	38.50	80.91	4
India	16	15	—	476	126	1	2	1	31.73	81.23	7
Kenya	1	1	—	130	130	—	—	1	130.00	100.00	—
New Zealand	28	28	4	1132	110	2	7	3	47.17	80.74	10
Pakistan	15	13	1	328	121*	1	—	1	27.33	79.61	4
Sri Lanka	15	15	1	546	130	1	5	1	39.00	81.01	4
South Africa	31	30	2	925	115*	2	4	2	33.04	70.72	9
West Indies	33	32	1	1084	102	2	8	1	34.97	73.69	17
Zimbabwe	7	7	3	302	87	—	3	—	75.50	82.07	4

Innings	Inn	NO	Runs	HS	0s	50	100	Avrge	Stk/Rt	Ct
First	90	3	3447	130	4	22	7	39.62	80.22	36
Second	63	9	1938	115*	6	10	4	35.89	73.83	23

Batting at Each Venue

Venue	M	Inn	NO	Runs	HS	0s	50	100	Avrge	Stk/Rt	Ct
in Australia											
Adelaide	8	6	1	235	104	—	1	1	47.00	87.36	3
Brisbane	7	7	—	230	102	—	1	1	32.86	77.44	—
Hobart	5	5	1	123	66*	—	1	—	30.75	86.62	2
Melbourne	25	24	2	516	57	1	2	—	23.45	63.55	10
Perth	7	7	1	308	130	1	1	1	51.33	70.64	2
Sydney	26	25	1	834	107	2	6	1	34.75	76.51	14
in England											
Birmingham	1	1	—	113	113	—	—	1	113.00	92.62	—
Leeds	1	1	—	11	11	—	—	—	11.00	28.21	—
Lord's	2	2	—	109	95	—	1	—	54.50	91.60	1
Manchester	1	1	—	56	56	—	1	—	56.00	88.89	1
The Oval	1	1	—	25	25	—	—	—	25.00	100.00	—
in India											
Ahmedabad	1	1	—	37	37	—	—	—	37.00	77.08	—
Bangalore	1	1	—	4	4	—	—	—	4.00	30.77	—
Chandigarh	2	2	—	37	37	1	—	—	18.50	72.55	1
Chennai	1	1	—	110	110	—	—	1	110.00	98.21	—
Delhi	2	2	—	107	87	—	1	—	53.50	75.89	—
Faridabad	1	1	—	16	16	—	—	—	16.00	47.06	—
Indore	1	1	—	50	50	—	1	—	50.00	73.53	—
Jaipur	1	1	—	30	30	—	—	—	30.00	47.62	—
Kanpur	1	1	—	6	6	—	—	—	6.00	54.55	—
Kochi	1	1	—	28	28	—	—	—	28.00	90.32	1
Mumbai	1	1	—	126	126	—	—	1	126.00	93.33	—
Nagpur	1	1	1	76	76*	—	1	—	—	69.72	1
Visakhapatnam	1	1	—	130	130	—	—	1	130.00	100.00	—
in New Zealand											
Auckland	5	5	—	209	83	—	2	—	41.80	86.01	2
Christchurch	2	2	—	122	65	—	2	—	61.00	77.22	—
Dunedin	2	2	—	108	60	—	1	—	54.00	100.93	—
Hamilton	1	1	—	108	108	—	—	1	108.00	82.44	—
Napier	1	1	—	42	42	—	—	—	42.00	77.78	—
Wellington	3	3	—	96	85	1	1	—	32.00	69.57	3
in Pakistan											
Faisalabad	1	1	—	38	38	—	—	—	38.00	66.67	—
Lahore	3	3	—	53	38	—	—	—	17.67	70.67	—
Multan	1	1	—	0	0	1	—	—	0.00	0.00	—

Venue	M	Inn	NO	Runs	HS	0s	50	100	Avrge	Stk/Rt	Ct
Peshawar	1	1	—	43	43	—	—	—	43.00	81.13	—
Rawalpindi	1	1	1	121	121*	—	—	1	—	90.30	—
in Sri Lanka											
Colombo (PIS)	5	5	—	191	61	—	3	—	38.20	79.25	1
Colombo (PSS)	2	2	—	55	31	—	—	—	27.50	79.71	2
Colombo (SSC)	3	3	—	55	23	—	—	—	18.33	67.90	1
in South Africa											
Bloemfontein	2	2	—	16	13	—	—	—	8.00	32.00	1
Cape Town	2	1	—	71	71	—	1	—	71.00	71.72	1
Centurion	1	1	—	0	0	1	—	—	0.00	0.00	1
Durban	1	1	—	3	3	—	—	—	3.00	17.65	1
East London	1	1	1	21	21*	—	—	—	—	46.67	1
Johannesburg	1	1	—	14	14	—	—	—	14.00	70.00	—
Port Elizabeth	3	3	1	192	115*	—	1	1	96.00	92.75	1
Verwoerdburg	1	1	—	0	0	1	—	—	0.00	0.00	—
in United Arab Emirates											
Sharjah	7	7	2	229	81	—	2	—	45.80	79.24	3
in West Indies											
Kingstown	1	1	—	26	26	—	—	—	26.00	70.27	—
Bridgetown	2	2	—	78	49	—	—	—	39.00	113.04	3
Georgetown	2	2	—	77	70	—	1	—	38.50	110.00	2
Kingston	1	1	—	67	67	—	1	—	67.00	101.52	—
Port-of-Spain	3	3	—	33	17	1	—	—	11.00	76.74	—

Country	M	Inn	NO	Runs	HS	0s	50	100	Avrge	Stk/Rt	Ct
Australia	78	74	6	2246	130	4	12	4	33.03	73.74	31
England	6	6	—	314	113	—	2	1	52.33	85.33	2
India	15	15	1	757	130	1	3	3	54.07	80.02	3
New Zealand	14	14	—	685	108	1	6	1	48.93	82.43	5
Pakistan	7	7	1	255	121*	1	—	1	42.50	78.95	—
Sri Lanka	10	10	—	301	61	—	3	—	30.10	76.98	4
South Africa	12	11	2	317	115*	2	2	1	35.22	71.56	6
Sharjah	7	7	2	229	81	—	2	—	45.80	79.24	3
West Indies	9	9	—	281	70	1	2	—	31.22	98.60	5

Batting position	Inn	NO	Runs	HS	0s	50	100	Avrge	Stk/Rt
1/2	59	3	2628	130	3	14	8	46.93	78.21
3	34	2	1197	121*	3	8	2	37.41	74.12
4	20	2	589	107	1	3	1	32.72	74.84
5	36	3	920	67	3	7	—	27.88	83.64
6	3	1	45	34*	—	—	—	22.50	88.24
9	1	1	6	6*	—	—	—	—	66.67

How dismissed:	Inns	NO	Bwd	Ct	LBW	Stp	RO	HW
	153	12	34	68	8	9	22	—

Centuries

Highest score: 130 Australia *v.* Sri Lanka, Perth, 1995–96

Score	Team	Opponent	Venue	Season
108	Australia	New Zealand	Hamilton	1992–93
113	Australia	England	Birmingham	1993
107	Australia	South Africa	Sydney	1993–94
121*	Australia	Pakistan	Rawalpindi	1994–95
130	Australia	Sri Lanka	Perth	1995–96
130	Australia	Kenya	Visakhapatnam	1995–96
126	Australia	India	Mumbai	1995–96
110	Australia	New Zealand	Chennai	1995–96
102	Australia	West Indies	Brisbane	1996–97
115*	Australia	South Africa	Port Elizabeth	1996–97
104	Australia	New Zealand	Adelaide	1997–98

Domestic Limited-Overs Career

Debut: 1985–86 New South Wales *v.* Victoria, Sydney

Season	M	Inn	NO	Runs	HS	0s	50	100	Avrge	Stk/Rt	Ct
1985–86	1	1	—	13	13	—	—	—	13.00	48.15	—
1986–87	2	2	—	50	46	—	—	—	25.00	64.10	1

Season	M	Inn	NO	Runs	HS	0s	50	100	Avrge	Stk/Rt	Ct
1987–88	4	4	—	129	38	—	—	—	32.25	79.14	2
1988–89	3	2	—	68	51	—	I	—	34.00	76.40	—
1989–90	3	3	—	82	50	I	I	—	27.33	62.60	3
1990–91	4	4	—	155	64	—	2	—	38.75	70.14	I
1991–92	4	4	I	159	112	—	—	I	53.00	82.81	3
1992–93	4	4	—	98	55	—	I	—	24.50	88.29	2
1993–94	2	2	—	101	68	—	I	—	50.50	150.75	I
1994–95	—	—	—	—	—	—	—	—	—	—	—
1995–96	4	4	2	93	43*	—	—	—	46.50	65.96	3
1997–98	3	3	—	153	76	—	2	—	51.00	106.99	2
Total	**34**	**33**	**3**	**1101**	**112**	**I**	**8**	**I**	**36.70**	**80.78**	**18**

Opponents	M	Inn	NO	Runs	HS	0s	50	100	Avrge	Stk/Rt	Ct
Queensland	7	7	I	169	40*	—	—	—	28.17	88.48	5
South Australia	5	5	—	235	76	—	3	—	47.00	85.77	2
Tasmania	6	5	—	160	68	I	2	—	32.00	93.57	2
Victoria	9	9	I	423	112	—	2	I	52.88	79.07	5
Western Australia	7	7	I	114	51	—	I	—	19.00	59.38	4

Innings		Inn	NO	Runs	HS	0s	50	100	Avrge	Stk/Rt	Ct
First		22	—	708	112	I	6	I	32.18	89.39	9
Second		11	3	393	64	—	2	—	49.13	68.83	9

Batting at Each Venue

Venue	M	Inn	NO	Runs	HS	0s	50	100	Avrge	Stk/Rt	Ct
Adelaide	2	2	—	105	55	—	2	—	52.50	80.15	2
Brisbane	6	6	I	153	40*	—	—	—	30.60	87.43	5
Melbourne	2	2	I	60	43*	—	—	—	60.00	72.29	I
North Sydney	7	7	—	330	112	I	3	I	47.14	104.10	3
Perth	7	7	I	114	51	—	I	—	19.00	59.38	4
Sydney	10	9	—	339	64	—	2	—	37.67	72.90	3

Batting position	Inn	NO	Runs	HS	0s	50	100	Avrge	Stk/Rt
1/2	I	—	16	16	—	—	—	16.00	51.61
3	2	—	32	32	I	—	—	16.00	60.38
4	26	3	939	112	—	7	I	40.83	85.21
5	I	—	51	51	—	I	—	51.00	70.83
6	3	—	63	46	—	—	—	21.00	60.00

How dismissed:	Inn	NO	Bwd	Ct	LBW	Stp	RO	HW
	33	3	4	18	2	I	5	—

Highest score: 112 New South Wales *v.* Victoria, North Sydney, 1991–92

BOWLING
First-Class Career
Debut: 1985–86 New South Wales *v.* Tasmania, Hobart

Season	Country	M	Balls	Mdns	Runs	Wkts	Avrge	5	10	Best
1985–86	Australia	7	748	27	352	11	32.00	—	—	4–130
1985–86	Zimbabwe	2	258	14	110	2	55.00	—	—	1–25
1986–87	Australia	I	66	4	32	I	32.00	—	—	1–2
1987–88	Zimbabwe	2	6	—	3	—	—	—	—	—
1987–88	Australia	10	276	7	158	6	26.33	—	—	3–49
1988	England	3	72	—	75	—	—	—	—	—
1988–89	Australia	11	258	7	163	I	163.00	—	—	1–46
1989	England	24	704	19	415	14	29.64	—	—	3–23
1989–90	Australia	12	789	20	465	15	31.00	—	—	2–7
1990	England	22	1146	33	771	12	64.25	I	—	5–37
1990–91	Australia	8	186	5	138	2	69.00	—	—	2–15
1990–91	West Indies	9	560	21	271	12	22.58	—	—	4–80
1991–92	Australia	12	587	28	258	7	36.86	—	—	2–11
1992	England	16	1108	31	671	22	30.50	—	—	3–38
1992–93	Sri Lanka	5	240	6	129	2	64.50	—	—	2–77
1992–93	Australia	9	210	2	131	4	32.75	—	—	2–21
1992–93	New Zealand	3	108	6	45	I	45.00	—	—	1–12
1993	England	16	727	28	403	6	67.17	—	—	3–26

Season	Country	M	Balls	Mdns	Runs	Wkts	Avrge	5	10	Best
1993–94	Australia	10	807	45	261	12	21.75	—	—	2–24
1993–94	South Africa	6	234	9	119	—	—	—	—	—
1994–95	Pakistan	4	180	3	106	2	53.00	—	—	2–63
1994–95	Australia	9	618	21	308	10	30.80	I	—	5–40
1994–95	West Indies	7	216	9	146	4	36.50	—	—	2–39
1995	England	16	1535	66	789	17	46.41	—	—	4–76
1995–96	Australia	11	570	21	219	7	31.29	—	—	2–19
1996–97	India	2	209	3	130	7	18.57	I	—	6–68
1996–97	Australia	7	144	5	85	2	42.50	—	—	2–54
1996–97	South Africa	5	120	6	68	1	68.00	—	—	1–34
1997	England	13	282	10	150	4	37.50	—	—	1–16
1997–98	Australia	11	738	25	318	4	79.50	—	—	2–26
1997–98	India	4	228	1	161	2	80.50	—	—	1–44
Total		**277**	**13930**	**482**	**7450**	**190**	**39.21**	**3**	**—**	**6–68**

Country	M	Balls	Mdns	Runs	Wkts	Avrge	5	10	Best
Australia	118	5997	217	2888	82	35.22	I	—	5–40
England	110	5574	187	3274	75	43.65	I	—	5–37
India	6	437	4	291	9	32.33	I	—	6–68
New Zealand	3	108	6	45	1	45.00	—	—	1–12
Pakistan	4	180	3	106	2	53.00	—	—	2–63
Sri Lanka	5	240	6	129	2	64.50	—	—	2–77
South Africa	11	354	15	187	1	187.00	—	—	1–34
West Indies	16	776	30	417	16	26.06	—	—	4–80
Zimbabwe	4	264	14	113	2	56.50	—	—	1–25

Team	M	Balls	Mdns	Runs	Wkts	Avrge	5	10	Best
AUSTRALIA	78	3774	143	1806	45	40.13	I	—	5–40
Australian XI	36	1346	40	779	21	37.10	I	—	6–68
Essex	80	4565	149	2721	65	41.86	I	—	5–37
New South Wales	83	4245	150	2144	59	36.34	—	—	4–130

Wickets taken:	Wkts	Bwd	Ct	C&B	LBW	Stp	HW
	190	30	119	7	31	2	1

Batsmen dismissed:	Wkts	1/2	3	4	5	6	7	8	9	10	11
	190	37	29	18	20	20	16	17	11	11	11

Five Wickets in an Innings

Best bowling: 6–68 Australian XI *v.* Indian Board President's XI, Patiala, 1996–97

Wkts	Team	Opponent	Venue	Season
5–37	Essex	Northamptonshire	Chelmsford	1990
5–40	Australia	England	Adelaide	1994–95
6–68	Australian XI	Indian Board Pres. XI	Patiala	1996–97

Test Career

Debut: 1990–91 Australia *v.* England, Adelaide

Season	Opponent	Venue	M	Balls	Mdns	Runs	Wkts	Avrge	5	10	Best
1990–91	England	Australia	2	36	1	26	—	—	—	—	—
1990–91	West Indies	West Indies	5	390	18	183	8	22.88	—	—	4–80
1991–92	India	Australia	4	222	9	89	1	89.00	—	—	1–36
1992–93	Sri Lanka	Sri Lanka	3	138	3	94	2	47.00	—	—	2–77
1992–93	West Indies	Australia	5	132	2	84	4	21.00	—	—	2–21
1992–93	New Zealand	New Zealand	2	90	5	27	1	27.00	—	—	1–12
1993	England	England	6	336	17	161	1	161.00	—	—	1–43
1993–94	New Zealand	Australia	3	288	18	94	5	18.80	—	—	1–7
1993–94	South Africa	Australia	3	108	6	30	1	30.00	—	—	1–20
1993–94	South Africa	South Africa	3	180	9	86	—	—	—	—	—
1994–95	Pakistan	Pakistan	3	162	2	93	2	46.50	—	—	2–63
1994–95	England	Australia	5	318	10	157	8	19.63	I	—	5–40
1994–95	West Indies	West Indies	4	84	3	48	1	48.00	—	—	1–9
1995–96	Pakistan	Australia	3	294	12	97	2	48.50	—	—	1–6
1995–96	Sri Lanka	Australia	3	150	5	73	2	36.50	—	—	1–15
1996–97	India	India	1	108	—	62	1	62.00	—	—	1–62
1996–97	West Indies	Australia	5	48	1	31	—	—	—	—	—
1996–97	South Africa	South Africa	3	48	1	38	1	38.00	—	—	1–34

Season	Opponent	Venue	M	Balls	Mdns	Runs	Wkts	Avrge	5	10	Best
1997	England	England	6	42	3	16	1	16.00	—	—	1–16
1997–98	New Zealand	Australia	3	126	5	54	—	—	—	—	—
1997–98	South Africa	Australia	3	282	12	114	2	57.00	—	—	2–28
1997–98	India	India	3	192	1	149	2	74.50	—	—	1–44
Total			**78**	**3774**	**143**	**1806**	**45**	**40.13**	**1**	**—**	**5–40**

Opponents			M	Balls	Mdns	Runs	Wkts	Avrge	5	10	Best
ENGLAND			19	732	31	360	10	36.00	1	—	5–40
INDIA			8	522	10	300	4	75.00	—	—	1–36
NEW ZEALAND			8	504	28	175	6	29.17	—	—	1–7
PAKISTAN			6	456	14	190	4	47.50	—	—	2–63
SRI LANKA			6	288	8	167	4	41.75	—	—	2–77
SOUTH AFRICA			12	618	28	268	4	67.00	—	—	2–28
WEST INDIES			19	654	24	346	13	26.62	—	—	4–80

Innings				Balls	Mdns	Runs	Wkts	Avrge	5	10	Best
First				1404	50	679	17	39.94	—	—	2–21
Second				630	26	312	4	78.00	—	—	1–3
Third				534	19	253	6	42.17	—	—	1–8
Fourth				1206	48	562	18	31.22	1	—	5–40

Bowling at Each Venue

Venue	M	Balls	Mdns	Runs	Wkts	Avrge	5	10	Best
in Australia									
Adelaide	8	384	16	189	8	23.63	1	—	5–40
Brisbane	7	252	11	115	2	57.50	—	—	1–6
Hobart	3	282	9	98	2	49.00	—	—	1–7
Melbourne	7	378	13	142	4	35.50	—	—	2–28
Perth	7	270	13	135	7	19.29	—	—	2–21
Sydney	7	438	19	170	2	85.00	—	—	1–21
in England									
Birmingham	2	120	7	48	1	48.00	—	—	1–43
Leeds	2	30	1	10	—	—	—	—	—
Lord's	2	138	5	71	—	—	—	—	—
Manchester	2	—	—	—	—	—	—	—	—
Nottingham	2	42	4	15	—	—	—	—	—
The Oval	2	48	3	33	1	33.00	—	—	1–16
in India									
Bangalore	1	24	—	24	—	—	—	—	—
Calcutta	1	108	1	77	1	77.00	—	—	1–77
Chennai	1	60	—	48	1	48.00	—	—	1–44
Delhi	1	108	—	62	1	62.00	—	—	1–62
in New Zealand									
Christchurch	1	30	1	12	—	—	—	—	—
Wellington	1	60	4	15	1	15.00	—	—	1–12
in Pakistan									
Karachi	1	18	1	4	—	—	—	—	—
Lahore	1	48	—	26	—	—	—	—	—
Rawalpindi	1	96	1	63	2	31.50	—	—	2–63
in Sri Lanka									
Colombo (PIS)	1	24	—	11	—	—	—	—	—
Colombo (SSC)	1	114	3	83	2	41.50	—	—	2–77
Moratuwa	1	—	—	—	—	—	—	—	—
in South Africa									
Cape Town	1	78	4	34	—	—	—	—	—
Centurion	1	42	1	34	1	34.00	—	—	1–34
Durban	1	66	3	38	—	—	—	—	—
Johannesburg	2	42	2	18	—	—	—	—	—
Port Elizabeth	1	—	—	—	—	—	—	—	—
in West Indies									
Bridgetown	2	174	6	92	4	23.00	—	—	4–80
Georgetown	1	12	—	18	—	—	—	—	—
Kingston	2	144	8	57	1	57.00	—	—	1–25
Port-of-Spain	2	48	2	18	2	9.00	—	—	1–9
St John's	2	96	5	46	2	23.00	—	—	1–8

Country	M	Balls	Mdns	Runs	Wkts	Avrge	5	10	Best
Australia	39	2004	81	849	25	33.96	I	—	5–40
England	12	378	20	177	2	88.50	—	—	1–16
India	4	300	I	211	3	70.33	—	—	1–44
New Zealand	2	90	5	27	I	27.00	—	—	1–12
Pakistan	3	162	2	93	2	46.50	—	—	2–63
Sri Lanka	3	138	3	94	2	47.00	—	—	2–77
South Africa	6	228	10	124	I	124.00	—	—	1–34
West Indies	9	474	21	231	9	25.67	—	—	4–80

Wickets taken:	Wkts	Bwd	Ct	C&B	LBW	Stp	HW			
	45	3	29	2	11	—	—			

Batsmen dismissed:	Wkts	1/2	3	4	5	6	7	8	9	10	11
	45	13	8	4	4	2	3	6	3	2	—

Best bowling: 5–40 Australia *v.* England, Adelaide, 1994–95

Sheffield Shield Career
Debut: 1985–86 New South Wales *v.* Tasmania, Hobart

Season	M	Balls	Mdns	Runs	Wkts	Avrge	5	10	Best
1985–86	6	748	27	352	11	32.00	—	—	4–130
1986–87	I	66	4	32	I	32.00	—	—	1–2
1987–88	10	276	7	158	6	26.33	—	—	3–49
1988–89	9	132	2	93	—	—	—	—	—
1989–90	11	726	17	429	12	35.75	—	—	2–22
1990–91	4	138	4	104	2	52.00	—	—	2–15
1991–92	7	305	16	143	6	23.83	—	—	2–11
1992–93	3	78		47	—	—	—	—	—
1993–94	3	316	15	115	5	23.00	—	—	2–24
1994–95	3	228	10	115	2	57.50	—	—	2–11
1995–96	5	126	4	49	3	16.33	—	—	2–19
1996–97	2	96	4	54	2	27.00	—	—	2–54
1997–98	4	204	4	109	—	—	—	—	—
Total	**68**	**3439**	**114**	**1800**	**50**	**36.00**	**—**	**—**	**4–130**

Opponents	M	Balls	Mdns	Runs	Wkts	Avrge	5	10	Best
Queensland	18	1592	46	809	28	28.89	—	—	4–130
South Australia	12	234	3	153	3	51.00	—	—	2–19
Tasmania	12	503	21	244	4	61.00	—	—	2–31
Victoria	14	719	34	284	8	35.50	—	—	2–15
Western Australia	12	391	10	310	7	44.29	—	—	2–11

Innings	Balls	Mdns	Runs	Wkts	Avrge	5	10	Best
First	1031	32	554	9	61.56	—	—	2–15
Second	1132	34	632	17	37.18	—	—	4–130
Third	317	12	154	7	22.00	—	—	2–22
Fourth	959	36	460	17	27.06	—	—	2–11

Bowling at Each Venue

Venue	M	Balls	Mdns	Runs	Wkts	Avrge	5	10	Best
Adelaide	6	144	2	91	I	91.00	—	—	1–18
Albury	I	96	4	40	—	—	—	—	—
Bankstown	I	96	4	54	2	27.00	—	—	2–54
Brisbane	9	820	19	463	13	35.62	—	—	4–130
Devonport	2	144	6	54	I	54.00	—	—	1–5
Hobart (Bel)	3	197	6	128	I	128.00	—	—	1–42
Hobart (TCA)	I	—	—	—	—	—	—	—	—
Melbourne	6	282	16	108	4	27.00	—	—	1–14
Newcastle	5	216	9	89	3	29.67	—	—	2–34
North Sydney	I	12	—	9	—	—	—	—	—
Perth	8	258	5	220	4	55.00	—	—	2–11
Sydney	25	1174	43	544	21	25.90	—	—	3 49

Wickets taken:	Wkts	Bwd	Ct	C&B	LBW	Stp	HW
	50	9	35	—	5	I	

Batsmen dismissed	Wkts	1/2	3	4	5	6	7	8	9	10	11
	50	8	8	3	7	8	6	2	1	3	4

Best bowling: 4–130 New South Wales *v.* Queensland, Brisbane, 1985–86

International Limited-Overs Career
Debut: 1988–89 Australia *v.* Pakistan, Adelaide

Season	Tournament	Venue	M	Balls	Mdns	Runs	Wkts	Avrge	5	Best	Stk/Rt	RPO
1988–89	World Series Cup	AUS	7	—	—	—	—	—	—	—	—	—
1989–90	World Series	AUS	1	—	—	—	—	—	—	—	—	—
1990–91	World Series	AUS	10	294	2	191	12	15.92	—	4–37	24.50	3.90
1990–91	West Indies v. Australia	WI	5	165	—	146	8	18.25	—	3–34	20.63	5.31
1991–92	World Series	AUS	5	54	—	46	—	—	—	—	—	5.11
1991–92	World Cup	ANZ	5	30	—	40	—	—	—	—	—	8.00
1992–93	Sri Lanka v. Australia	SL	3	6	—	6	—	—	—	—	—	6.00
1992–93	World Series	AUS	10	213	—	159	9	17.67	1	5–24	23.67	4.48
1992–93	New Zealand v. Australia	NZ	5	30	—	34	1	34.00	—	1–5	30.00	6.80
1993	England v. Australia	ENG	3	30	—	33	—	—	—	—	—	6.60
1993–94	World Series	AUS	11	246	—	184	6	30.67	—	2–26	41.00	4.49
1993–94	South Africa v. Australia	SAF	8	192	1	168	4	42.00	—	1–26	48.00	5.25
1993–94	Austral-Asia Cup	UAE	2	42	—	41	—	—	—	—	—	5.86
1994–95	Singer World Series	SL	3	24	—	19	—	—	—	—	—	4.75
1994–95	Wills Triangular Series	PAK	6	143	—	131	4	32.75	—	2–43	35.75	5.50
1994–95	World Series	AUS	4	66	1	46	2	23.00	—	2–43	33.00	4.18
1994–95	New Zealand Centenary	NZ	4	84	1	57	2	28.50	—	1–19	42.00	4.07
1994–95	West Indies v. Australia	WI	4	58	—	65	4	16.25	—	3–42	14.50	6.72
1995–96	World Series	AUS	10	306	—	215	6	35.83	—	2–30	51.00	4.22
1995–96	World Cup	IPS	7	288	1	229	5	45.80	—	3–38	57.60	4.77
1996–97	Singer World Series	SL	4	132	1	130	4	32.50	—	3–24	33.00	5.91
1996–97	Titan Cup	IND	4	120	1	86	2	43.00	—	2–38	60.00	4.30
1996–97	CUB Series	AUS	7	51	1	38	1	38.00	—	1–11	51.00	4.47
1996–97	South Africa v. Australia	SAF	4	21	—	16	—	—	—	—	—	4.57
1997	England v. Australia	ENG	3	48	—	44	1	44.00	—	1–28	48.00	5.50
1997–98	CUB Series	AUS	9	246	—	178	7	25.43	—	2–39	35.14	4.34
1997–98	New Zealand v. Australia	NZ	4	30	—	30	—	—	—	—	—	6.00
1997–98	Triangular Cup	IND	5	48	—	45	—	—	—	—	—	5.63
1997–98	Coca-Cola Cup	UAE	5	66	—	46	1	46.00	—	1–26	66.00	4.18
Total			**158**	**3033**	**9**	**2423**	**79**	**30.67**	**1**	**5–24**	**38.39**	**4.79**

Opponents	M	Balls	Mdns	Runs	Wkts	Avrge	5	Best	Stk/Rt	R/O
England	12	222	1	180	7	25.71	—	4–37	31.71	4.86
India	16	234	—	201	4	50.25	—	2–38	58.50	5.15
Kenya	1	30	—	23	—	—	—	—	—	4.60
New Zealand	28	624	3	470	16	29.38	—	3–20	39.00	4.52
Pakistan	15	194	1	179	4	44.75	—	2–43	48.50	5.54
Sri Lanka	15	276	—	256	2	128.00	—	1–23	138.00	5.57
South Africa	31	675	2	525	16	32.81	—	2–26	42.19	4.67
West Indies	33	682	1	508	27	18.81	1	5–24	25.26	4.47
Zimbabwe	7	96	1	81	3	27.00	—	3–24	32.00	5.06

Innings		Balls	Mdns	Runs	Wkts	Avrge	5	Best	Stk/Rt	R/O
First		1568	4	1274	45	28.31	1	5–24	34.84	4.88
Second		1465	5	1149	34	33.79	—	3–29	43.09	4.71

Bowling at Each Venue

Venue	M	Balls	Mdns	Runs	Wkts	Avrge	5	Best	Stk/Rt	R/O
in Australia										
Adelaide	8	144	—	93	3	31.00	—	2–25	48.00	3.88
Brisbane	7	198	—	144	4	36.00	—	2–30	49.50	4.36
Hobart	5	72	—	50	1	50.00	—	1–37	72.00	4.17
Melbourne	25	654	1	471	24	19.63	1	5–24	27.25	4.32
Perth	7	75	—	63	2	31.50	—	2–26	37.50	5.04
Sydney	26	339	3	249	9	27.67	—	3–29	37.67	4.41
in England										
Birmingham	1	18	—	21	—	—	—	—	—	7.00
Leeds	1	12	—	16	—	—	—	—	—	8.00
Lord's	2	36	—	28	1	28.00	—	1–28	36.00	4.67
Manchester	1	12	—	12	—	—	—	—	—	6.00

Venue	M	Balls	Mdns	Runs	Wkts	Avrge	5	Best	Stk/Rt	R/O
The Oval	1	—	—	—	—	—	—	—	—	—
in India										
Ahmedabad	1	30	—	24	—	—	—	—	—	4.80
Bangalore	1	—	—	—	—	—	—	—	—	—
Chandigarh	2	78	—	54	2	27.00	—	2–38	39.00	4.15
Chennai	1	48	—	43	1	43.00	—	1–43	48.00	5.38
Delhi	2	—	—	—	—	—	—	—	—	—
Faridabad	1	48	1	34	—	—	—	—	—	4.25
Indore	1	18	—	14	—	—	—	—	—	4.67
Jaipur	1	60	1	38	3	12.67	—	3–38	20.00	3.80
Kanpur	1	—	—	—	—	—	—	—	—	—
Kochi	1	18	—	21	—	—	—	—	—	7.00
Mumbai	1	60	—	44	1	44.00	—	1–44	60.00	4.40
Nagpur	1	30	—	30	—	—	—	—	—	6.00
Visakhapatnam	1	30	—	23	—	—	—	—	—	4.60
in New Zealand										
Auckland	5	132	1	104	2	52.00	—	1–19	66.00	4.73
Christchurch	2	24	—	24	1	24.00	—	1–5	24.00	6.00
Dunedin	2	—	—	—	—	—	—	—	—	—
Hamilton	1	12	—	20	—	—	—	—	—	10.00
Napier	1	—	—	—	—	—	—	—	—	—
Wellington	3	—	—	—	—	—	—	—	—	—
in Pakistan										
Faisalabad	1	—	—	—	—	—	—	—	—	—
Lahore	3	101	—	92	3	30.67	—	2–43	33.67	5.47
Multan	1	30	—	20	—	—	—	—	—	4.00
Peshawar	1	36	—	39	1	39.00	—	1–39	36.00	6.50
Rawalpindi	1	12	—	15	—	—	—	—	—	7.50
in Sri Lanka										
Colombo (PIS)	5	90	1	78	3	26.00	—	3–24	30.00	5.20
Colombo (PSS)	2	—	—	—	—	—	—	—	—	—
Colombo (SSC)	3	72	—	77	1	77.00	—	1–36	72.00	6.42
in South Africa										
Bloemfontein	2	21	—	16	—	—	—	—	—	4.57
Cape Town	2	54	—	50	1	50.00	—	1–50	54.00	5.56
Centurion	1	—	—	—	—	—	—	—	—	—
Durban	1	18	—	14	—	—	—	—	—	4.67
East London	1	—	—	—	—	—	—	—	—	—
Johannesburg	1	—	—	—	—	—	—	—	—	—
Port Elizabeth	3	66	—	52	2	26.00	—	1–26	33.00	4.73
Verwoerdburg	1	54	1	52	1	52.00	—	1–52	54.00	5.78
in United Arab Emirates										
Sharjah	7	108	—	87	1	87.00	—	1–26	108.00	4.83
in West Indies										
Kingstown	1	—	—	—	—	—	—	—	—	—
Bridgetown	2	82	—	76	6	12.67	—	3–34	13.67	5.56
Georgetown	2	54	—	59	2	29.50	—	1–23	27.00	6.56
Kingston	1	42	—	38	1	38.00	—	1–38	42.00	5.43
Port-of-Spain	3	45	—	38	3	12.67	—	2–6	15.00	5.07

Country	M	Balls	Mdns	Runs	Wkts	Avrge	5	Best	Stk/Rt	R/O
Australia	78	1482	4	1070	43	24.88	1	5–24	34.47	4.33
England	6	78	—	77	1	77.00	—	1–28	78.00	5.92
India	15	420	2	325	7	46.43	—	3–38	60.00	4.64
New Zealand	14	168	1	148	3	49.33	—	1–5	56.00	5.29
Pakistan	7	179	—	166	4	41.50	—	2–43	44.75	5.56
Sri Lanka	10	162	1	155	4	38.75	—	3–24	40.50	5.74
South Africa	12	213	1	184	4	46.00	—	1–26	53.25	5.18
Sharjah	7	108	—	87	1	87.00	—	1–26	108.00	4.83
West Indies	9	223	—	211	12	17.58	—	3–34	18.58	5.68

Wickets taken:	Wkts	Bwd	Ct	C&B	LBW	Stp	HW				
	79	17	51	5	2	4	—				

Batsmen dismissed:	Wkts	1/2	3	4	5	6	7	8	9	10	11
	79	15	8	7	9	9	9	8	6	5	3

Best Bowling: 5–24 Australia *v.* West Indies, Melbourne, 1992–93

Domestic Limited-Overs Career
Debut: 1985–86 New South Wales *v.* Victoria, Sydney

Season	M	Balls	Mdns	Runs	Wkts	Avrge	5	Best	Stk/Rt	RPO
1985–86	1	54	1	28	1	28.00	—	1–28	54.00	3.11
1986–87	2	36	—	37	—	—	—	—	—	6.17
1987–88	4	114	3	62	5	12.40	—	3–23	22.80	3.26
1988–89	3	—	—	—	—	—	—	—	—	—
1989–90	3	113	—	86	2	43.00	—	1–26	56.50	4.57
1990–91	4	84	1	66	3	22.00	—	2–26	28.00	4.71
1991–92	4	150	1	134	3	44.67	—	2–26	50.00	5.36
1992–93	4	66	—	65	2	32.50	—	2–23	33.00	5.91
1993–94	2	—	—	—	—	—	—	—	—	—
1994–95	—	—	—	—	—	—	—	—	—	—
1995–96	4	84	1	60	—	—	—	—	—	4.29
1996–97	—	—	—	—	—	—	—	—	—	—
1997–98	3	28	—	31	2	15.50	—	2–31	14.00	6.64
Total	**34**	**729**	**7**	**569**	**18**	**31.61**	**—**	**3–23**	**40.50**	**4.68**

Opponents	M	Balls	Mdns	Runs	Wkts	Avrge	5	Best	Stk/Rt	R/O
Queensland	7	172	—	132	8	16.50	—	3–23	21.50	4.60
South Australia	5	138	1	111	3	37.00	—	2–23	46.00	4.83
Tasmania	6	132	1	107	1	107.00	—	1–17	132.00	4.86
Victoria	9	186	5	121	4	30.25	—	2–26	46.50	3.90
Western Australia	7	101	—	98	2	49.00	—	1–26	50.50	5.82

Innings		Balls	Mdns	Runs	Wkts	Avrge	5	Best	Stk/Rt	R/O
First		437	4	344	10	34.40	—	3–23	43.70	4.72
Second		292	3	225	8	28.13	—	2–26	36.50	4.62

Bowling at Each Venue

Venue	M	Balls	Mdns	Runs	Wkts	Avrge	5	Best	Stk/Rt	R/O
Adelaide	2	78	—	70	3	23.33	—	2–23	26.00	5.38
Brisbane	6	172	—	132	8	16.50	—	3–23	21.50	4.60
Melbourne	2	24	—	19	—	—	—	—	—	4.75
North Sydney	7	120	1	108	2	54.00	—	2–26	60.00	5.40
Perth	7	101	—	98	2	49.00	—	1–26	50.50	5.82
Sydney	10	234	6	142	3	47.33	—	1–17	78.00	3.64

Wickets taken:	Wkts	Bwd	Ct	C&B	LBW	Stp	HW			
	18	5	9	3	1	—	—			

Batsmen dismissed:	Wkts	1/2	3	4	5	6	7	8	9	10	11
	18	2	—	3	4	1	3	3	1	1	—

Best bowling: 3–23 New South Wales *v.* Queensland, Brisbane, 1987–88

D.P. Waugh
(Right-hand batsman, right-arm medium/off-spin bowler)

BATTING AND FIELDING
First-Class Career
Debut: 1995–96 New South Wales *v.* Queensland, Sydney

Season	M	Inn	NO	Runs	HS	0s	50	100	Avrge	Ct
1995–96	1	2	—	22	19	—	—	—	11.00	1
Total	**1**	**2**	**—**	**22**	**19**	**—**	**—**	**—**	**11.00**	**1**

Batting position	Inn	NO	Runs	HS	0s	50	100	Avrge
5	2	—	22	19	—	—	—	11.00

How dismissed:	Inn	NO	Bwd	Ct	LBW	Stp	RO	HW
	2	—	—	2	—	—	—	—

Highest score: 19 New South Wales *v.* Queensland, Sydney, 1995–96

Domestic Limited-Overs Career
Debut: 1995–96 New South Wales *v.* Tasmania, Hobart

Season	M	Inn	NO	Runs	HS	0s	50	100	Avrge	Stk/Rt	Ct
1995–96	2	2	—	43	28	—	—	—	21.50	72.88	—
1996–97	1	1	—	4	4	—	—	—	4.00	40.00	—
Total	**3**	**3**	**—**	**47**	**28**	**—**	**—**	**—**	**15.67**	**68.12**	**—**

Opponents	M	Inn	NO	Runs	HS	0s	50	100	Avrge	Stk/Rt	Ct
Queensland	1	1	—	4	4	—	—	—	4.00	40.00	—
Tasmania	1	1	—	15	15	—	—	—	15.00	44.12	—
Western Australia	1	1	—	28	28	—	—	—	28.00	112.00	—

Innings	Inn	NO	Runs	HS	0s	50	100	Avrge	Stk/Rt	Ct
First	3	—	47	28	—	—	—	15.67	68.12	—
Second	—	—	—	—	—	—	—	—	—	—

Batting at Each Venue

Venue	M	Inn	NO	Runs	HS	0s	50	100	Avrge	Stk/Rt	Ct
Brisbane	1	1	—	4	4	—	—	—	4.00	40.00	—
Hobart	1	1	—	15	15	—	—	—	15.00	44.12	—
Sydney	1	1	—	28	28	—	—	—	28.00	112.00	—

Batting position	Inn	NO	Runs	HS	0s	50	100	Avrge	Stk/Rt
1/2	1	—	15	15	—	—	—	15.00	44.12
6	2	—	32	28	—	—	—	16.00	91.43

How dismissed:	Inn	NO	Bwd	Ct	LBW	Stp	RO	HW
	3	—	1	—	—	—	2	—

Highest score: 28 New South Wales *v.* Western Australia, Sydney, 1995–96

BOWLING
First-Class Career

Has not bowled in first-class cricket.

Domestic Limited-Overs Career
Debut: 1995–96 New South Wales *v.* Tasmania, Hobart

Season	M	Balls	Mdns	Runs	Wkys	Avrge	5	Best	Stk/Rt	RPO
1995–96	2	—	—	—	—	—	—	—	—	—
1996–97	1	6	—	4	—	—	—	—	—	4.00
Total	**3**	**6**	**—**	**4**	**—**	**—**	**—**	**—**	**—**	**4.00**

Index

Please note: for most Pakistani and some Indian names, the author has followed the indexing style of Wisden Cricketers' Almanack.